I0802883

EARLY CHILDHOOD EDUCATION SERIES

NANCY FILE & CHRISTOPHER P. BROWN, EDITORS

Culturally Responsive Teaching for Infants and Toddlers: Strategies to Strengthen Development and Learning
MARIE L. MASTERSON

Addressing Stress With Self-Compassion: A Guide for Early Childhood Teachers
DAVID P. BARRY

Teacher Well-Being in Early Childhood: A Resource for Early Care and Education Professionals
ANGELA C. BAUM & KERRIE L. SCHNAKE

Pro-Blackness in Early Childhood Education: Diversifying Curriculum and Pedagogy in K–3 Classrooms
GLORIA SWINDLER BOUTTE, JARVAIS J. JACKSON, SAUDAH N. COLLINS, JANICE R. BAINES, ANTHONY BROUGHTON, & GEORGE LEE JOHNSON

Seven Crucial Conversations in Early Childhood Education: Where Have We Been and Why Does It Matter?
NANCY FILE, NANCY E. BARBOUR, & ANDREW J. STREMMEL, EDS.

Supporting Korean American Children in Early Childhood Education: Perspectives From Mother-Educators
SOPHIA HAN, JINHEE KIM, SOHYUN MEACHAM, & SU-JEONG WEE

Relationship-Based Care for Infants and Toddlers: Fostering Early Learning and Development Through Responsive Practice
SUSAN L. RECCHIA, MINSUN SHIN, & ELENI LOIZOU

Infants and Toddlers at Work: Using Reggio-Inspired Materials to Support Brain Development, Second Edition
ANN LEWIN-BENHAM

Leading Anti-Bias Early Childhood Programs: A Guide to Change, for Change, 2nd Ed.
LOUISE DERMAN-SPARKS, DEBBIE LEEKEENAN, & JOHN NIMMO

We Are the Change We Seek: Advancing Racial Justice in Early Care and Education
IHEOMA U. IRUKA, TONIA R. DURDEN, KERRY-ANN ESCAYG, & STEPHANIE M. CURENTON

Young Investigators: The Project Approach in the Early Years, 4th Ed.
JUDY HARRIS HELM, LILIAN G. KATZ, & REBECCA WILSON

Emotionally Responsive Teaching: Expanding Trauma-Informed Practice With Young Children
TRAVIS WRIGHT

Rooted in Belonging: Critical Place-Based Learning in Early Childhood and Elementary Teacher Education
MELISSA SHERFINSKI WITH SHARON HAYES

Transforming Early Years Policy in the U.S.: A Call to Action
MARK K. NAGASAWA, LACEY PETERS, MARIANNE N. BLOCH, & BETH BLUE SWADENER, EDS.

Music Therapy With Preschool Children on the Autism Spectrum: Moments of Meeting
GEOFF BARNES

On Being and Well-Being in Infant/Toddler Care and Education: Life Stories From Baby Rooms
MARY BENSON MCMULLEN

Principals as Early Learning Leaders: Effectively Supporting Our Youngest Learners
JULIE NICHOLSON, HELEN MANIATES, SERENE YEE, THOMAS WILLIAMS JR., VERONICA UFOEGBUNE, & RAUL ERAZO-CHAVEZ

Resisting the Kinder-Race: Restoring Joy to Early Learning
CHRISTOPHER P. BROWN

Reshaping Universal Preschool: Critical Perspectives on Power and Policy
LUCINDA GRACE HEIMER & ANN ELIZABETH RAMMINGER, WITH KATHERINE K. DELANEY, SARAH GALANTER-GUZIEWSKI, LACEY PETERS, & KRISTIN WHYTE

Pre-K Stories: Playing with Authorship and Integrating Curriculum in Early Childhood
DANA FRANTZ BENTLEY & MARIANA SOUTO-MANNING

Ready or Not: Early Care and Education's Leadership Choices—12 Years Later, 2nd Ed.
STACIE G. GOFFIN & VALORA WASHINGTON

For a complete list of series titles, visit https://www.tcpress.com/ece

continued

Early Childhood Education Series, *continued*

Teaching STEM in the Preschool Classroom
Alissa A. Lange et al.

High-Quality Early Learning for a Changing World
Beverly Falk

Guiding Principles for the New Early Childhood Professional
Valora Washington & Brenda Gadson

Leading for Change in Early Care and Education
Anne L. Douglass

When Pre-K Comes to School
Bethany Wilinski

Continuity in Children's Worlds
Melissa M. Jozwiak et al.

The Early Intervention Guidebook for Families and Professionals, 2nd Ed.
Bonnie Keilty

STEM Learning with Young Children
Shelly Counsell et al.

Courageous Leadership in Early Childhood Education
Susi Long et al., Eds.

Teaching Kindergarten
Julie Diamond et al., Eds.

The New Early Childhood Professional
Valora Washington et al.

Teaching and Learning in a Diverse World, 4th Ed.
Patricia G. Ramsey

In the Spirit of the Studio, 2nd Ed.
Lella Gandini et al., Eds.

Exploring Mathematics Through Play in the Early Childhood Classroom
Amy Noelle Parks

Becoming Young Thinkers
Judy Harris Helm

The Early Years Matter
Marilou Hyson & Heather Biggar Tomlinson

Thinking Critically About Environments for Young Children
Lisa P. Kuh, Ed.

Standing Up for Something Every Day
Beatrice S. Fennimore

FirstSchool
Sharon Ritchie & Laura Gutmann, Eds.

Early Childhood Education for a New Era
Stacie G. Goffin

Everyday Artists
Dana Frantz Bentley

Multicultural Teaching in the Early Childhood Classroom
Mariana Souto-Manning

Inclusion in the Early Childhood Classroom
Susan L. Recchia & Yoon-Joo Lee

Moral Classrooms, Moral Children, 2nd Ed.
Rheta DeVries & Betty Zan

Defending Childhood
Beverly Falk, Ed.

Starting with Their Strengths
Deborah C. Lickey & Denise J. Powers

The Play's the Thing
Elizabeth Jones & Gretchen Reynolds

Twelve Best Practices for Early Childhood Education
Ann Lewin-Benham

Big Science for Growing Minds
Jacqueline Grennon Brooks

What If All the Kids Are White? 2nd Ed.
Louise Derman-Sparks & Patricia G. Ramsey

Seen and Heard
Ellen Lynn Hall & Jennifer Kofkin Rudkin

Connecting Emergent Curriculum and Standards in the Early Childhood Classroom
Sydney L. Schwartz & Sherry M. Copeland

Infants and Toddlers at Work
Ann Lewin-Benham

Educating and Caring for Very Young Children, 2nd Ed.
Doris Bergen et al.

Beginning School
Richard M. Clifford & Gisele M. Crawford, Eds.

Emergent Curriculum in the Primary Classroom
Carol Anne Wien, Ed.

Enthusiastic and Engaged Learners
Marilou Hyson

Powerful Children
Ann Lewin-Benham

Supervision in Early Childhood Education, 3rd Ed.
Joseph J. Caruso with M. Temple Fawcett

Guiding Children's Behavior
Eileen S. Flicker & Janet Andron Hoffman

The War Play Dilemma, 2nd Ed.
Diane E. Levin & Nancy Carlsson-Paige

Playing to Get Smart
Elizabeth Jones & Renatta M. Cooper

The Emotional Development of Young Children, 2nd Ed.
Marilou Hyson

Young Children Continue to Reinvent Arithmetic—2nd Grade, 2nd Ed.
Constance Kamii

Bringing Learning to Life
Louise Boyd Cadwell

Bringing Reggio Emilia Home
Louise Boyd Cadwell

Culturally Responsive Teaching for Infants and Toddlers

Strategies to Strengthen Development and Learning

Marie L. Masterson

Teachers College Press
Teachers College, Columbia University

Teachers College Press cannot be held responsible for damage, mishap, or injury incurred during the use of or because of the activities in this book. Appropriate and reasonable caution and adult supervision of children involved in activities and corresponding to the age and capability of each child involved is recommended at all times. Do not leave children unattended at any time. Observe safety and caution at all times.

Published by Teachers College Press,® 1234 Amsterdam Avenue, New York, NY 10027

Front cover design by Holly Grundon / BHG Graphics. Photograph by Compassionate Eye Foundation/David Oxberry/Getty Images.

Library of Congress Cataloging-in-Publication Data

Names: Masterson, Marie L. author
Title: Culturally responsive teaching for infants and toddlers : strategies to strengthen development and learning / Marie L. Masterson.
Description: New York, NY : Teachers College Press, [2025] | Series: Early childhood education series | Includes bibliographical references and index. | Summary: "This book equips educators with the knowledge, dispositions, and skills to create high-quality learning environments for infants and toddlers. It includes teaching tips, activities, and reflection questions"—Provided by publisher.
Identifiers: LCCN 2025004652 (print) | LCCN 2025004653 (ebook) | ISBN 9780807787601 paperback | ISBN 9780807787618 hardcover | ISBN 9780807783351 ebook
Subjects: LCSH: Multicultural education—Activity programs | Early childhood education—Activity programs | Culturally relevant pedagogy
Classification: LCC LC1099 .M375 2025 (print) | LCC LC1099 (ebook) | DDC 372.2101—dc23/eng/20250401
LC record available at https://lccn.loc.gov/2025004652
LC ebook record available at https://lccn.loc.gov/2025004653

ISBN 978-0-8077-8760-1 (paper)
ISBN 978-0-8077-8761-8 (hardcover)
ISBN 978-0-8077-8335-1 (ebook)

Printed on acid-free paper
Manufactured in the United States of America

My deepest thanks are extended to colleagues who shared their insights with me, including Erin Cetera, Meishi Haslip, Jana Howard, Phillis Mills, and Sherry Rocha. The greatest expression of gratitude is extended to my father, Gordon Mumma, and to my children, David, James, Sara, and Stephen, who understand the remarkable influence of context and culture and the critical need for children to be nurtured in gardens of joyful discovery, with teachers who inspire their love of learning, nourish their creativity, and empower the richness and meaning of their lives.

Contents

Culturally Responsive Teaching for Infants and Toddlers

Introduction

Whether you are beginning your teaching career, are a veteran teacher, or are supporting early childhood programs through coaching and leadership development, this book is for you. Whatever the type of early childhood program, you have the capability to radically impact the quality of teaching and influence the experiences of families and children through inclusive and collaborative teaching.

The purpose of this book is to help infant and toddler teachers design curriculum and implement teaching practices that promote children's self-identity, self-agency, and love for learning. It presents an expanded view of child development that is anchored in the multiple contexts of family, community, culture, and language. The contexts of children and families are valued and honored as essential anchors for teaching and are the foundation for learning about and from children to create meaningful and joyful learning experiences.

With more than half of children under age 3 enrolled in nonparental care on a weekly basis, there is increasing demand for high-quality programming (Banghart et al., 2020; NCES, 2019). Yet many early childhood programs have little curriculum specifically developed for infants and toddlers (Smith & Osborn, 2024). In addition, the quality of care for infants and toddlers remains low and variable (Mangione et al., 2016; Perlman et al., 2017). Teachers need additional resources to adequately support the development and learning of infants and toddlers (Simons et al., 2022).

Importantly, deficits in quality impact equity and access for families in underresourced communities (Bichay-Awadalla & Butotsky-Shearer, 2022). Families experiencing neighborhood violence, poverty, and other stressors are least likely to have access to high-quality programs (Levine Coley et al., 2021). Many states continue to have "child care deserts," where there are fewer than one licensed infant and toddler slot for every three children under age 3, with low-income counties offering the fewest options (Jessen-Howard et al., 2020).

In order to address the critical nature of the current infant and toddler child care landscape, this book seeks to overcome these inequities by providing focused encouragement, a wealth of effective strategies, and key insights and action steps for increased impact to support the work of all who advocate for and teach our youngest children. Given the rapid development of children's brains in the first 3 years, the need for security in relationships, and the need for rich cognitive learning experiences, early childhood educators have the opportunity to make a difference. High-quality programs invite families as full partners in authentic learning communities, offering connections to resources and opportunities, and empowering children with a strong start in life.

The release of the updated Statement on Developmentally Appropriate Practice (NAEYC, 2020) and the book *Developmentally Appropriate Practice in Early Childhood Programs Serving Children From Birth Through Age 8,* 4th edition (2022) calls for resources that show how context, culture, and compassion influence family engagement and how child-centered practices can nourish and strengthen development and learning during the infant and toddler years. In each chapter of this book, you will find a relational approach to teaching that results in a safe, vital learning community where families, children, and teachers can thrive.

As you explore each section, consider how the examples and stories are similar or different from those you have observed. What do families experience when they enroll their infant or toddler in a program? What cultural expectations and norms may be invisible or remain unaddressed? In what ways do family cultures and contexts influence their priorities and values? How do your own perspectives and beliefs impact communication, child care, approaches to teaching, and decision-making? When these questions become a regular part of daily planning and reflection, you will develop deeper understanding of yourself and others, be able to honor the strengths and insights of families, and apply these insights to teaching decisions.

Each chapter will include:

- *Learning Goals.* Chapter goals focus on important concepts for each chapter.
- *Real-Life Scenarios.* Teaching stories bring practical concepts and strategies to life.
- *Research Revisited.* Easy-to-read facts and explanations anchor teaching reflection.
- *Strategy Toolboxes.* Tips and strategies provide action steps for planning, organization, communication, decision-making, and teaching.
- *Overcoming Practical Challenges.* Common problems are addressed with practical explanations and effective solutions.
- *From My Experience.* Insights from personal stories provide unique perspectives, ideas, and suggestions.
- *For Your Information.* Resources for additional exploration introduce important connections to experts, professional organizations, research, and additional strategies for practice.

- *Q&As From the Field.* A question-and-answer format responds to frequent questions experienced in infant and toddler classrooms related to chapter content.
- *Reflection Questions.* Key thought prompts encourage application of chapter concepts and strategies that promote professional reflection and meaningful discussion with colleagues for use in communities of practice, group study, and self-study.

Each chapter guides you through a personal and professional journey to explore the cultural beliefs, norms, and experiences that contribute to your own life and motivations for teaching. You will develop deeper understanding of the impact of teaching decisions, investigate the role of cultural safety, consider teacher stories, and encounter multiple ways families participate in the life of programs. You will view the perspectives of children and explore the ways curriculum, authentic relationships, rich and meaningful learning, and responsive caring routines strengthen children's emerging skills, capabilities, and self-agency. Importantly, you will discover a wealth of scenarios and practical examples that reflect professionals like you who celebrate the remarkable curiosity, creativity, and resilience of children. You will find encouragement and inspiration to add to your toolbox of strategies and ideas as you invite children into relationships of belonging and affirmation and positively influence their lives.

CHAPTER 1

Exploring Child Development Through the Lens of Culture

This chapter explores the deeply embedded and often hidden beliefs and assumptions that anchor child care and teaching practices with infants and toddlers. It explores the key components of culture that influence teacher perceptions, expectations, and ways of teaching and responding to children. Practical action steps honor the diverse needs of infants and build on the expanding skills, curiosity, and energy of toddlers.

Learning Goal 1: Describe childrearing beliefs and practices that are situated in the unique contexts of families, vary across cultures, and can become powerful resources to strengthen teaching.

Learning Goal 2: Examine the cultural contexts of development and learning, including teacher approaches to planning, classroom routines, meaningful learning, communication, goal setting, and individualized teaching.

Learning Goal 3: Evaluate the benefits of inclusive practices for infants and toddlers, building on individual differences as strengths and creating caring and equitable learning communities where all children and families can thrive.

EXPLORING THE IMPACT OF CULTURE

In Ms. Cailie's toddler room, 30-month-old Luan arrives in the morning and sits quietly next to the books. She doesn't interact with her peers but watches them carefully. Knowing that Chinese is spoken in Luan's home, Ms. Cailie has learned simple prompts, like kěyǐ bāng nǐ mā *for "Can I help you?" She uses picture cards with words in Chinese and English, like* shuǐ *for water and* yùshì *for bathroom. Luan seems happy, smiling at funny moments, sitting next to teachers, and playing next to other children. She comes to the table for a snack but doesn't seem to be interested in the food. Ms. Cailie thinks Luan has eaten breakfast and simply isn't hungry.*

When Celeste, an experienced coaching consultant, visits the classroom to evaluate spaces and materials, she notices Luan sitting quietly while other children are eating. She asks, "Have you talked with the mother to see if Luan is hand-fed at home?" Ms. Cailie looks surprised. "What do you mean?" Celeste responds, "It's likely that Luan is hungry and is waiting for you to feed her."

This is an established and respected program with a focus on creative arts and unstructured play. The room has a beautiful library with picture books that represent the children's cultures and backgrounds. Music played at naptime represents the languages and cultures of the children. Dramatic play spaces incorporate food items, homemaking activities, and doll care items that represent the diversity of children's lives. But the teachers don't know that Luan's behavior is related to cultural variations in feeding practices. Ms. Cailie meets with Luan's mother, Jasmine, to learn more. She begins to assist Luan with feeding and also encourages her to take independent bites of muffins and other finger foods.

Ms. Cailie also learns that Luan's family does not like her to drink cold water, as traditional Chinese medicine teaches them that warm water is a healthier option. This request is easily accommodated. Jasmine hopes Luan will have some academic skill instruction. Ms. Cailie provides materials for letter recognition as an option during free play. Luan's family expects her to show obedience and follow instructions, but the program encourages children to make their own decisions. To adapt, Ms. Cailie encourages helping activities that engage Luan in showing responsibility. Jasmine is invited to read with the children at the Chinese New Year and Unity of Mankind Day. She provides books that reflect traits valued in a diverse community.

This successful and trusting collaboration is the result of Ms. Cailie's sincere willingness to learn about and honor other perspectives. She is committed to incorporating cultural diversity as an asset and develop a deeper level of cultural knowledge (Bennett et al., 2018). Like Ms. Cailie, when you learn about families, you will also develop greater insight about yourself.

The language and expressions of the home, the smells and tastes of food, and the timing, rhythm, and ways that adults lead and respond to children imprint lasting patterns for living and relating to others. Culture frames the familiar ways of being that are unique to each family. Cultural and linguistic anchors are perhaps the most important ingredients for children's developing sense of self and their early roots of security and well-being.

Culture influences the way people solve conflict and manage stress. Culture impacts the formality or informality of relationships and styles of communicating that seem familiar and normal. These norms become the unspoken rules and expectations that are viewed as acceptable and appropriate that people hold for themselves and for others (UNICEF, 2021).

Some cultural differences or norms are visible—like the way people dress, the way people greet others, and the amount of personal space that makes them feel comfortable. Personal space means how closely someone stands to another during an interaction. But in the infant and toddler classroom, norms are often invisible. Hidden differences can interfere with communication between teachers and add complex dynamics and challenges to interactions between teachers and families.

Teachers can identify and explore the many strengths and benefits of diversity and the ways development and learning are strengthened through the positive contributions of families, communities, and cultures (Edyburn et al., 2019). The unique contexts of families are called *funds of knowledge* and are assets that need to be valued and integrated between home and the program (Vélez-Ibáñez & Greenberg, 2005). The concept of *funds of identity* (Esteban-Guitart, 2021) adds to the understanding of funds of knowledge by focusing on the lived experiences of families, their social contexts, and reflective understanding of their identities.

Assumptions about culture influence children's adjustment to early childhood programs. "Children who find themselves in an unfamiliar environment—such as a classroom that reflects a culture different from their home culture—are likely to feel confused, isolated, alienated, conflicted, and less competent because what they've learned so far in their home culture simply doesn't apply" (Kaiser & Rasminsky, 2019, p. 22). For very young children, expectations in group settings may be unfamiliar and provoke anxiety. When ways of nurturing and responding to children are congruent with those of families, children experience familiarity, reassurance, and comfort.

As you reflect on your teaching experiences, how do you notice cultural norms and values reflected in the lives of infants and toddlers and in their families? How do families' unique cultural ways of being impact your classroom decisions? In what ways might cultural norms be hidden in infant and toddler programs? These questions can guide your thinking as you explore the ways family and program values and approaches may differ.

Does your program reflect many diversities in language, race, culture, socioeconomic status, family structure, gender, ability, and age? Does your program represent a single race, culture, or language? Even when programs are monocultural, conversations about the cultural contexts of staff, families, and children provide a needed anchor for teaching.

REFOCUSING IDEAS ABOUT TEACHING

Ms. Nona sits on the floor in front of Marianna in the young toddler classroom. "You can do it!" She encourages the 18-month-old. "Pull your sweater off by yourself." Marinna tugs one arm out of the sweater and then another and grins triumphantly. Ms. Nona cheers. "You pulled your sweater off! Let's take your sweater to your cubby." Ms. Nona lifts Marinna up so she can reach and says, "Can you put your sweater in the cubby?" She pats the cubby, and Marinna pushes the sweater onto the shelf.

When Marianna's mother, Ms. Farina, comes to take Marianna home, she puts the sweater on her daughter. "Momma will help you. Give me your hand." Ms. Nona says, "Marianna pulled off her sweater all by herself today." Ms. Farina responds, "I don't like her to take off her clothes or she will do it all the time. I prefer to dress her."

Across the room, Ms. Nona hears Sebastian start to cry. Ms. Angie, another teacher in the young toddler classroom, sees he did not get the truck he wanted. She takes Sebastian gently by the hand and says, "Let's get another truck. Do you want the red fire truck or the blue dump truck? The red fire truck has a siren." She makes a siren sound and cranks up the ladder. Sebastian stops crying and reaches for the truck. Ms. Angie adds, "Look. Here is the ladder. Can you turn the lever around to make the ladder go up?" Sebastian pulls the truck on his lap and turns the lever.

Ms. Nona has worked with Marianna to encourage independence in dressing. She wishes Marianna's mother wouldn't do for her child what the child is capable of doing alone. She also experiences strong feelings when her coteacher helps Sebastian. She is not sure why Ms. Angie steps in so fast and doesn't give Sebastian time to work things out for himself. She also is unsure how to talk about the differences she sees.

Where do ideas about teaching children originate? Most teachers recognize there are cultural differences that impact infant and toddler teaching, but they tend to attribute differing ways of child caring and teaching to someone's personality or training rather than to their culture.

Most people feel strongly about "their own" way of being raised, because these norms and values reflect what was done to them and what they do at home. Without purposeful examination, these differences can become hidden barriers to communication, can impact teachers' stress levels, and can affect decision-making. For these reasons, the cultural contexts of the children, their families, and the teachers must be explored and understood.

Differences in childrearing approaches may result in conflicting goals. Just as Ms. Nona holds strong ideas about independence for Marianna, her family prefers she remain highly dependent. They believe prolonged dependence provides opportunity to teach and transmit important manners and values. To complicate the matter, culture often guides behavior at the unconscious level so that ways of approaching caregiving and behavior typically happen without evaluation (De Gioia, 2013). In fact, "culturally defined beliefs are so powerful that parents sometimes act on them as much as or more than on what their senses tell them about their own children" (Bornstein, 2015, p. 5).

While Ms. Nona and Ms. Angie differ in their ideas about how to support Sebastian in solving problems, they have an important opportunity to explore the cultural norms and values that influence the way they plan materials and respond to children's needs. In the next sections, you will dig deeper to see what these differences look like and how cultural variations are part of everyday decisions and communication.

REFRAMING CHILD DEVELOPMENT

Two-year old Sienna pulls the bowl of water closer across the table to dip in her paint brush. Water sloshes over the bowl and splashes onto the paper. Her freshly painted blue lines ooze together. Sienna grunts in frustration. Phebe, the child sitting next to Sienna, looks up, startled. She says, "Look out!" as the water splashes on her.

Ms. Caitlin, the children's teacher, places her hand gently on Sienna's shoulder. "What will help you clean up? Paper towel?" She offers a paper towel. Sienna presses the paper towel with both hands to blot the spilled water. "Great!" says Ms. Caitlin. "You are learning to clean up by yourself. It feels good to be a helper." Next, Ms. Caitlin hands a paper towel to Phebe. "Can you wipe up your splash?" Phebe pats her damp tummy with the towel. "All better!" she says.

As the children dip their brushes in fresh water and slide the brushes over their paper, Ms. Caitlin's coteacher, Ms. Blaire, speaks quietly, "I told them to be careful with the water. They are making a mess. They need help instead of trying to do it themselves."

Ms. Blaire values obedience and thinks children should follow directions. She feels this activity makes a mess, even though the children enjoy it. Ms. Caitlin values independence, creativity, and initiative. She wants the children to make their own decisions and learn from their mistakes. While these differences seem straightforward, strongly held beliefs can make communication between teachers complicated. Differences reflect ideas about what is in the best interest of children.

To complicate the matter, culture contributes subtle and unique factors that differ greatly across cultures and also within members of specific groups (AACAP, 2019). A single family may represent the interplay of many cultures, languages, and experiences that are part of different contexts and contributions to their lives (CDE, 2016). In fact, there are greater differences within cultures than across cultures (Deater-Deckard et al., 2018; Taras et al., 2016). These differences often are the result of socioeconomic status, specific geographic locations, and other societal factors.

In addition, culture develops and shifts over time and influences every part of life, not just customs and beliefs (Keller, 2017). Variation in child development is linked to differences in childrearing practices, including the amount of restriction or stimulation and support that are provided for specific skills (Karasik & Robinson, 2022). Researcher Caterina Bembich (2016) states, "Caregivers follow different cultural scripts in parenting, which have an adaptive value within their specific sociocultural context" (73). Teachers learn about intracultural variation within contexts to avoid stereotypes and consider each child and family as individuals.

To add to the challenge, children display a wide range of individual differences in the emergence of skills. One infant may crawl sooner than other children and develop more advanced verbal skills. A toddler may develop fine motor dexterity and easily handle art materials more quickly than other children in a group. Emerging skills develop in unique ways and are impacted by day-to-day variations in health, the consistency of routines, and other biological and environmental factors.

Finally, developmental skills may emerge inconsistently within a single child, known as asynchronous development (NAGC, 2019). While areas of development are interdependent, some skills may jump ahead of others. For example, a toddler may be cognitively and verbally advanced but need a great deal of emotional support. Asynchronous development can lead to unrealistically high expectations from teachers about a child's physical, emotional, or regulatory development.

To understand and build on family contexts, teachers must observe and learn about parenting practices without assuming all members of a specific cultural background use the same approaches. Teachers can observe the ways families interact with children and become more intentional in learning about and recognizing these patterns. Over time, with awareness and reflection, a deeper and more nuanced understanding about children's unique strengths and assets will emerge.

Research Revisited: Investigating Development in Context

The anchors for infant and toddler research have widened to include a greater range among universals of development than previously recognized. Early studies on child development were focused on European cultures that valued individualism and cognitive competence. Cultures that placed value on community and social development were not represented (Oudgenoeg-Paz et al., 2020). Absent a broader context for understanding development, children were often improperly judged or labeled. The National Association for the Education of Young Children (NAEYC) Statement on Developmentally Appropriate Practice (2020) requires educators to adopt a broader and more complex view of child development in the context of the family, culture, and community.

Knowledge about the impacts of childrearing practices on development has also expanded. For example, when the guidelines for sleeping in the United States changed in 1994 from placing infants on their stomachs to sleeping on their backs, other motor skills, like rolling, sitting, crawling, and standing, were delayed (Karasik et al., 2015; Pelligra et al., 2014). In cultures where infants are cradled, carried, or bound, the onset of children's crawling is delayed. In the same way, language acquisition, physical, and social development differ across cultures (Karasik & Kuchirko, 2022).

Developmental science now includes "advances in cultural psychology and growing awareness of how the structure and meaning of child-adult interactions are situated in particular linguistic and ethic traditions, including middle-class

Anglo-heritage families" (Fuller et al., 2020, p. 32). Teachers must be able to identify cultural, linguistic, and developmental contributions to child development and honor individual characteristics and variations as strengths.

Importantly for teachers, "judgments and decisions about planning and instruction may be based less on professional knowledge and more on their own beliefs about a topic" (Gardner-Neblett et al., 2021, p. 56). Teachers may respond to children based on the way they themselves were raised, on their previous experience in a classroom, or on their personal beliefs about child development or discipline (Castle et al., 2016). For these reasons, it is important to identify your values, beliefs, professional knowledge, and personal experiences to explore how they influence your perceptions of children's capabilities and potential.

HONORING FAMILY LIFE STRUCTURES

In a large urban program, Ms. Chen, the early education program director, sets a family meeting to welcome a new mother and baby Nouri. She expects to greet just one parent to review the program handbook and give a tour. On the morning of the meeting, seven family members arrive. Ms. Chen must find a meeting space large enough to include everyone in the extended family. Over the months, different family members pick up Nouri at the end of the day, always stopping to talk with the infant teacher and the director.

Ms. Chen has learned that styles of caring for children differ very much from one family to another. In Nouri's family, her development is supported by multiple caregivers, all of whom contribute equally. In the same infant classroom, 12-week-old Raoul is cared for by his mother. Raoul has a babysitter who stays with him on days when he needs to be absent from the program, and his father helps on the weekend. Four-month-old Maureen lives with her grandmother and is dropped off at the program daily by her aunt. Ms. Chen appreciates all of the family members that love and care for the children.

Without exploring family life structures, program leaders and teachers may assume the mother is the primary caregiver and incorrectly address a father, aunt, or other family member. In the same way, a teacher may assume a child has a two-parent traditional family. While teachers may think of race, color, nationality, ethnic origin, religion, age, ability, and gender as diversities, infant and toddler teachers uniquely interact with families that involve multiple structures. These include traditional, single-parent, blended, two parents of the same gender, grandparents raising grandchildren, extended, and unconventional families, such as multiple families that live together. Families may be experiencing complex cultural transitions, such as adjusting to immigration or geographical relocation. They may hold beliefs and values that are much different from the teacher and use practices different than the program.

Just as important is promoting full inclusion of children and families with disabilities, so that all encounter positive messages of pride, identity, belonging, and participation in a caring community (Wise Lindeman & McKendry Anderson, 2018). Inclusive, caring communities provide a compassionate, caring place for everyone to belong.

EXAMINING APPROACHES TO CARING

Ms. Ana tries to comfort 7-month-old Emmie. The child has been fussy for over 20 minutes, but Ms. Ana can't seem to soothe her. It is past the time Emmie's mother says she will normally fall asleep. Ms. Ana tries to walk and sing, but still, Emmie seems stressed. Finally, Ms. Ana places Emmie in the crib with her small stuffed bunny soother blanket. Emmie immediately stops crying. Within a minute, she is asleep. Ms. Ana says to her coteacher, Ms. Izzy, "I don't know why Emmie wouldn't fall asleep when she was so tired. I'm glad she likes her bunny."

These teachers routinely cuddle or sway with infants to calm them. They rock or pat the children's backs gently to assist with their transition to sleep. They don't realize that Emmie's family always lays her in the crib to fall asleep. They have done this since Emmie was born. Because Emmie is so tired, she wants to fall asleep, but the singing, swaying, and walking of her teacher stimulates instead of calms her.

Ways of responding to children's signals, verbal and nonverbal exchanges, physical closeness, and emotions are culturally determined (Farkas et al., 2017). Comforting approaches include how well adults understand children's nonverbal cues, whether they anticipate children's needs, how quickly they step in when children are distressed, styles of touching, ways of holding, strategies for coregulation, and expectations about self-soothing and independence. Teachers will need to develop sensitivity to each child to understand their ways of being and recognize the kind of support each one needs.

Ways of Comforting. Comforting responsiveness relates to the way adults respond to children's physical and emotional needs. It includes the length of time the adult waits before stepping in and the ways physical and emotional needs are met. When a teacher helps a child take deep breaths, talks about solutions to a problem, and assists the child in reengaging in a new activity, this is an example of co-regulation, which is essential for the development of self-soothing (Paley & Hajal, 2022). "By using their voice, movements, affects, gestures, and intonations, parents and primary caregivers can help infants and young children know that they are 'felt with' and 'attuned to'" (para. 6).

Level of Physical Contact. Close physical contact in non-Western cultures takes place between an infant and caregiver 79%–99% of each day, yet in Western cultures, infants may be in physical contact only 18% of the day (Bigelow & Rankin Williams, 2020). Where are infants when not being held? Often, they spend extended time in carriers, car seats, swings, high chairs, and cribs. Referred to as "container baby syndrome," extended time with limited movement can impact the development of rolling, sitting, and standing (Grisez, 2018). Close proximity with caregivers increases oxytocin and supports sensitive responding and nurturing, along with awareness of nonverbal cues, which boosts children's experience of safety (Yoshida & Funato, 2021). Important physical connections strengthen physical, emotional, and social development.

Support for Emotion Expression. The encouragement of emotion expression or emotional control and arousal is culturally specific (Denham et al., 2017; Lim, 2016). Culture influences the way adults identify and express feelings (Curtis et al., 2020). Infants are sensitive to cultural differences as early as 11 months, noticing body language, differentiating and attaching meaning to facial expressions, and internalizing rules and expectations for emotion expression (Liu, 2021). Culture determines whether adults use emotion talk and whether they encourage or minimize conversations about emotions (Denham et al., 2017). Infants learn by observing these subtle differences.

Verbal and Nonverbal Soothing. In Western cultures, adults use extensive verbal soothing, with eye contact, hugging, and kissing to demonstrate care. Family members will walk up and down to soothe a crying infant or distract a child through songs, objects, and games. In contrast, face-to-face verbal interaction and smiling are not typical practices in non-Western cultures (Lancy, 2015). While verbal soothing may be valued in Western cultures, caregivers are more likely wait until a child shows active signs of distress before intervening.

In non-Western cultures, caregivers are more highly attuned and anticipate physical and emotional needs before children become distressed. When physical contact is valued, verbal interaction and smiling are less frequent. When this is the case, teachers may interpret the family's lack of verbal soothing as a lack of emotional connection, when their physical responsiveness is actually a strong sign of emotional involvement.

To ensure children experience culturally sensitive teaching, you will continue to learn about each child and explore the unique cultural assets and values of families. Over time, you will become more aware of the specific contexts of each child and be able to apply these understandings in practical ways to ensure children's ongoing adjustment, comfort, and sense of security.

Research Revisited: Exploring Attachment From a Cross-Cultural Perspective

The foundational message of attachment theory is that early relationships create a working model for future relationship patterns (Cassidy et al., 2013). While it is generally agreed that infants need warmth and affection, the way attachment between infants and caregivers forms and the way caregivers communicate with and respond to children varies greatly (Strand, 2020). While cultural differences are present, families across all cultures show sensitivity in caring for children, even though expressed in different ways (Mesman et al., 2018).

Expression of affection and approaches to feeding, sleeping, and play depend on each family's context (Keller et al., 2018; Vu et al., 2020). Recognition and response to infants' signals, verbal and nonverbal exchanges, physical closeness, and sharing of emotions are culturally determined (Farkas et al., 2017). These variations depend on single or multiple child care arrangements, cultural goals, and other situational patterns (Lansford, 2022). Geographic setting and socioeconomic status greatly impact parent beliefs and practices, especially when families are focused on survival (Mesman et al., 2016).

Attachment goals also relate to the extent to which adults control children's experiences and respond to their initiations and needs. For example, American families tend to provide a safe setting and within that prepared space promote autonomy and individuality (Choi et al., 2021). American mothers "try to promote autonomy, assertiveness, verbal competence, and self-actualization in their young children, whereas traditional Japanese mothers try to promote emotional maturity, self-control, social courtesy, and interdependence in theirs" (Bornstein, 2015, p. 4). Japanese mothers encourage dependence in feeding and dressing. They promote close physical proximity, including co-sleeping and co-bathing, and direct an infant's gaze to reinforce dependence on the mother for feeding and dressing (Behrens & Umemura, 2020). Understanding and honoring differences can help teachers more accurately interpret children's initiations and responses, and more clearly understand attachment in context.

SETTING GOALS FOR SOCIALIZATION

Two-and-a-half-year-old Natalia stands quietly next to her mother while her 7-month-old sister is handed to Ms. Sophie in the infant room. While Ms. Lee, the girl's mother, is talking with Ms. Sophie, Natalia stands very still. She keeps one hand on her mother's leg and looks up. She seems to be listening quietly to her mother. When Ms. Lee turns to leave, she says goodbye to Ms. Sophie but doesn't address Natalia. Natalia leaves quietly behind her.

A few minutes later, when the Smith family comes to bring 5-month-old Leah to Ms. Sophie's room, 2½-year-old Esther runs over to the toys. She wiggles the white plastic cows on the shelf and makes them "moo." When it is time to leave, Esther shakes her head and protests. Ms. Smith lets her stay a few more minutes to play with the barn animals before leaving. Ms. Sophie wonders what Ms. Lee does differently to have Natalia be so compliant. But she also notices how interested Esther is in exploring and watching everyone. She thinks it is great that Esther shows initiative.

One of these girls is oriented almost entirely to her mother, but the other mother is oriented almost entirely toward her child. This interesting dynamic represents a difference in cultural childrearing practices. In some cultures, children take part in the daily activities of adult life, whereas, in other cultures, infant care takes place within separate boundaries (Keller, 2016). On one end of the spectrum, children are required to go along with the work patterns or life routines of adults. On the other end, adults follow children's needs and make them the central focus.

In non-Western cultures, the goals of socialization include interdependence, obedience, conformity, and respect for authority. Infants are held facing outward, helping them learn about others and about the wishes of others (Johnson et al., 2013; Keller, 2018). In Western cultures, families promote autonomy, self-reliance, and initiative with the goal of independence. Children are faced inward, helping them to learn about themselves.

Understanding and honoring cultural differences can help teachers evaluate children's behaviors without value judgment and adjust their own interactions to best promote learning and development.

UNDERSTANDING EXPECTATIONS FOR BEHAVIOR

During the family conference, Ms. Lopez lets 10-month-old Layla explore the buckles on her purse. Leyla sits happily on the floor and reaches in to pull out her mother's keys. Then she lifts out everything else: the makeup case, a comb, a small tube of lotion, sunglasses, and a business card case. Finally, she chews happily on the pacifier she finds tucked into a side picket. Ms. Ava, Leyla's teacher, offers a basket of rattles and small toys. "It's okay," Ms. Lopez comments. "Leyla likes to play with my things."

Ms. Ava feels a mobile toddler should play with children's toys, while Ms. Lopez doesn't restrict Leyla from exploring her personal items. As with most aspects of child care, Ms. Ava understands that ways of guiding and structuring boundaries may be different for the teacher than for the family. She sees that some families encourage free exploration or restrict the use of spaces where children play. She notices that some families follow the behaviors of the child, while others expect the child to fit in with the family's activities. Ms. Ava recognizes a range of differences as appropriate and enjoys observing the families with their children.

Early boundaries and expectations set the pattern for how adults will respond to children's behavior choices in the future. Families may expect children to be submissive to elders and conform to rules, while other families take a more democratic approach to behavior (Schröder et al., 2012). Whatever the approach, the important anchor for behavior guidance is *consistency*, as infants and toddlers internalize expectations by observing behaviors that are modeled and encouraged regularly over time.

Children's developing social skills are part of the intricate, complex interdependence of developmental skills, such as the role of physical, verbal, and cognitive development in emotion regulation. Teachers and families may hold unrealistic expectations about what infants and toddlers can handle and may not recognize the underlying capabilities and individual variations that are a natural part of early development. All infants and toddlers depend on individualized, assisted support (co-regulation) that includes encouragement and authentic caring that align with their unique ways of being. Behavior guidance is addressed in detail in Chapter 6.

From My Experience: *When children need support, I consider how they must feel away from their families and missing that connection. It makes me pause and spend time really seeing through their eyes.*

INVESTIGATING IDEAS ABOUT HEALTH AND WELLNESS

Ms. Narvaez brings a homemade container of calendula and chamomile balm for her 20-month-old daughter, Beatriz. She asks Beatriz's teacher, Ms. Jenn, to use it during diapering. Ms. Jenn is not sure if it is allowed or how to facilitate the conversation. She knows this cultural practice represents the mother's spiritual and emotional responsibility for her child.

Ms. Jenn reaches out to her licensing representative and learns that if the container is labeled with the child's name, date, and ingredients, it may be stored safely. Some guidelines state that medicines and ointments may only be used for a 90-day duration before needing to be replaced, with new written permission given. Other programs don't typically use ointments or lotions on a child's skin unless diaper rash is present and it is prescribed by a doctor. Without labeled ingredients and written permission, the program may be liable for a child's adverse reaction. These issues must be discussed locally with the program director and a licensing representative. With greater knowledge and understanding of cultural differences, program staff can expand their thinking about, acceptance of, and advocacy for a wider range of health and safety practices.

Ms. Jenn and the program staff partner with licensing and local health agencies to learn more about the medical beliefs and practices of the community.

They recognize that caring routines often require careful investigation and planning on the part of teachers (Yildiz et al., 2018). At times, they find they ignore a child's mild sniffle, only to discover that a family is upset that they are not notified. Sometimes, families downplay a child's illness, even when the teachers feel it may be significant. The teachers learn to ask families directly what physical symptoms are a concern and when the family wants to be notified.

Among many cultural and religious traditions, evil eye bracelets and azabache anklets are worn by infants for protection against disease, spirits, and the hostile intent of others. Religious traditions may include Karnavedha (ear piercing) and other jewelry that are believed to bring blessing or protection.

Superstitions related to health and safety are also prevalent. A family in an urban setting explained to their infant's teacher that when the baby is ill, they hold a frog in front of her mouth and nose. They believe the frog's breath removes the illness. Because the teachers understand the context of the family's community and culture, they listen with respect.

When culturally determined beliefs and practices are present, the most important value is for teachers to be active learners, listening and responding in ways that honor the family. Strategies for integrating family goals in caring routines are explored in depth in Chapter 4.

GUIDING PLAY

Fifteen-month-old Aiden joins the classroom at the beginning of the day. His mother, Charlotte, helps him with handwashing and then spends time with him before she leaves for work. She sits on the floor, places four balls on top of a ramp system, and hands Aiden the plastic hammer. Aiden pounds the balls vigorously to push them through the holes at the top of the ramps. The hammer flies out of his hand, and the balls pop off the ramp. Charlotte retrieves the hammer and ball and says, "Aiden, do it like this." She shows him how to push the ball through the hole and then guides his fingers to do the same. Aiden looks for the hammer but cannot see it tucked behind his mother's back.

Charlotte offers him a small basket. "Put the balls in the basket, Aiden, so they don't roll away after they go down the ramp." When Aiden sees the basket, he carefully takes each ball from the top of the ramp and places it inside the basket. He tucks the basket handle over his arm and marches away. "Aiden, the balls go on the ramp." Charlotte wants him to come back, but he is busy placing the balls into a toy dump truck.

Play provides opportunities for children to explore the world around them. How does the ball fit through the hole? What makes the ball go faster? How many balls can fit in the basket? Play helps infants and toddlers coordinate their fingers and bodies, find their balance, and test their strength. Play helps them integrate their previous understanding about how things work with new and interesting discoveries. Importantly, play allows children to test their initiative, make choices, and see how adults and other children respond.

While play seems like a typical childhood pastime, cultural values and beliefs are active and influential in the ways adults set goals for play and interact with children.

Charlotte might have encouraged Aiden to try again with the hammer. She might have joined him in putting the balls in the basket. But she had a strong sense that the balls should be used on the ramp. The level of control, support, and flexibility during play interactions depend on the adult's beliefs and values about the nature of the child's responsibility and the role of the parent (Faircloth & Murray, 2015).

Where autonomy is valued, children are more likely to be free to select activities, spaces, and ways of playing. In cultures where conformity is valued, adults are more likely to lead, using higher amounts of control, while interactions are still within the context of caring relationships (Lansford, 2022; Xiong et al., 2022).

Some teachers may feel more comfortable with adults leading and children following. For example, the teacher may feel there is one best way to play with stacking cups by demonstrating first and then showing the child how to do it. The teacher may rearrange the cups and tell the child how to do it. "The big red cup goes on the bottom. Put it here. Get the green cup. It goes on top. No, not that one. Get the big one. There it is. Good." This approach communicates a specific way toys and materials should be used.

Other teachers may believe children should take the lead, with adults taking a supportive role. For example, the child may be encouraged to experiment by playing with the cups in different ways, such as putting balls in and out of the cups, trying the cups on as hats, and making noises into the cups to experiment with sounds. The child may knock down stacked cups and laugh at the sound they make when they fall. This teacher may say to the child, "Oh, that made a big racket. A racket is a big noise. Let's do it again. Which cup goes on the bottom?" "What cup will you stack next?" This teacher's approach communicates permission to experiment and enjoy play.

At home, families may encourage children to take reasonable risks during active play, like climbing on a low ledge or testing skills on playground equipment. Children may use the slide going down head first at the park or in the backyard. Why does this matter? At the program, children may need guidance to sit and slide down feet first. A toddler who jumps on the furniture at home may need gentle guidance to sit on chairs and use furniture for designed purposes in the program. Use simple words to explain that children are allowed to do things differently at home, but here, to be safe, the rules are to go down the slide feet first and to sit when in chairs. Without considering the full picture, a teacher may attribute the children's actions to challenging behavior rather than to the need to differentiate expectations with assistance in the program.

In contrast, children whose activities are highly structured at home may be unsure how to explore independently in a child-centered classroom. A teacher may assume children know how to join in. They may misunderstand a child's reserve and fail to recognize the need to provide support for a child who does not engage. Understanding these differences can help you become more sensitive and responsive to the behaviors you observe.

Cultural beliefs also impact family expectations. Families may anticipate a more formal program setting and feel concern when they observe their toddler engaging in active play-based activities. They may hold strong views about cleanliness and feel upset when their child gets dirty outdoors or has residue from an art project on clothing. Understanding these perspectives can help you respond sensitively—and be consistent in offering smocks for art activities or coveralls for outdoor play.

Taking stock of your own personal beliefs about children's play can guide self-reflection. During child-centered play, teachers used to more adult direction may need to practice asking open-ended questions, giving children freedom to experiment, and encouraging exploration. Rather than consider one way as "better" or "right," the goal is to develop a more complex understanding about the dynamics present and respond appropriately to plan for, support, and communicate about play.

Strategy Toolbox: Incorporating Cultural and Linguistic Diversity

When you observe infants playing, what should you see? When you listen to teachers interacting with toddlers during play, what should you hear? Offering diverse materials in the classroom, such as books and displays, is an important first step. Children need to recognize themselves in the images and materials they enjoy. The following action steps offer additional tips for observing, listening to, and learning about children as you help them take pride in their families and themselves.

- Make connections to families. "You have beautiful curls, just like your momma." "You like to dance, just like your daddy." "You like to laugh, just like your grandmother." Ask questions that connect picture books to children's lives. "Do you go for a walk with your momma?" "Do you go to the zoo with your brother?"
- Greet children in their home language, and use familiar names for family members. "Buenos dias, Ana y Tia Sofia. Bienvenidas a dia feliz en nuestro salón de clases." (Good morning, Anna and Aunt Sofia. Welcome to a happy day in our classroom.)
- Sing lullabies/songs and do finger plays children enjoy at home. See Chapter 2 for strategies to engage families in reading, singing, and playing games.
- Select books with pictures and stories that reflect home activities children enjoy.

- Display photos and images that represent children's community activities.
- Laminate photos of families and display at children's eye level or provide them in a soft basket for exploration.
- Use familiar words in home languages for self-care, like diaper, ointment, and bottle.
- Talk personally with children about family members, pets, and home life. With preverbal infants, narrate your own actions and talk about how the child does the activity at home.
- Ask toddlers where they go with their families, how they help families at home, and what they enjoy playing with their families.
- Use mealtimes to connect with children personally, remaining attuned to their verbal and nonverbal cues. What foods do they enjoy? What delights them and makes them laugh? Talk about their daily events and experiences.

EMBRACING ABILITIES AS STRENGTHS

Anna, at 2½ years old, asks for milk at snack time: "Oooo." Ms. Judith responds, "Yes, milk." She uses sign language for milk, and Anna signs back. After snack time, Ms. Judith helps some of the children put on hats, and they laugh at themselves in the mirror.

Ms. Brenda takes Anna's hand gently and asks if she wants to snuggle. Henry joins them in the cozy corner. It is located in a quiet area of the room, with pillows, soft toys, and a low sofa. Ms. Brenda offers Henry and Anna their "stuffies"—favorite stuffed animals. She gives Anna a pacifier and Henry a blanket. Ms. Judith turns on a playlist of soft, classical lullabies. She offers quiet activities, including books and play dough to the other children, while Ms. Brenda prepares Henry and Anna for a nap.

Anna fits in with the other children. They don't notice the gentle adaptations the teachers make to support her sensory needs. They don't realize that Anna becomes overwhelmed by stimuli, such as noise and transitions. Twice a week, Anna works with an occupational therapist and a speech therapist due to developmental and speech delays. These are part of her individualized family service plan (IFSP), where family members, teachers, and therapists work together to help Anna thrive. The occupational therapist suggests ways to calm, comfort, and reorient her attention toward experiences that feel safe to her. The teachers ask questions like, "How does your body feel? What does your body need?" "What do your hands feel like playing with now?" They support Anna's choices about play materials, clothing, and activities. Directions are simple, with advanced notice and predictable routines and schedules. This approach helps her develop awareness of her body and confidence in her ability to make positive, self-guided choices.

Ms. Brenda keeps instructions simple and affirms Anna's sensory needs, like attachment to a pacifier. The teachers ensure Anna feels comfortable and competent. These approaches are highly effective for all toddlers, but they are uniquely designed for Anna. Ms. Brenda and Ms. Judith attended meetings with specialists to understand the specific ways they can support her. They work closely with Anna's family to discuss her progress and daily activities.

OVERCOMING PRACTICAL CHALLENGES: STAYING CURRENT WITH CHILDREN'S EMERGING SKILLS

The children you teach are at different stages of development, even when they are the same age. All teaching for infants and toddlers requires individualized curriculum, with coordinated support between families and teachers. What approaches incorporate individual goals?

- **Prepare materials to offer a range of challenges.** For example, provide chunky puzzles with a few pieces and simple shapes, along with peg and knob choices and those with more challenge. Offer simple colors and high-contrast images, along with more complex pictures. Consider the skills required and support needed for successful engagement.
- **Talk with individual children.** Rather than focusing exclusively on giving instructions or describing an activity to the group, focus on personal conversations.
- **Personalize support for each child.** Adjust your approaches. For example, with one child, model how to fit a block into a shape sorter and then ask the child to try. With another child, you may offer a greater level of support by doing it together. "Help me push the block into the square hole," and then guide the child's hand.
- **Keep track of children's progress.** Write up-to-date notes that describe children's communication, activities, and emerging skills. Use this information for planning and ongoing conversation with families. See Chapter 3 to learn more about individualizing teaching.

Strategy Toolbox: Teaching With Individual Goals

Children from diverse backgrounds communicate and show their competence in many ways. Teachers have an ethical responsibility to recognize individual variation for infants and toddlers who are typically developing and for those with intellectual or developmental disabilities or delays. Use strategies that protect children's developing sense of self and safeguard their well-being. Daily interactions are designed to encourage and support children where they are and where they are headed. Try the following strategies:

- **Focus on safety, security, and belonging.** While supporting skill development, keep the big picture in mind. How can you help this child feel loved, supported, and secure?
- **Use strengths-based communication.** Monitor your language to eliminate deficit-based thinking, expectations, and messages. For example, replace the words "weaknesses" and "challenges" with "areas for support" and "areas of opportunity."
- **Identify areas of competence.** What are this child's interests and pleasures? How can you incorporate these in ways that encourage new skills? Keep track of activities the child enjoys and positive interactions with others.
- **Individualize support for activities.** Modifications adjust individual learning goals, while accommodations adjust the way learning is supported (McGlynn & Kelly, 2019). For example, a learning goal for Anna is to engage successfully three times a week with art materials. Accommodations include taping down paper so it doesn't slip when coloring and adding art tools with larger sizes and easier grips.
- **Make decisions with input from families.** Seek family perspectives about what is happening at home and their priorities for children's skills in the program. Families are your best thought and planning partners.

SUPPORTING DEVELOPMENT WITH AN INDIVIDUALIZED FAMILY SERVICE PLAN (IFSP)

Ms. Ginny coos in response to 9-month-old Jasmine, rubs her tummy, and smiles. "How's my sweet girl today?" She pulls a soft scarf gently back and forth, letting it brush Jasmine's arms. As she places it in Jasmine's hand, she says, "The scarf is soft. Does that feel nice?" Jasmine brings the scarf to her mouth. Ms. Ginny helps Jasmine sit up, supporting her back and tummy. "Look at you, sitting up. You are getting so big!" When Jasmine drops the scarf, Ms. Ginny offers a soft teether, which Jasmine sucks happily.

Jasmine has Down syndrome and participates in the infant classroom. Ms. Ginny enjoys supporting Jasmine's physical development. Jasmine doesn't yet push up with her arms, but with the assistance of a soft bolster enjoys "Pat-a-Cake" over and over. Ms. Ginny assists Jasmine in rolling gently from side to side and sings "Row, Row, Row Your Boat" in time to the gentle motion. Ms. Ginny provides soft books and toys that can be easily grasped and will land gently when dropped. For oral stimulation, Jasmine is offered a variety of teethers and rattles to grasp and chew.

Ms. Ginny keeps a record of communication with Jasmine's mother. Jasmine is given breast milk in a bottle and takes feedings in small amounts. Ms. Ginny and Jasmine's family exchange a daily sheet to track Jasmine's schedule, including details about feeding, napping, routines, and activities.

In addition to collaborating with Jasmine's teachers, the family works with the local children's hospital to coordinate a schedule of screenings, therapies, and evaluations. Jasmine's mother picks her up twice a month to take her to physical therapy, speech and language therapy, and occupational therapy. These services build on her strengths and provide additional support for weaker areas of development. Jasmine's mother, Ms. Ginny, and the social worker meet monthly to coordinate an individualized family service plan (IFSP) to ensure Jasmine has all the supports she needs while in the program.

Working with infants and toddlers with disabilities calls for specific training when cognitive, physical, or communicative disorders require adaptations and supports during caring routines. This is where families can be guides, showing what and how routines need to be carried out, demonstrating equipment, timing, and other modifications that make experiences feel safe, comfortable, and positive for children. All work together to overcome barriers, including support staff, specialists, program leaders, teachers, and families.

Early childhood programs must make reasonable modifications to integrate children with developmental delays and disabilities. Early intervention provides funding and reimbursement for nursing and medical services, certain therapies, and family education, but it does not cover the direct costs of child care. Infants and toddlers with disabilities are protected by the Individuals with Disabilities Education Act (IDEA), the Americans with Disabilities Act (ADA), and Section 504 of the Rehabilitation Act. ADA ensures that child care programs cannot exclude children with disabilities unless there would be a direct threat to the health or safety of others or a fundamental alteration of the program. For guidance and resources, see ADA.gov: https://www.ada.gov/resources/child-care-centers/

Infants and toddlers with disabilities and their families receive early intervention services under the Individuals with Disabilities Education Act (IDEA) Part C. IDEA Part C provides assistance for children with disabilities or significant delays in development, including early intervention services. When Part C services begin, an IFSP is created to address the specific services needed for infants and toddlers with developmental delays or disabilities. A team that includes the family, the early childhood teacher, a disability services coordinator, and specialists, such as a social worker or therapist, and medical personnel work together to ensure each child is consistently provided optimal opportunities for learning and development.

The purpose of the IFSP is to provide comprehensive support for the family and child together and to ensure coordination of care and learning. The IFSP summarizes the child's development based on evaluations, data, and input from the family. It describes focus skills and goals and outlines the services that will be provided, along with a transition plan for future transfer to public school (Centers for Disease Control, 2024b).

Children should be included to the maximum degree possible in the daily routines, activities, spaces, materials, and interactions of daily events. They should feel as though they are an important and cherished part of the classroom community, included and engaged just like every child. Children with physical disabilities should find adaptive spaces to participate with others in the classroom and on the playground.

The most important focus of the IFSP is the child. What schedule works best with their active play and rest cycles? What skills do they have that can be strengthened? What relationships and activities do they enjoy most? What activities are tailored to their interests that strengthen developmental skills? What strengths and unique traits are encouraged?

Once children are 3 years old and through the age of 21, they receive special education and related services under IDEA Part B (U.S. Department of Education, 2024). As they participate in public education, an individualized education plan (IEP) is developed to ensure the least restrictive environment, related services and modifications, and open channels of communication, including regular meetings with the family and IEP team. In this way, each child receives comprehensive services with the full engagement of families in decision-making, leading to inclusive practices and positive social, learning, and developmental outcomes.

CULTURALLY APPROPRIATE SCREENING

A hallmark of the infant and toddler years is the range of variation in individual development. Very young children are influenced by cultural practices and social contexts, by the day-to-day priorities and schedules of adults, by health factors, and by the stability of schedules, routines, and caregivers. For this reason, many disabilities or delays in development can remain hidden without early screening and family and teacher awareness.

While inclusive practices can meet individual developmental and learning needs for infants and toddlers, only 34.2% of children overall and 28.5% of children from low-income families are screened (Cole et al., 2023). Critically, the percentage of infants and toddlers with disabilities from birth to 2 years old who received early intervention services under IDEA Part C during 2021 was only 6.8%. Only 11% of children with access to Early Head Start were screened (Zero to Three, 2022). Screening is the important first step to identify the need for additional evaluation and services.

When you work with children from a different culture, ethnicity, or language than your own, you may need assistance from a cultural broker. A cultural broker is a person who shares the language and culture of families and ensures a bridge between program and family communication (Massing et al., 2016). A cultural or linguistic broker is a "conduit—moving between the family and program to bring knowledge and understanding of cultural practices from one to the other" (7). This person provides ongoing resources and participates in meetings with families to facilitate two-way understanding. Cultural and linguistic brokers should have a history of experience with the specific cultural groups or tribal backgrounds of the families, including communities of color and immigrants and/or refugees. They have understanding of culturally appropriate assessments, services, and programs. Cultural brokers may be identified through the local school district and through local social service and community agencies that are partnering with the early education program.

What are some first steps? Review your program policies to include the schedule for screenings and a description of screening types (language, vision, cognitive, social, fine and gross motor skills, and language/speech development). Describe clear procedures for securing a cultural or linguistic broker who shares families' home language and cultures. Communicate that all families receive screening results, along with information about additional resources and services. Work with a cultural broker to review the screening tools and family questionnaires to ensure these fit with the families' cultural practices. Ensure the cultural broker attends all family meetings to answer questions and to advocate on behalf of the family.

Unfortunately, lack of cultural knowledge and understanding about the implications of screening processes can result in over-referral or overrepresentation of children from diverse backgrounds. Lack of awareness perpetrates bias related to school readiness, leads to ongoing trauma for families, and promotes deficit-based teaching (Cronk, 2023). For these reasons, teachers must learn about and advocate for inclusive and equitable practices for every child.

Q&As FROM THE FIELD: ALIGNING PRACTICES

Question 1: A family asked me to carry out sleeping routines without talking to the child. This is so contrary to the way I interact with the other children. I rock them, pat their backs, and assist them with the transition from being awake to sleeping. It doesn't feel right to me to ignore a child. How can I adjust my emotional response when I want to rock a child to sleep but the family asks me to lay her down without support?

Answer: Remember that the goal is to create cultural coherence—consistency—between the home and the program setting. It will help to learn more about the family and ask them to show you how they place their daughter in the crib. You may find that they actually do use subtle ways of comforting and have a very specific routine. You will likely find that the child responds well to the procedure the family models for you.

In Chapter 2, you will discover questions to guide your conversations with families. Once you invite input, you may find other families also use sleeping routines that vary. As long as safety guidelines are followed, embracing family differences can be a remarkable learning experience as you discover a range of procedures that feel comforting to each child.

Question 2: How do I get my coworkers onboard with culturally responsive practices? My program wants me to do everything the same with all children. I wish I had a study or growth group in my program. I have heard those are called a community of practice.

Answer: The best approach is to start by talking informally with your colleagues about what you are learning. Begin by focusing on topics you all agree on, such as safety and supervision, creating a predictable schedule, and communicating with families about program requirements. Then take a big-picture approach that is inviting and interesting, such as asking how others think the program can be more welcoming and inclusive for every family. Share some ideas you are trying in your classroom, and ask what others have been doing. Talk about a challenge you experience, and ask for input. You may find others also want to meet regularly to share common experiences and grow professionally in a community of practice. You can also share resources that address specific topics for infants and toddler teaching from the National Association for the Education of Young Children (NAEYC) and Zero to Three websites. Chapter 8 provides more information to guide your professional growth.

FOR YOUR INFORMATION: SERVING CHILDREN WITH DISABILITIES

The following resources can help you learn more about early screening, early intervention, and resources for teachers and families:

- Toolkit for Working with Culturally and Linguistically Diverse Children: https://agesandstages.com/wp-content/uploads/2021/04/cultural-diversity-toolkit.pdf

- The Decision Tree—Child Indicator Seeds for Success: https://www.veipd.org/main/pdf/decisiontree/cultural_diversity_developmental_screening_tools_young_children_june_2016_decision_tree.pdf
- Cross-Cultural Lessons: Early Childhood Developmental Screening and Approaches to Research and Practice: https://www.ualberta.ca/community-university-partnership/media-library/community-university-partnership/resources/publications/crossculturalhandbook.pdf
- Ages and Stages Questionnaire (ASQ), Tips for Screening Children from Diverse Cultures: https://agesandstages.com/
- Overview of Early Intervention: https://www.parentcenterhub.org/ei-overview/
- The Administration for Children and Families Office of Child Care (ACF-OCC) State and Territory Resources: https://childcare.gov/state-resources-home
- The Council for Exceptional Children, Division for Early Childhood (DEC) Recommended Practices: https://www.dec-sped.org/dec-recommended-practices
- The American Speech-Language-Hearing Association (ASHA): https://www.asha.org/public/speech/development/01/
- Centers for Disease Control Developmental Milestone Resources for Early Childhood Educators: https://www.cdc.gov/ncbddd/actearly/Information-for-Early-Childhood-Educators.html

The following resources will guide your exploration of state and federal guidelines and resources for children with disabilities and their families.

- The Child Welfare Information Gateway provides a comprehensive list of state and national organizations that support children with disabilities: https://www.childwelfare.gov/organizations/
- IDEA (Individuals with Disabilities Education Act) explains legal rights: https://sites.ed.gov/idea/about-idea/
- IDEA Infant and Toddler Coordination Association provides state resources: https://www.ideainfanttoddler.org/state-contacts.php
- The National Down Syndrome Society offers helpful information: https://ndss.org/resources/early-intervention
- Head Start provides tips for the Individualized Family Service Plan: https://headstart.gov/publication/individualized-family-service-plans-ifsps-tips
- PACER Center provides information about resources and services: https://www.pacer.org/ec/early-intervention
- The Devereau Center for Resilience Children offers information for working with infants and toddlers: https://centerforresilientchildren.org/infants/about-resilience/

- The Office of Disability Rights (2022) explains people first language: https://odr.dc.gov/page/people-first-language

REFLECTION QUESTIONS

Consider your personal views and teaching experiences as you think about the impact of cultural assets and strengths.

1. What were the key messages you received growing up about your own culture? What values and practices were important?
2. How did your cultural background impact your sense of belonging in your family, school, and community?
3. How are perceptions and expectations of children and families impacted by previous cultural experiences?
4. What cultural practices or family requests have you observed, and how have you responded?

CHAPTER 2

Building Trust Through Meaningful Communication With Families

This chapter shows how family engagement can energize and inform teaching and create a caring and vital learning community. It presents stories that show how teachers become aware of their own contexts to avoid bias that can harm, rather than support, family engagement and children's learning. It explores the visible and invisible barriers to inclusive participation and presents strategies to overcome communication challenges and connect with families' priorities and goals.

Learning Goal 1: Understand the dynamic nature of family engagement and the role of the teacher as active agent in facilitating reciprocal communication and trust.
Learning Goal 2: Recognize the visible and invisible forms of family engagement and explore strategies to incorporate family goals and priorities, cultures, languages, and experiences to nurture the strengths of children.
Learning Goal 3: Provide cultural safety through strengths-based strategies that embrace the life values, knowledge, and social contexts of families as essential to creating settings, materials, activities, and interactions that foster security, belonging, self-identity, and continuity for each child.

LISTENING TO FAMILY VOICES

Naila recently enrolled her 7-month-old infant daughter, Sarah, in the neighborhood child care program. During a morning family coffee connection event, Naila talks with other families.

> I never let my babies cry at home. I make sure everything they need is taken care of and anticipate their needs. One day, I accidently kept my daughter Sarah's blanket with me on the way to work. So, I returned to the program. I found Sarah

> was crying—but no one was helping her. I wanted to say, "Feed her this way, don't give her this, give her that." But I didn't say anything. I just gave them the blanket and left.

The others listen intently. Kim responds,

> I know how you feel. All our children slept with me at home. We never did get a crib for Charisa. Co-sleeping is how we were raised. When they had to go to child care, I remember thinking I didn't want them to be mistreated. But I never thought about how they would have to sleep in a crib—alone and in a completely new way. So, when they told me Charisa was crying at naptime, I didn't know what to say.

Alyssa shares,

> Before I returned to work after my second child, Liam, I visited the classrooms. I stayed several mornings to show the infant teachers the way we use cloth diapers and prepare breast milk, and how my daughter, Karalee, goes to sleep. In the toddler classroom, I wanted them to help my 2-year-old son learn to hold a cup, since we do that for him at home. I did not want them to make him use utensils for certain foods, since he uses his fingers at home. The mornings I stayed in the classrooms allowed me to go back to work without fear.

The mothers who shared these stories identify as Hispanic, African American, and Pakistani. Two of them were unable to explain what they wanted to their children's teachers and remained worried. The third was direct about what her children needed. Yet all three experiences reflect an important responsibility for teachers. Frequently, families do not speak up when they have a concern. They don't want to upset the person who will be caring for their child. They also may not be sure how to explain what they need.

These examples illustrate the hidden dynamics that exist in programs that are often overlooked. The situations may be considered from two perspectives—that of the family and that of the teachers. On the morning Alyssa returned with the blanket for Karalee, the teachers were distracted by a sick child and were contacting the family to come and get him. The teachers had tried every way they could to comfort Karalee but were unaware of the sleeping practices used at home. They didn't think the parent was withholding information and didn't realize she may be embarrassed to explain that her child had never slept in a crib.

Alyssa was determined to ask for what her son Liam needed. As a result, the teachers had to adjust and learn new ways to support the children. They had to be flexible and welcoming to allow the family to visit the classroom. They had to take time to listen, watch, and ask questions about how to feed the children. These examples illustrate the critical need for teachers to invite families to share their stories. Teachers must take the initiative to explore hidden dynamics and really listen to family voices.

Teachers establish authentic relationships with families for the purpose of sharing information and making decisions (NAEYC, 2020). "Also essential is deep knowledge of each child, based on what the teacher has learned from close observation and from the family about the individual child's interests, skills, and abilities and about practices of importance to the family" (3). The NAEYC Position Statement on Developmentally Appropriate Practice (2020) requires that educators take responsibility for establishing trusting relationships, making sure that the timing and ways of communicating work for each family. Teachers honor all the ways families contribute and include family ideas, values, and goals as they design learning experiences for each child. They seek to understand and build on family cultures, languages, and contexts as strengths and assets that are valued and integrated in decision-making (Reyes et al., 2016).

REMOVING BARRIERS TO FAMILY ENGAGEMENT

Mirna hugs her 2-year-old daughter, Nika, as she comes through the kitchen door. "Thank you for bringing her home, Alex." Mirna's brother, Alex, brings Nika to and from their cousin's child care. He responds, "Ms. Emmy said Nika played with baby dolls today." To Nika, he says, "Adijo, Nika. Do Sutra." Mirna likes that Alex tells Nika "Goodbye until tomorrow" in Croatian.

Mirna helps Nika wash her hands and climb up on the stool at the kitchen counter. Mirna cuts potatoes into cubes. Nika picks up the pieces with her fingers and drops them into a pot of cold water. She leans over the pot to watch the cubes sink. Mirna says, "Baka will stay for dinner. She will read to you before bed." After dinner, Nika's grandmother gives Nika a bath and tucks her in. They read Lijepo sanjaj, zlato moje (Sweet Dreams, My Love) *by Shelley Admont. Mirna helps Nika's brother with homework and then comes to say goodnight to Nika.*

Nika's teacher, Ms. Emmy, learns about the close relationships in this extended bilingual family by visiting the home. While Mirna does not come to the program or attend meetings or events, Ms. Emmy stays in regular contact. She shares pictures, notes, and videos that show what Nika is learning and doing. She asks questions about activities Nika enjoys at home. Ms. Emmy understands the many ways this family provides a rich context for Nika's growth and development.

Family engagement focuses on the visible and invisible ways that families participate with programs to support children's development and learning (McWayne et al., 2018). This includes all interactions between early childhood programs and their families. It involves family participation at home, at school, and in the community. This mindset is anchored in a strengths-based philosophy that values cultural and linguistic differences.

Traditional family engagement requires that families come to the program. Activities are visible when families visit the program, meet with teachers, and participate in classroom activities. They drop off and pick up children, participate in conferences, and attend program events. Teachers may assume families care or are invested only when they are able to be present in person.

Nontraditional forms of engagement include the way families help children learn at home. The participation is invisible when they instill values, reinforce respect for teachers, and include children in family and community activities (Coba-Rodriguez et al., 2020). Nika's teachers understand how important the family's role is in strengthening Nika's self-identity, love of learning, language development, and social skills. The program staff know about, recognize, and give value to visible *and* invisible family contributions.

Biased perceptions and views about families begin in early childhood programs during the infant and toddler years. Yet researchers find that bias is less likely to be recognized in early childhood programs than in other settings. This is known as the "bias blind spot," where teachers may recognize bias in others (and other places) but not in themselves (Blackson et al., 2022). In fact, bias infiltrates the work of early childhood programs in a unique way because ways of caring for children, beliefs about teaching, staff communication, perceptions of families, and expectations are linked to culturally determined beliefs. Often, teachers do not recognize that the norms of the program are hidden from families. Families may not speak up due to embarrassment about differences, fear of retaliation, or simply not knowing how to explain differences.

Biases include unspoken assumptions about the causes of children's behavior, developmental progress, or academic capability. Assumptions can be very subtle, and teachers may not recognize them immediately. This is why active reflection is so important. For example, teachers may assume a family from a specific culture cannot speak English or is uneducated. They may judge families as uncaring when they do not attend program events. They may assume a well-dressed child comes from a "better home" than a poorly dressed child. They may feel more appreciative of families whose ways of caring for a child are like their own. Just as importantly, teachers may not have developed a sensitive ear to bias or notice disparaging comments or stereotypical depictions in conversations of the program. They must actively pursue hidden beliefs, values, and practices and observe, listen to, and learn from families. The following dynamics are often invisible or present barriers to participation.

- Families whose values, beliefs, or behaviors do not fit with expectations and norms may be left out of engagement essential to children's successful adjustment, development, and learning (Hoffman et al., 2020).
- Families of children with disabilities may encounter language and communication barriers (Rossetti et al., 2020).

- Families who do not speak English as a first language may be unfamiliar with priorities of the classroom, may be hesitant to ask questions, and may be prevented from engagement by economic barriers (Andrade-Guirguis & Plotka, 2019).
- Some families believe it is their responsibility to be involved in education, whereas others think it is the teacher or caregiver's sole authority to instruct children (Calzada et al., 2015). These differences may cause the teacher to misinterpret family commitment.
- Child care that is offered only during typical work hours is less likely to be inclusive for Black, Hispanic, and low-income workers, who are more likely to work during nontraditional hours (Hector Bruder, 2022).
- A hidden power differential exists when teachers have information about children and care for them daily, which places the family in the position of "outsider" unless teachers overcome the imbalance (Einarsdottir & Jónsdóttir 2019; Miller, 2018).
- Teachers may lack knowledge about the linguistic contexts families have or hold deficit beliefs and assumptions about language development and linguistic diversity (Choi et al., 2021; Zheng et al., 2021).
- Communication styles and language differences may cause family concerns to remain hidden (Andrade-Guirguis & Plotka, 2019). Families may see teachers as authority figures or feel it is disrespectful to speak up.
- A color-blind approach removes open and purposeful conversations about race, ethnicity, and diversity, so that "the silence surrounding the topic[s]" leave children and their families without opportunity to discuss critical issues that impact program participation (Vittrup, 2016, p. 38).
- Lack of understanding about the experiences of immigrant families leads to misdiagnosis to special education and low expectations for children, pointing out a critical need for training of early childhood teachers (Keys Adair, 2019).
- Lack of access to high-quality, affordable infant and toddler care situates families from underresourced communities with few options for programs that offer vital services to promote health, safety, and high-quality learning (Jessen-Howard et al., 2020).
- Visible barriers to participation include lack of transportation, parking limitations, lack of access outside of work hours, and the difficulty of eligibility and enrollment processes (Greenberg et al., 2016).
- Nontraditional barriers to engagement include family health, major or toxic stress experienced by the family or community, and trauma. Teachers must also be sure families have the knowledge they need to navigate the program (WIDA, 2022).

If not actively explored, barriers may remain hidden, resulting in family exclusion. Issues must be explicitly overcome, leading to humility, trust, and authentic dialog with colleagues, families, and children. As you reflect on your program, consider the practices, norms, and barriers that may remain hidden or unexamined. Seek new opportunities for growth that fit with the unique context of your program. Work together with families to create positive change.

Research Revisited: Removing Bias in Infant and Toddler Teaching

Researchers have documented critical areas of bias that impact interactions with young children. Are the following areas surprising to you, or have you observed these mindsets?

- Thinking children should obey and perceiving those who are not compliant as difficult or less intelligent (Clegg et al., 2017). Similarly, treating compliant children as more intelligent than those who are active or nonconforming (Wen et al., 2019).
- Believing Black boys are more responsible for their behavior than white children and assuming signs of misbehavior, even before anything happens (NASP, 2017).
- Suspending Black students at twice the rate of white students (Harper et al., 2019).
- Underrepresenting African American, Hispanic American, and Native American students by at least 50% in gifted programs (National Association for Gifted Children, 2024).
- Subjecting young children from ethnically and racially diverse backgrounds to higher rates of punitive discipline and expulsion, leading to lowered cognitive performance in elementary school (Sabol et al., 2021; Skiba, 2013).
- Identifying Black students as having disabilities 40% more often and American Indian students as 70% more often than their peers (Gopalan, 2019; Harper, 2017).
- Assuming people with disabilities are not as capable as others (Dunn, 2021).
- Lowering teacher expectations, support, and expectations about child achievement for children of color (Kim & Calzada, 2019; Wright & Counsell, 2018).

Bias may not be intentional, but it is an automatic, stereotypical response or association made about an individual or group of individuals that can affect teachers' understanding, actions, or decisions (Staats, 2016). Bias may imply that one's own way of thinking has more value than that of others. It may demonstrate lack of knowledge and respect for others' experiences.

Explicit bias reflects attitudes or beliefs people hold at a conscious level (NASP, 2017). Explicit bias results in judgments about a family's educational level based on their language, accent, or physical attributes. For example, a teacher judges the way a child is dressed and comments negatively about the family to a program director. A teacher thinks a parent should "get their child in line" when a child is misbehaving, and complains to a coteacher that the family doesn't use the guidance strategies the program provided.

Implicit bias includes subtle and often unrecognized stereotypes and ideas that unintentionally or unconsciously influence expectations and interactions with children and families. For example, a teacher may assume all people from a specific culture look alike. They may make conversation more frequently during drop-off and pickup with families who share their own background, unaware they are selectively giving positive attention. They may not recognize the bias, may ignore it, or may not speak up to correct it.

ENSURING CULTURAL SAFETY

Mario's family has just moved to the city to live with relatives. They have come from Puerto Rico after a hurricane. Mario's Aunt Camila works at Sunshine School and brings 2-year-old Mario with her. Mario is crying a lot, and his teacher, Ms. Anahi, seeks his aunt's advice. She explains that Mario should be exploring all the toys and play areas, but he sits quietly and doesn't interact.

Camila suggests lap reading when Mario first comes in, along with a cuddle blanket and Mario's teddy bear, before introducing other toys or activities. As a result, Ms. Anahi reads Besos for Baby: A Little Book of Kisses *and* Te Quiero com Eres: I Love the Way You Are *each morning after greeting Mario. She sees that Mario begins to come to her to read. After several days, he begins to explore other books and toys and imitate the other children's play. Ms. Anahi invites Mario's family to visit and schedules private time with them. She wants to hear about their experiences in Puerto Rico and learn more about Mario.*

An important goal for infants and toddlers is to experience cultural safety. Cultural safety is the "acknowledgement of and attendance to a child's needs and cultural frames of reference, even if they are not fully understood" (Fulcher, 2002). This strengths-based approach embraces the life values, knowledge, and social networks of families. It honors the personal stories of families through authentic engagement and deep listening.

Teachers who foster cultural safety approach families with an attitude of curiosity, empathy, and respect—essential for honoring multiple diversities

(Richardson & Romano, 2014). In this way, providing cultural safety is the foundation for effective teaching. Teachers can support each child's relationship with their family and promote families' relationships with each other (Johnson & Peterson, 2019). Teachers become informed and sensitive interpreters of children's communication and interactions with the setting, with other children, and with adults.

The following practices promote cultural safety.

Ask for feedback. Seek feedback from families and staff about the program handbook and policies with the goal of removing barriers to participation. Gather feedback in person, through small group discussions, and through the use of formal and informal surveys.

Make cultural safety visible. Place your program's commitment to cultural safety in the program mission statement and family handbook. Let families know that yours is a welcoming program, and you will help children celebrate and learn about differences.

Present consistent and respectful messages. Honor and take pride in children's diversities during conversations.

- "All children are welcome here."
- "It's okay to be different."
- "Our program is a welcoming place for all staff, families, and children."
- "We are an inclusive and caring program and embrace all diversities and abilities."

Explore bias with colleagues. Hold regular, safe conversations to talk about teaching experiences. Place intercultural learning and opportunities for shared reflection on meeting agendas.

Speak up. Say something when you hear an undermining comment made by staff, families, or others that conveys judgment or reflects stereotypical thinking. Respond by saying,

- "We have an inclusive and equitable program that ensures respect for all diversities."
- "We use affirming words and messages in our program."
- "We use person-first language in our program to refer to children with disabilities."

Reframe problems as opportunities to learn. Ask questions to learn more. "What would you like me to know?" "How can I support you or your child?"

Monitor your own concerns. When you wonder if families have a concern, schedule a conversation. "Let's talk about what's going on." Seek to make visible issues that may be hidden from view. The more you know, the more you can influence outcomes and meet real needs.

Take time to think and reflect. Explore your own cultural beliefs and practices, including biased perceptions and stereotypical views. Ask for feedback from colleagues about your interactions with others: "What do you think? How did I come across?" "Was I really listening and hearing what families were saying? Did I miss anything?" You may want to try journaling or meeting regularly with colleagues. Reflection requires openness to new insights and willingness to take action.

Be an advocate. Participate in your state or local early childhood system. Seek to promote cultural coherence and learning.

Through these actions, you will develop deep relationships of caring with families as you support children's well-being. By learning about and responding to these complex issues, your program will be a place of healing and support—a place of cultural safety.

DEVELOPING CULTURAL HUMILITY

Ms. Velasco drops 19-month-old Nathalie off at the program. She has three other children in tow. Ms. Ruby greets them. Ms. Velasco looks worried and says, "I'm sorry we are late. I had to wait for the director to submit papers." Ms. Ruby reassures her. "Please don't worry. We can talk for a few minutes later today when you pick up Nathalie."

When Ms. Velasco returns later in the day, she is alone. Ms. Ruby tells her, "I'm glad to see you. Nathalie is a delight. She played with the puppets and enjoyed dancing. She took a long nap." A smile of relief shows on Ms. Velasco's face. Ms. Ruby invites her in. "We can sit here while Nathalie plays. Won't you tell me about yourself?" Ms. Velasco explains, "We lost our home when my husband passed away after a long illness. We live with my mother—where my other children are this afternoon." As Ms. Velasco shares her story, Ms. Ruby wants to know more. "Tell me more about Nathalie. How has she adjusted to the new setting and routines?"

As Ms. Ruby listens, she realizes she has much to learn about the ways families show courage, determination, and love to their children during difficult times of challenge and change. She realizes the family is well educated and learns that Nathalie's father was a musician. She knows she can help Nathalie and her family develop a sense of connection and belonging within the program community.

Ms. Ruby is determined not to judge the late arrival, the children's clothing, the baby's crying, or the mother's accent. She believes she can develop a genuine, reciprocal relationship of support and care. She knows that over time, she will come to know and become an active partner in supporting this family's strengths and assets. Through these actions, Ms. Ruby embodies cultural humility.

Cultural humility recognizes the unique cultural experiences of others and the ways these impact their lives. One way to define cultural humility is "a lifelong process of self-reflection and self-critique whereby the individual not only learns about another's culture, but one starts with an examination of her/his own beliefs and cultural identities" (Yeager & Bauer-Wu, 2013, p. 2). This personal journey requires the ongoing practice of self-reflection to explore the dynamics that impact one's own emotional reactions and choices. The Connecticut Conference of Municipalities (2020) notes that cultural humility "challenges us to learn from those we work with and serve, reserve judgment, and actively bridge cultural divides" (45). Cultural humility requires sensitivity and openness while eliminating power imbalances and committing to supportive interactions with others (Campinha-Bacote, 2018).

The lens of cultural humility honors families as children's primary teachers and supports their competence and connection with children. The following strategies can inspire personal reflection and meaningful action.

- **Embrace collaboration.** Move from thinking about family engagement as something families do to a journey of teachers learning from families to deepen understanding and to enhance collaboration.
- **Demonstrate sensitivity.** Recognize the impact of culture shock and other traumatic life events, including social and financial stress, neighborhood violence, displacement, and chronic stress. Surround families with a circle of community resources and supports.
- **Give positive feedback.** Demonstrate appreciation for the influence families have on children's development at home. Let them know when their toddler is helpful and caring or when their infant reflects special family characteristics. "I notice the way Elijah's face lights up when you come in. I can see the close bond you share."
- **Share an attitude of gratitude.** Give families written notes to thank them for all they do to teach and care for children at home. "Dear Ms. Manning. I want you to know how much we enjoy having Daniel in our program." Get help from someone who can translate to the family's home language when needed.
- **Make affirmation visible.** Display welcome and good morning signs in families' home languages, with photos of the children at play posted where families can enjoy and talk about them during drop-off and pickup exchanges.
- **Create connections.** Introduce new families to others who share similar life experiences, cultures, and languages. Offer coffee and donuts on a regular schedule to encourage relationships.

- **Share resources.** Offer information about community events, maps to parks, and suggestions for educational and play activities. Ask families to share their positive community experiences on a web-based or program-located community events board.
- **Open opportunities.** Create frequent but uncomplicated "open door" events at times convenient for families, such as informal family chats, coffee connections, and purposeful play events like music and reading hours. Instead of long, highly structured or lecture-type meetings, aim for brief, informal meetings where families receive maximum social benefit in minimum time.
- **Be available.** Offer multiple opportunities for families to reach you by phone, email, and text. Set aside specific times each week to invite calls and meetings. Be sure classroom visits and conferences are scheduled during times that support the unique work schedules of families.

OVERCOMING PRACTICAL CHALLENGES: ELIMINATING POWER IMBALANCES

A hidden power imbalance exists when teachers have inside information and control over children's care. At the same time, families have cultural, linguistic, and social knowledge critical to children's development and learning (Einarsdottir & Jónsdóttir, 2019; Miller, 2018). Power is shared when families are full collaborators in planning and decision-making. The following steps can ensure power differentials are minimized and families are included:

- **Seek family feedback.** Let families know your goal is to learn from them through their experiences and perceptions about the children. Ask families to give formal and informal feedback about their experiences. Use data from surveys to make positive changes.
- **Be transparent about decisions and plans.** Involve families in conversations about decisions that impact current and future program planning.
- **Consider family perspectives.** View yourself, your classroom, and your program through the eyes of families. Ask, "What do families need to see and hear from me to feel heard and included?"
- **Explore your own cultural beliefs and experiences.** Identify an interaction in a school or early childhood setting when you felt uncomfortable or left out. What assumptions did others make about you at that time? What does being an "insider" and "outsider" mean to you?

- **Brainstorm to evaluate multiple perspectives.** When you wonder about how to improve family experiences, ask colleagues, "If we try this, what impacts/outcomes will happen?" "Are there other options and choices we have not considered?" "Are we missing hidden dynamics that need to be addressed?"
- **Involve families in the leadership and guidance of the program.** Include families in planning and decision-making on the parent board, advisory board, and through formal and informal focus groups to gain insight and perspective.
- **Use reflective practice with colleagues.** On a regularly scheduled basis, reflect on what families experience and identify what can be changed and adapted to remove barriers and become more inclusive. Plan specific positive action steps to create positive change.

FOCUSING ON RELATIONSHIP-BASED TEACHING

During a group family meeting, Ms. Noemi, the teacher of the younger toddler group, asks, "What is something special or important you remember doing as a child?" Mr. Ramerez answers, "Playing on my apartment balcony with a bowl of wooden animals my father carved." Ms. Kimura raises her hand and offers, "My family let me play with wind chimes and a koto—a Japanese plucked instrument. I sat in my mother's lap and felt happy." Ms. Parker nods, "I remember baking kolaczki with my grandmother and older sisters."

There is a moment where the group is still. Ms. Soriano reflects, "How wonderful to think about the way our childhoods made us who we are." Ms. Noemi agrees. "Yes. It is an honor to learn about each other. I hope each of you will provide photos that show something special your child does with you. I will print and laminate these to guide our conversations with the children."

In the classroom, Ms. Noemi plays with 14-month-old Mila. She selects a laminated photo from the basket and asks, "Who is this? Is this Mila?" Mila puts the photo up to her nose. Ms. Noemi asks, "I see Mila and a dog. Are you hugging your dog?"

Thirteen-month-old Anthony crawls over. Ms. Noemi pulls him gently onto her lap. "Is this you, Anthony? Is this your Nonno?" She points to the photo of Anthony with his grandfather. After they play with the photos, Ms. Noemi reads The Baby and Me *by Christianne Jones and* You're So Nice, Baby: Teaching Positive Affirmations to Children, *by Molly Dresner to Mila and Anthony.*

When Ms. Noemi learns about families and invites them to contribute photos, she understands more about their values and dreams for their children. By asking the families about a special formative experience, she also conveys the importance of creating a classroom that is an extension of and reflection of their lives. Relationship-based teaching happens when teachers and family work together to create the most integrated and individualized approach to teaching. It ensures the most productive and positive experiences for each child (Mortenson & Barnett, 2015).

Rather than position the teacher as the authority or provider of information, professional guidelines show how important it is to invite families to be authentic partners with teachers in strengthening the development, learning, and security of each child. The NAEYC Position Statement on Developmentally Appropriate Practice (2020) prioritizes family engagement in "Guideline 2: Engaging in Reciprocal Partnerships with Families and Fostering Community Connections." Teachers develop respectful, reciprocal relationships that position families as the most important source of information and include them in decision-making by prioritizing their choices and goals.

USING CULTURALLY RESPONSIVE COMMUNICATION

Ms. Jordan looks up from play and sees 7-month-old Oliver's mother, who arrives to take her son to a doctor's appointment. Ms. Jordan greets her warmly. "Good morning, Marguerite. Oliver is having a happy morning. He is scooting around so well. We had fun playing peek-a-boo with the hippopotamus. And he is waving bye-bye!" She gives Oliver to his mother and encourages him, "Wave bye-bye, Oliver! See you tomorrow."

Marguerite is quiet as she takes Oliver and places him in the car seat carrier. She adjusts his shirt sleeves to cover his wrists, closes his neck snap, and pulls up his knit booties. She pulls a soft blanket from her bag, folds it into a rectangle, and tucks it neatly around him. As she lifts the carrier and turns to go, she says quietly, "See you tomorrow." As Marguerite and Oliver leave, Ms. Jordon wishes she had been more careful when she dressed Oliver after his diaper change. She wonders if Marguerite was upset that his clothing was askew.

Later, Ms. Jordan comments to her coteacher, Ms. Lizzy, "I'm worried because Marguerite was so quiet." Ms. Lizzy responds, "I think her way of interacting with Oliver is just different than the active games we play. I think she was focused on getting to the appointment. Ms. Jordan agrees. "Next time, I'll try not to overwhelm her with my enthusiasm when I know she is on a deadline."

Communication challenges and complexities are part of everyday teaching. It may be instinctive to attach meaning to someone's body language, tone of voice, or actions. But even simple exchanges during the departure transition require thoughtful self-awareness and reflection. Marguerite takes pride in her child's clothing, as she takes him to the doctor. Ms. Jordan genuinely wants to share her joy about Oliver's accomplishments. Ms. Lizzy wisely notices the differences in communication styles. Both teachers take time to share their thinking and to grow in their understanding.

Communication differences impact interactions in a variety of ways. Families may ask for help directly or indirectly to get what they want and need. A family that communicates indirectly may say, "I think Hazel is tired." The teacher may simply respond, "Oh, well she had a great day today." But what the family means is "I notice Hazel seems tired. How long is she sleeping during naptime? I'm worried she's getting sick." But because details are omitted, the teacher does not recognize the family's concern or ask follow-up questions. She may delay talking with the family to elicit more information.

On the other hand, a family that is direct may ask, "How are you putting Hazel to sleep?" A direct response from the teacher is "We pat Hazel's back and tuck her in at 1:30. Does she seem rested to you?" But a teacher who is not used to a direct communication style may feel defensive—wondering if the family is questioning her competence. Navigating communication with sensitivity requires reflection about the best ways to seek and confirm information from others.

Communication differences also impact interactions with children. Teachers may offer an indirect suggestion to a toddler, such as "It's time to clean up," and wonder why the child goes on playing. The teacher doesn't realize the family speaks directly to the child, saying something like "Shepherd, put the blocks in the basket. I will hold the basket." Children can and do differentiate between settings, but teachers must be aware of the differences as they help children adapt.

Becoming culturally responsive during communication requires an increasingly sophisticated view about the ways culture and language contribute to the structures and dynamics of families, childrearing, child care, and teaching. Over time, you will develop a deep understanding of the developmental patterns of the children, the language and cultural contexts of families, and the ways each child and family are special and unique. The following tips can help:

- **Shift perspectives.** View your program, your classroom, and yourself through the eyes of families. An empathy lens helps you see their point of view.
- **Be inclusive.** When communicating with families, consider what they need to hear and see from you to feel included, listened to, and like they belong.
- **Identify barriers.** What invisible barriers are present in information, practices, or access? What practical questions can help families express their concerns and feel safe?
- **Invite contact.** Do you know the best time and way to reach out to families? Do they know when and how to reach you?
- **View questions as opportunities.** When families wonder about procedures, progress, or plans, this is the perfect time to learn more. What insights can families share? Are there hidden concerns that you can identify and address? What will feel reassuring and collaborative to the family?

Strategy Toolbox: Facilitating Reciprocal Communication

The following are communication strategies to help you establish reciprocal conversation.

1. **Keep learning.** Learn all you can about the traditions and practices of the families in your care. When you meet privately with them, welcome them and ask open-ended questions:
   - "I'm so glad you came. I'm glad we can spend time talking together."
   - "What do you enjoy doing at home with your child? What are some ways you do this?"
   - "Tell me about your child. What would you like me to know?"
2. **Listen more than talk.** When a family has a concern, the temptation is to provide answers or solutions before gathering information. Even when you feel sure about an issue, ask for clarification.
   - "Can you tell me more about the issue? What else would you like me to know?"
   - "Do you have suggestions I can use to support your child? What would you like me to do?"
   - When a family asks questions, it is always best to gather data before you offer information or draw conclusions. Say, "Thank you for bringing this to my attention. I will observe your child over the next few days to see how they are managing this situation."
   - When you are asked for a direct answer, consider saying, "I need some time to think about the best plan of action and appreciate your suggestions." Or "Thank you for sharing these suggestions. Let's talk together about what might work best."
3. **Use neutral language.** When you want to discuss a concern that you observe in the classroom, use emotionally neutral, descriptive language.
   - Emotionally loaded language sounds like "Sara has trouble going to sleep."
   - Neutral language describes only the observed behavior. "Sara yawns and rubs her eyes at 11:00. I place her in the crib in the way you demonstrated, but she is still awake at 11:15."
   - Emotionally loaded language sounds like "Winnie seems upset when I feed her."
   - Neutral language gives specific information. "Winnie begins to be fussy at 10:45. When I give her the bottle, she pushes the nipple out with her tongue and cries a little."
4. **When you have a concern, ask if the family sees the issue at home.** Elicit information about the family's experience with the same circumstances. "Do you notice Lucy stays awake after you put her in the

crib?" If the family says this is not the case, ask, "What would you do if Lucy stayed awake?"

- Ask for more ideas and strategies. "What else do you think we can do? "What would you like me to try?"

5. **Communicate positive expectations, which lead the way to success.** When you identify the need to support emerging skills, affirm the shared goal:
   - "This is a great opportunity for us to rethink the level of challenge Liam needs."
   - "I'm glad we can work together to support Kai's artistic skills."
   - "Let's use the next few weeks to play puzzles with Samir. I am confident this will have a big impact."
6. **Plan action steps.** Agree on one action step you will take in the program and one the family will take at home. "I will work with Melinda on sitting during mealtime, and you can try it for a few minutes at home each day." This is a simple way to ask for support.
7. **Use active reflection before, during, and after conversations.**
   - Before you get started, have clear goals. Answer the question, "What do I want to accomplish?"
   - During a conversation, ask yourself, "Am I really listening? Have I put aside my own agenda to hear what the family wants to tell me?"
   - After your time together, consider, "What went well? What could I have said or done differently?" "What follow-up steps do I need to take?"

DEVELOPING A STRENGTHS-BASED MINDSET

Ms. Kaylee meets with 2-year-old Saimi's mother. "I'm delighted to talk with you about Saimi. She loves to play with the water toys outside. Her favorite activity is pushing a baby doll in the stroller. She enjoys the other children." "She seems happy," responds Ms. Dupree. Ms. Kaylee seeks Ms. Dupree's input. "I am wondering if you notice Saimi stays awake during naptime at home? Can you tell me more about how you put her down at home?" Ms. Dupree explains that they place Saimi to sleep in a completely darkened room with a sound machine at home. Ms. Kaylee says, "That is good to know. We can be sure the area where Saimi sleeps is darkened."

Ms. Kaylee makes the intentional choice to use strengths-based language. She might have said, "Saimi has trouble going to sleep." But she knows that the word "trouble" has negative connotations that can invite resistance. Instead, she chooses a positive approach: "I'm wondering what you notice . . ." to invite shared engagement.

When almost 3-year-old Everett shows little interest in books and keeps wiggling away, Ms. Kaylee is tempted to say to his father, "I'm worried that Everett doesn't like to read." Instead, she invites collaboration. "I am happy to send a copy of the books I am reading here for you to read at home." This plan allows her to send books home without directly asking if the family has books at home. The family may respond that they have books, but they would like to have books from the program, as well.

Affirming language applies to all areas of communication: sharing progress, asking for insights, and discussing goals. Positive verbal messages have an indelible influence and ensure families feel safe and included—part of the team. Carefully chosen words invite families to look for their children's strengths and to support positive and collaborative goals.

From My Experience: *When I meet with families, I realize I need to ask the right questions and be a good listener. When I say, "Tell me about your child," families share important information I really need to know." Now I prepare with positive notes about the child's progress. I bring just one issue I want to work on and ask the family how they see it at home. I always find they are on the same page—wanting the best for their child.*

INVITING FAMILY ENGAGEMENT

Mr. Elio sits with 2½-year-old Liam and Dhalia at the play dough and sensory table. They squish play dough through their fingers. Dhalia stuffs dough into an extruder and watches the stringy piece press back out. "What's that?" Liam asks Dhalia. "Making pisgetties," she says. Mr. Elio says, "You're making spaghetti?" Dhalia says, "Pisgetties for mama."

Liam uses the handgrip roller to make a flat pathway in some dough. He pushes a car back and forth over the flat surface. "Making tracks," he says and lines up plastic child figures on top. "Look out!" He takes one figure and shoves another one over. "Oh no! Gotta get 'em up."

Dhalia rubs a pizza cutter back and forth, flattening some dough. She picks it up and cuts off bits with scissors. Liam tries but needs help getting the scissors onto his fingers. Mr. Elio says, "That's the way. The handle goes over your thumb and fingers. Open and close it. Good. Now try with the dough." At first, Liam struggles. But he is excited to cut when Mr. Elio holds the piece of dough.

Mr. Elio is pleased Liam wants to use scissors after he sees Dhalia using them. He notices Liam's mildly aggressive figure play, but sees how he picks up and brushes off the figure that was knocked over. He knows that through play, Liam practices regulating his body and emotions. He notes the fine motor skills just emerging as Liam works with the scissors. Mr. Elio is also interested in Dhalia's intent focus while making dinner for her mother. He writes what the children say on a notecard, along with some comments about his observations. He plans to use this information to communicate with the children's families about their play.

Connecting families to the classroom is the primary goal for Mr. Elio. He takes notes, photos, and videos as an important way to communicate with and include families. He enjoys inviting them to see and talk about their children's progress. He knows what he shares and what he learns help him be a more effective teacher.

Family engagement always begins with a comprehensive orientation, a family handbook review, time for families to observe in classrooms, and follow-up meetings to build trust, gather information, and answer questions. When programs are not physically accessible to families, in-person home visits or virtual meetings using a video chat software like Zoom, Skype, or FaceTime are effective as long as the technology is available to families. The following priorities will enrich and extend the approaches you are already using:

- **Schedule regular family meetings.** After an initial meeting when the family enrolls, a follow-up meeting should occur 10 ten days to 2 weeks later. The meeting may take place in the program or in the home. Set ongoing touch-base meetings to keep communication strong.
- **Talk in person.** Reserve email, texts, and app messages for brief, positive information updates rather than discussion about children. Make a phone call to arrange face-to-face meetings at times that work for families. Respond to questions by phone, video chat, or in person rather than by email.
- **Reserve drop-off and pickup times for brief, positive information.** When families ask questions about their child during pickup or drop-off exchanges, be sure to set a private meeting rather than discuss children while they and others are present. A brief comment about what the children ate or the duration of a naptime are okay. But families may want to ask about a child's behavior or a more complex issue. Respond with "Let's talk together personally. Would it be okay for me to call you at 12:30 today?"
- **Use exchanges to celebrate children.** Thank families for the opportunity to teach their children. Share a sweet, funny, or kind thing children did. This exchange encourages families to look for and reinforce positive traits, and children hear affirming messages about themselves.
- **Make the most of technology.** Digital applications (apps) can help teachers and families communicate daily and provide security and privacy for shared information. While your program may use software to share messages, post photos and videos, and exchange daily

information about the schedule, naps, meals, and routines, don't let technology take the place of personal interaction and connection.

- **Elicit daily updates from families.** Ask families to fill out a brief form on arrival or elicit responses by text, email, or app. The goal is to invite daily feedback about two essential questions: (1) Is there anything you want us to know about your child today? (2) Is there anything special you want us to do today to support your child? This information can be incredibly helpful to you and establishes trust and open communication.
- **Make positive "just want you to know" calls.** Each month, give each family a brief personal phone call—in addition to scheduled meetings. During the call, share a milestone, something sweet a child did or said, a book the child enjoyed with you, or a character or personality trait you appreciate about the child. Keep a call list to be sure all families receive a call. Phone calls can be made when children are napping.
- **Facilitate interfamily connections through "family chats."** In addition to morning coffee events and conversation groups, plan bimonthly family chats. Introduce families to each other. Invite their suggestions for focus topics. Common requests include nutrition for picky eaters, positive guidance, and sleep issues. Invite a community liaison such as a nurse, social worker, doctor, or child psychologist to answer questions. Provide time for families to share their stories. The goal is to facilitate connections among families and develop relationships with community organization and resources.
- **Encourage family leadership.** While families contribute to the program advisory board and provide regular feedback, encourage expanded roles through participation in collaborative community advocacy for children, decision-making about family events, and participation in the life of the classroom.

GETTING ORGANIZED AND KEEPING RECORDS

Ms. Reyna lifts 6-month-old Tala from the crib after her nap, changes her diaper, and settles into the rocking chair. She has a bottle warmed, but Tala wants to play. Ms. Reyna sings "Sampung Mga Daliri," a Tagalog song that means 10 fingers. She points to Tala's fingers, hands and feet, nose, and teeth as she sings. When Ms. Reyna wiggles her tongue, Tala mimics the action by sticking out her own tongue. Ms. Reyna sings until Tala is ready for her bottle.

After feeding, Ms. Reyna pats Tala on the back to burp her and then moves with her to the floor. She offers a sensory ball with knobs. Tala grasps the ball with both hands and sucks on it. It squishes and squeaks in her mouth. Ms. Reyna takes a second ball and squeezes it. "Squeak, squeak!" Ms. Reyna mimics the ball's sounds in a funny high voice.

Tala's family has come to the United States from the Philippines, like several families in the program. The teachers have worked with a cultural broker to connect new families with community resources and services. Ms. Reyna and the other teachers are excited to learn new finger plays and songs. They invite the families to spend time in the classrooms, singing and playing with the children. The collaboration between the teachers, families, children, and community experts has been a success.

Ms. Reyna has worked hard to learn some of the words, songs, and finger plays that support Tala. She listens to a digital file of music recorded by the family and enters notes about Tala's progress in her portfolio. Over the next few weeks, she plans to update the portfolio and add entries to the classroom volunteer calendar for the following month.

Accurate record-keeping is required by state and local licensing agencies and quality improvement initiatives, including documents that support effective family communication. You may enter data directly into apps or keep a clipboard that documents the diapering schedule, food consumption, napping times, and other personal notes. Even when you use digital records, you will need an up-to-date physical filing system. Paper documents with personally identifiable information must be secured in a locked file. Digital documents must be password protected. Figure 2.1 is a list of documents you will be required to keep up-to-date.

Figure 2.1. Family Records Checklist

Program, family, and child records. Records kept in the classroom include:

- ❑ Copy of the program family handbook
- ❑ Program calendar
- ❑ Parent/legal guardian contact information and methods of contact
- ❑ Authorized transportation, including people with permission to transport the child and any designated transportation company
- ❑ Family permission forms for trips, special outings, or events
- ❑ Medical and allergy forms
- ❑ Accident report forms and completed records
- ❑ Individualized feeding plans
- ❑ Procedures and permissions for medications as allowed by licensing
- ❑ Attendance forms, such as sign-in/sign-out sheets or a child care attendance tracking app
- ❑ Home-visiting records
- ❑ Family conference notes, meeting agendas, and record of visits to the classroom, like sign-in forms or emails
- ❑ Family-reported developmental screening and language surveys
- ❑ Developmental screening and home language survey permissions, results, and follow-up information and referrals indicated
- ❑ Child portfolios
- ❑ Family resources related to screening, child development, early intervention, literacy supports, and developmental disability services

(*continued*)

Figure 2.1. (*continued*)

Health, nutrition, and safety information. The information below must conform to your state and local licensing requirements:

- ❑ Posted safety and emergency plans and procedures
- ❑ Meal and snack plans or meal-tracking software
- ❑ Cleaning checklists (e.g., sanitizing of the bathroom, meal surfaces, toys, etc.)
- ❑ Ratio chart and break schedules

Program records. While your program office will house family records, you may retain copies in your classroom:

- ❑ Signed program contract and payment records
- ❑ Enrollment records, including photo permissions and family information
- ❑ Birth certificates
- ❑ Current physical examination and health forms
- ❑ Accident/incident forms
- ❑ Family home language surveys
- ❑ Child screening records
- ❑ Documentation of family involvement in decision-making (i.e., parent boards, advisory boards, and other program contributions)

In addition to the records above, you will need to schedule and maintain records for conferences that take place at least twice a year. This includes notices of offering conferences and attendance sheets. Consider holding conferences within 2 weeks of each child's birthday and again 6 months later on a rolling basis. This makes sense for families as well as for your schedule.

Daily lesson plans are posted on the door or an entryway bulletin board, as well as provided digitally to families. Individualized learning goals and supports are shared privately, rather than on posted lesson plans. In addition to filing and managing lesson plans, you will need to update and manage your portfolio system. Some programs require digital portfolio records like child-generated examples, photographs, videos, anecdotal notes, and checklists. You may use a developmental tracker or checklist to support assessment and communication. Organized family conference and communication management, along with teaching records management, will benefit all areas of teaching and keep you in compliance with program and licensing requirements.

ASKING FAMILIES TO DEMONSTRATE AND EXPLAIN WHAT THEY DO

Eight-month-old Adrian reaches into a soft container and throws objects out one by one. He pulls out a plush elephant, a ball, a rattle, and a sensory teether with little fabric tabs. He crawls over to the teether, rolls onto his back, and puts it into his mouth. Ms. Iris sits next to him watching, until Adrian drops the teether and crawls onto her lap. Ms. Iris helps him get settled and sings. "Mamma's hands go clap-clap-clap. Mamma's hands go tap-tap-tap, up and down. Yia Yia's hands go clap-clap-clap. Yia Yia's hands go tap-tap-tap, up and down. Adrian's hands go clap-clap-clap, Adrian's hands go tap-tap-tap, up and down." She helps Adrian clap his hands and moves them up and down.

This is a song Ms. Iris learned from the Cirillo family that Adrian enjoys at home. She uses all the names of Adrian's family in the song, ending with Adrian's name. Because Ms. Iris has watched them sing this song to Adrian, she knows just how the motions and verses go. She asks families to show her—not just tell her—what they do. Ms. Iris observes families carefully to see how they interact with children. She meets with them and uses a family survey to learn all she can about children's sleep, diapering or toileting, feeding, and play patterns.

The survey questions in Figure 2.2 are conversation starters to bring to light issues you and the family might not otherwise discuss. The questions may be used over time to dig deeper into family perspectives and to develop a true partnership of shared information and decision-making. The words in the questions may be personalized to use the child's specific name and adapted to fit with each family's unique situation and the age of the child. The goal is to ensure families have time to share details that are important to them and to ask questions.

Figure 2.2. Family Survey and Conversation Starters

Family Priorities

- ❑ What do you enjoy most about your child?
- ❑ What do you want us to know about your child?
- ❑ Who are some of your child's important family members and friends?
- ❑ Are there any recent changes in your family routine that may impact your child's needs?
- ❑ Do you have questions or concerns?

Child's Favorite Activities

- ❑ What toys, finger plays, songs, games, and activities does your child enjoy?
- ❑ What are your child's favorite interests and activities?
- ❑ What active play does your child enjoy?
- ❑ What dress-up or make-believe play does your child enjoy?
- ❑ What are your child's favorite books, and how do you read them to your child?
- ❑ Are you willing to record and teach the songs you sing to your child at home?

Diapering and Toilet Training

- ❑ When do you expect your child to begin toilet training?
- ❑ Where do you usually change your child's diaper?
- ❑ What techniques or routines are used during diapering/toileting procedures?
- ❑ Are there specific words, cues, or songs your child associates with diapering and toileting time?
- ❑ What special words or words in the home language are used for diaper ointments, the child's bottom, and other diapering processes?
- ❑ How do you ask to change a diaper or remind your child to visit the bathroom?

(*continued*)

Figure 2.2. (*continued*)

- ❑ What words of encouragement are used during diapering/toileting procedures?
- ❑ Is your child used to having a diaper changed by someone other than you?

Meal and Feeding Routines

- ❑ What meal routines are followed at home?
- ❑ Do you bottle-feed or nurse your child at home?
- ❑ How do you hold your baby and the bottle during feedings?
- ❑ Does your child self-feed fingerfoods and manage a spoon, or does an adult feed the child?
- ❑ Are there specific dietary restrictions or allergies that require attention or supervision?
- ❑ What family members are present and involved in mealtime activities?

Cultural Coherence

- ❑ What are some beliefs, cultural traditions, and childrearing practices that are valued?
- ❑ What are some character traits you value and want us to support in your child?
- ❑ What special traits, skills, and qualities do you see in your child?
- ❑ What would you like us to do to support your child while in a group setting?
- ❑ What emerging skills would you like us to notice, encourage, and support?

Sleeping Routines

- ❑ How does your child sleep at home? Does your child sleep in a bassinet, a crib, or with the parent(s)?
- ❑ Is your child rocked at home to fall asleep? If so, are they laid in the crib or on the bed while still awake, drowsy, or when fully asleep?
- ❑ What sleeping routines do you use with your child? What comfort items, songs, or rituals?
- ❑ Is your child nursed or given a bottle at home before falling asleep?
- ❑ When you lay your child down, do you give back pats or rubs?
- ❑ Do you allow your child to fall asleep after fussing for a few minutes? If not, how do you intervene in fussy behaviors?

Emotional and Physical Support

- ❑ How is your child comforted or reassured when they are upset?
- ❑ Are there any stresses or unpredictable changes the child has experienced?
- ❑ What health or developmental concerns can be supported?
- ❑ Do you tend to wait and let your child self-soothe, or do you step in right away to minimize frustration?
- ❑ How do you support your child's independence?
- ❑ Are there unique words or techniques used to comfort or soothe your child?
- ❑ How do you guide your child's behaviors? What do you do to support success in learning new skills?

Personal and Group Skills

- ❑ Describe your child's previous group experiences. Do they mostly play alone or show interest in others?
- ❑ How does your child manage being away from you?
- ❑ Are there specific activities that your child does not like/prefer, for example, touching wet or slippery things, having their nose wiped, getting into an outer coat or snowsuit, or getting into a high chair? How do you help them with this at home? How would you like us to help them in the classroom?

Revisit the family survey questions on a regular basis. As children's development and learning advance, you will need to check in with families to update your understanding of their perspectives. While the survey is detailed, start with the questions you currently use and gradually add on. Using these prompts will help you build authentic and meaningful relationships for information sharing and decision-making. You may discover other questions that are personal to each child—and that can guide families to share hidden or meaningful information to help you teach their child.

Keep learning from families. Seek to understand their strengths, contributions, and investment in their children's learning and development. Support them as children's first and best teachers. Let them know you depend on their insights, goals, and experiences to make teaching decisions.

Q&As FROM THE FIELD: NAVIGATING DIFFICULT CONVERSATIONS

Question 1: *I know we are supposed to take into account family requests and adaptations for the caring routines and teaching of children. But what do we do if the request goes against our program guidelines? Families want us to feed toddlers in the high chair and control what they select to eat, but our program practices family-style meals.*

Answer: It is important for the program handbook to provide a clear statement about the ways the program is committed to fair and equitable practices, with opportunities for families to share their goals and priorities. You can meet with colleagues to discuss ideas and beliefs you hold about what is "right" or "best" for children. Together, you can identify and remove biases related to family preferences.

Allowing a child additional weeks to remain in a high chair and following a family's dietary guidelines are important ways to individualize care. When requested by the family, these are important ways to support continuity between home and the program. Over time, the child can be transitioned to family-style meals. Conversations with the family—and if needed a cultural broker—can help you develop deeper understanding and appreciation of the multiple contexts of children's lives and family ways of childrearing.

Question 2: *Are there nonnegotiables and program practices that prohibit incorporating family requests?*

Answer: While most family requests can be incorporated, you will need to identify licensing standards that are nonnegotiables. Requirements include physical accessibility to the program for families and children with disabilities, adult–staff ratios, and other regulations that protect the health, safety, and well-being of children, families, and staff. The following are just some of the areas that are nonnegotiable:

- The safety of the building, spaces, furniture, and equipment where children play
- Securing of medical and immunization records and guidelines for the use of medications
- Sanitary procedures for handwashing, diapering, toileting, and stopping the spread of disease
- Guidelines for safe sleeping, such as laying an infant on their back and keeping the crib free from soft, plush, or stuffed items
- Guidelines for the use of swings, child carriers, and high chairs
- The prohibition of corporal punishment, withdrawal of care, verbal and emotional abuse, and isolation, and open access for families to a copy of the program's behavior guidance policy
- Nutrition guidelines and sanitary preparation of foods
- Health, safety, and cardiopulmonary resuscitation (CPR) training for adults
- Emergency procedures for the program and risk-management protocols

Each teacher and program should know where to locate state and local licensing requirements. To learn more, see https://childcare.gov/consumer-education/child-care-licensing-and-regulations.

FOR YOUR INFORMATION: RESOURCES FOR ADDITIONAL EXPLORATION

- To explore additional strategies for bridging cultural gaps and removing barriers, see https://wida.wisc.edu/about/news/it-takes-more-village-challenging-status-quo-and-establishing-inclusive-family.
- To learn more about family engagement in action, explore information and strategies from NAEYC at https://www.naeyc.org/resources/topics/family-engagement.

REFLECTION QUESTIONS

1. What are some reasons families encounter barriers to typical forms of participation? What barriers may be present in your program?
2. For what reasons might teachers overlook the importance of the ways family support infants and toddlers receive at home? What important details may be missed?

3. Which of the strategies for communication presented in this chapter do you currently use with families? What are some new strategies you want to try?
4. Cultural safety benefits families. How does providing cultural safety also benefit teachers?
5. What steps can teacher trainers, coaches, and program leaders take to place a priority on the cultural contexts of families and practices of cultural humility?

CHAPTER 3

Facilitating Play-Based Teaching

This chapter offers ideas to design individualized curriculum that strengthens children's emerging skills and supports learning through play. It shows how to apply what you learn through observation and documentation to create individualized play and lesson plans and prepare materials, activities, and spaces that support all areas of children's development. It provides stories and examples of intentional and responsive teaching during child-centered play where families are active partners and children form perceptions of themselves as capable and joyful learners.

Learning Goal 1: Recognize play as the primary process for learning, enjoying relationships with others, internalizing cultural values, forming personal identity, and developing self-agency through active engagement.

Learning Goal 2: Identify the types of play that facilitate learning and development, including strategies for planning, supervising, and adapting play experiences.

Learning Goal 3: Integrate observation, documentation, and assessment as intentional processes to learn from and about children and families, and use the resulting comprehensive data to plan curriculum that strengthens all areas of development and learning.

PROMOTING JOYFUL LEARNING

Ms. Zoe sits with Jasmine's mother, Alexis, on the floor watching 10-month-old Jasmine play. Jasmine scoots through the tunnel under the soft foam climber, pokes her head out, and laughs. Ms. Zoe and Alexis laugh, too. Jasmine smiles with delight. Ms. Zoe offers Jasmine a red cloth ball. "Bola roja." She shows Jasmine how to put the ball into the top of a clear, hollow tube. The ball rolls down the tube and comes out the bottom end.

Ms. Zoe helps Jasmine hold the tube. She pushes the ball into the tube and gives it a tap. When the ball rolls from the bottom, Jasmine says, "Uh oh!" Ms. Zoe repeats it.

"Uh Oh! Se cayó la pelota! The ball fell down!" Ms. Zoe comments to Alexis, "Jasmine loves the cloth balls. They are easy to hold."

While this looks like a typical day in the infant room, the shared playtime is a family conference. Ms. Zoe comes once a month on Saturday mornings to meet families who cannot come during the week. She shows Alexis what Zoe enjoys during play. She also learns what Zoe is doing at home.

What do you notice as you watch children play? Infants and toddlers are masters of discovery, motivated by curiosity to see how things work. Through play, children learn about their bodies and capabilities and the world around them. Play, in turn, stimulates their social, physical, emotional, and cognitive development (Dijkstra-de Neijs et al., 2023). Even when children appear to be randomly exploring, play strengthens development through clear learning goals (Toub et al., 2016). During play, children practice skills, coordinate hand movements, distinguish between textures and colors, try new ways to use objects, and solve problems.

Sheila Degotardi (2017) encourages teachers to view infants and toddlers not only as emotional beings but as critical thinkers, knowers, and naturally curious explorers—ready to be challenged, inspired, and engaged by the rich, meaningful experiences of play. She points out the need for sustained, shared interaction that helps children develop awareness of themselves and others.

During play, teachers use modeling and mirroring, where the adult and children take turns taking the lead in activities. Children associate positive play experiences with feelings of acceptance and affirmation, which become part of their developing self-identity. They learn that they can bring joy and satisfaction to themselves and to others.

Research Revisited: Ensuring Equity in Play

All children have a right to safe indoor and outdoor play spaces. "Play must be the right of every child. Not a privilege" (Souto-Manning, 2017, p. 785). Teachers must advocate for high-quality play experiences to overcome disparities children experience through lack of opportunities for play associated with race and socioeconomic status (Jordan, 2022). The NAEYC Position Statement on Developmentally Appropriate Practice, Principle Three, states, **"Play promotes joyful learning that fosters self-regulation, language, cognitive and social competencies as well as content knowledge across disciplines. Play is essential for all children, birth through age 8" (9).**

Outdoor playtime is diminishing dramatically in the lives of children due to increased screen time, concern about outdoor safety, perceptions about risky play, and lack of available spaces (Loebach et al., 2021). It is also impacted by long periods in car seats, strollers, and swings (Dinkel et al., 2019; Siddicky et al., 2020).

Extended time in reclined devices restricts children's ability to move freely and is often referred to as "container baby syndrome" (Nationwide Children's, 2018). For these reasons, early childhood programs play an important role in protecting active play and movement opportunities for young children (Bento & Dias, 2017).

Unstructured outdoor play is critical for physical development and sensory growth, as children run and jump on various surfaces, climb, and slide. Outdoor play promotes gross and fine motor skills, social development, and cognitive growth as children engage in problem solving, creativity, and investigation skills. The right to natural outdoor spaces for play and protection from physical harm are basic human needs that contribute to healthy child development and mental and physical well-being (Jones Harden & Slopen, 2022). The need for safe and protected play is a priority issue of equity in early childhood.

EXPLORING THE BENEFITS OF PLAY-BASED LEARNING

Griffin and Grace crawl over to the activity center. Both 11-month-olds pull themselves up and stand. Griffin's head pops up first. When Grace's face appears on the other side, they laugh at each other—big belly laughs. Ms. Dionne smiles. She sits next to them on the floor and demonstrates different ways to use the activity cube. "The beads make a train. See how the beads slide across the wire?" She makes the beads snake up and down until they reach the other side. Griffin tries to push the beads on his side, but they stick on the curved track. Ms. Dionne dislodges them. Grace maneuvers the beads up and over the wire, shaking the beads until they move forward. After a few minutes, Ms. Dionne notices their interest wanes. She introduces a hedgehog peg toy.

"I'm giving Harriet Hedgehog some hair." Ms. Dionne picks up a peg and presses it into a hole. Griffin reaches for a peg and pushes it into a hole on the hedgehog's back. Ms. Dionne knows Griffin's fine motor skills are a perfect match for this level of challenge. Grace scoops up several pegs, drops them into a cup, and dumps them back out. Ms. Dianne reaches over for a peg that escapes and hands it to Grace. Griffin pushes two more pegs into the holes."

Ms. Dionne keeps track of the puzzles and toys the children favor, rotating and introducing new options. While Ms. Dionne plans activities for the children, she doesn't force them to engage. She demonstrates and then watches to see how they respond. In addition to the activity cube and hedgehog pegs, she provides mallets with wooden pegboards and shape sorters. The children are free to crawl away and explore other activities.

Ms. Dionne also keeps a chart that tracks the children's development. She writes notes about the ways she observes their emerging skills. She reviews this information to plan new activities. She talks with her coteacher about activities that can benefit each child. The teachers recognize that the benefits of play depend on their effective planning.

Research Revisited: Recognizing the Benefits of Play

Play pays big benefits for children in the present with lasting impacts on lifelong learning, health, and well-being.

- **Play increases language, cognitive, and social skills.** Play helps children recognize word labels, determine categories, and understand concepts while providing scaffolding for social interactions, creativity, problem solving, teamwork, flexibility, and innovation (Yogman et al., 2018).
- **Play promotes emotion regulation.** Playfulness and playful interactions are associated with improved emotion regulation and lowered child negativity in early childhood (Menashe-Grinberg & Atzaba-Poria, 2017; Shorer et al., 2019).
- **Play increases self-regulation.** Active unstructured play for toddlers predicts better self-regulation at ages 4 and 5 and at ages 6 and 7 (Colliver et al., 2022).
- **Play decreases behavior challenges.** Warm and responsive parent-child play in infancy is associated with fewer behavior problems later in childhood (Schneider et al., 2022). Play increases self-regulation, lowers aggression, and boosts cognitive skills, which contribute to positive behaviors (Amodia-Bidakowska et al., 2020).
- **Play moderates stress and promotes resilience.** During play with caring adults, infants and toddlers develop self-agency, creativity, and ownership, which are coping skills necessary for resiliency (Housman, 2020).
- **Play increases self-agency and confidence.** Play offers opportunities for choice and autonomy, which add to self-agency and confidence (Goodhall & Atkinson, 2020).
- **Play boosts a range of cognitive skills.** Indoor and outdoor free play experiences are linked to better problem solving, literacy, math, and cognitive outcomes (Miller et al., 2022; Whitebread et al., 2017).
- **Play strengthens executive functioning and self-regulation.** Play offers opportunities to focus attention, control impulses, and hold information in mind (remember what happened, what needs to be done, and what happens next). These cognitive skills are part of executive function, which support behavior and learning (Center on the Developing Child, 2024).

UNDERSTANDING THE WAYS CHILDREN PLAY

Ms. Jana helps 2-year-olds Lola and Andre pull on knitted caps and mittens in front of the plexiglass wall mirror. She plays Waldteufel's Skater's Waltz *using virtual assistant technology and offers ribbon sticks. The children spin and raise and lower their arms to wave the ribbons.*

At the activity table, Ms. Demi helps 2½-year-old Jordan select a geoboard. He chooses a boat picture to put in the frame and takes a handful of large rubber bands from the container. "Are you making a sailboat today?" Ms. Demi asks. Jordan responds, "Sailboat." Madi sits next to Jordan and dumps the container of bristle blocks onto the table. She puts the blocks back into the container one by one. Ms. Demi says, "You are taking the bristle blocks out and putting them back in." Madi puts her hand in the container, completely focused on her movements.

On the carpet next to the table, Zachary rolls over and sits up. He rocks a plush giraffe back and forth in time to the skating music. Aadab puts her baby doll in a wagon and tries to cover her with an embroidered muslin blanket. Ms. Demi comes to help.

In this child-centered program, the toddlers freely choose play activities that interest them. Ms. Jana and Ms. Demi offer opportunities for active play, with alternate choices that are calming and comforting. They keep in mind the quickly changing abilities and interests of the children.

Most definitions of play describe adults who provide materials and supervision, with children who have autonomy in selecting activities and determining the way they play (Colliver et al., 2022). In the infant and toddler years, play is driven by children's quickly developing physical, cognitive, social, and language skills and their innate curiosity to explore and learn. Children are developing physical skills to manipulate objects and the social and regulatory skills to play with and near others. While there are increasing moments of time that children play alone, a teacher's direct supervision is always necessary.

Play is intrinsically rewarding, as infants learn to coordinate their attention and actions with others through turn-taking, language, and gestures (Thiele et al., 2021). Thiele and colleagues found that from 7 to 13 months of age, infants take an increasingly active role in interacting directly with others, as well as observing the interactions of others. During play, they experience positive emotions, pleasure, affection, and attachment (Barrish, 2020). With joyful engagement and positive relationships, play is satisfying and fun.

EXPLORING PLAY TYPES: WHAT CHILDREN ARE DOING

The way infants and toddlers engage in play depends on the preparation of spaces and materials, their developmental skills, and the play goals of the child and teacher. While five types of play are described, children combine and move between these types flexibly.

1. **Unstructured play.** During unstructured play, children match their play choices to their curiosity and stimulation needs. They may be active or quiet as they test their skills, copy the actions of others, and focus on self-selected materials and activities.

While the play is unstructured, it is not random. Teachers prepare appropriate challenges, build on children's interests and enjoyment, and are aware of children's physical capabilities. They monitor interest, assist as needed, and protect focused play from the interruption of other children. At times, teachers may reengage children or help them move on to other activities.

2. **Discovery, sensory, and fine motor play.** Discovery play is an early form of inquiry learning, where children explore, learn how things work, and test their ideas. Infants and toddlers are investigators—touching, tasting, feeling, smelling, listening, examining textures, comparing attributes, and making connections about how things are the same and different.

   Infants enjoy the sounds of rattles, the textures of scarves and plush animals, and the clicks and jingles of a sensory board. Items like teethers, rattles, dangling rings, and busy boxes are favorites for younger infants, with shape sorters, soft blocks, stacking cups, and flap books favorites of mobile infants.

   Toddlers enjoy painting with water, blowing bubbles, pouring water into funnels, and making tracks in sand tables. They enjoy open-ended materials like tubes, ramps, collage papers and fabrics, gears, balls, and containers that can be used in many ways. They engage quickly with natural collections and nature experiences and also enjoy beads, knob puzzles, shape sorters, geoboards, and sorting games.

3. **Imitation and pretend (symbolic) play.** Infants and toddlers learn through observation. They imitate what they see their families doing—eating, preparing food, going to the market, watering plants, washing clothes, and cleaning. Meaningful imitation play depends on thematic materials that are grouped together, like plush animals, brushes, small blankets, and bowls to reenact pet care.

   Emerging research has challenged the idea that infants and toddlers only engage in object play. With intentional concept and social modeling of teachers in a prepared setting, toddlers may engage in symbolic play sooner than previously thought (Fleer, 2023). They may use a block like a telephone or pretend a cup is a boat or car.

4. **Social play.** Infants and toddlers seek playful interaction and positive social–emotional connection with others. For infants, social interactions include individualized lap and floor playtime, along with personal conversations. Interactions with others are flexible, with one or more peers moving in and out of play, and with moments when the teacher quietly observes the child before reengaging.

   While toddlers play alone and often next to other children, they participate in social pretend play as early as 18 months (Luo et al., 2022). Some studies show that children at 27 months engage in social play about 31% of their total playtime, with about 33% of time spent in social-pretend play. Children begin to observe the play of others and interact more spontaneously over time, gradually learning to coordinate their play.

5. **Active physical play.** Active physical play is essential for infants and toddlers. See Chapter 7 for the positive impacts of active physical play on health, learning, and behavior. Teachers encourage active movement for infants during dancing and copycat movement games. During tummy time, floor play, and lap time, infants use active motor skills as they roll, reach, and grasp. Mobile infants need extended time for rolling, bending, climbing, cruising, pushing, pulling, throwing, dancing, and playing physical games.

   During indoor gross motor play, toddlers enjoy active games like follow the leader, hide-and-go-seek, freeze games, throwing beanbags, and bowling. During active play, children also use fine motor skills as they grip a ball, pick up objects, and grasp equipment. During outdoor activities, they need space and equipment for jumping, bouncing, spinning, swinging, lifting, rocking, hopping, scooting, peddling, and balancing.

   The healthy development of the body is coordinated by the proprioception, vestibular, and sensory systems, which depend on opportunities for active physical play.

   - *Proprioception* involves the brain and body system, as children coordinate their bodies, muscles and joints; understand where external objects are in relation to their bodies; and monitor their movement and actions (Holst-Wolf et al., 2016).
   - *Vestibular sense* provides information about head and body position and allows children to balance and orient themselves in space (Abbott, 2022). This coordination system is essential for children to activate and regulate their own bodies, as well as respond to external stimulation and physical demands.
   - *Sensory integration* involves the ways the brain and nervous system take information from the senses, organize it, and respond appropriately (AAP, 2019).

PLAY FACILITATION: WHAT THE TEACHER IS DOING

The hallmark of infant and toddler teaching is the flexible ways teachers and children work and play and learn together, taking turns as initiator and responder. At all times, teachers intentionally promote learning and development, encourage children to try new activities, and support social and emotional needs and well-being.

Child-Centered Play. During child-centered play, teachers follow the lead of infants and toddlers by noticing their interests, monitoring the pace and length of play, and ensuring that play is satisfying and enjoyable. Play is interactive and shared, with teachers responding to children's level of engagement. At times, teachers may step back to observe, and at times, they engage as play partners. Child-centered play offers a range of opportunities for child autonomy and teacher direction (Skene et al., 2022).

During child-centered play, teachers may encourage children to try new skills or help them invent new ways to play. The teacher may briefly demonstrate but is careful not to take over the activity. Infants and toddlers depend on assisted collaboration for problem solving.

Child-centered play depends on teacher preparation. For instance, a nonmobile infant can only play with materials a teacher makes available. Young toddlers may not yet be able to use materials without assistance. In this way, child-centered play for infants and toddlers is always individualized and is dependent on the intentional facilitation of teachers.

Teacher-Guided Play. Teacher guiding is like a mini-lesson, where the teacher models a specific skill for a specific purpose. The teacher may demonstrate how turning a knob opens a door, introduce how to use nesting cups, or show how Matryoshka dolls pull apart and fit together. Teachers lead play during routines like diaper changing, when they introduce a finger play or play peek-a-boo. Keep in mind that it may be the child who initiates and leads peek-a-boo, so teacher leading depends on the circumstances.

Teacher-led activities are brief and intentional and are adjusted to fit the interest and attention span of the children. During reading, the teacher sings an introduction or uses puppets to tell the story. During creative play, the teacher demonstrates how to use instruments or how to work with different art materials. Fine motor activities also require moments of teacher leading, as teachers model and assist with new activities and provide more challenging materials. During outdoor and nature play, teachers may have specific goals as they point out different kinds of bark, leaves, seed pods, or animals. At all times, teacher leading is congruent with the interest and engagement level of the children.

Strategy Toolbox: Considering Play From Children's Perspectives

The following questions can help you decide the best way to prepare for and support each child's play:

1. Which play activities spark a child's interest and joy?
2. How does the child show you they are interested in an activity or object?

3. What are the child's emerging skills? Which skills need focused support?
4. How does the child show you an activity is appropriately challenging?
5. What play activities do families suggest?
6. How will you organize and prepare materials ahead of time?
7. How will you respond when a child is quiet or alone to reengage them?
8. How do children show they need to shift to a new activity?
9. What signs do children give that they feel comfortable and safe during play?
10. What favorite imitation, pretend, sensory, discovery, fine motor, and big body play activities do children enjoy?
11. In what ways do you include unstructured, child-centered, and teacher-guided play across a continuum with the children you teach?
12. When does leading, following, or supporting children during play make sense for specific types of activities?

INVESTIGATING CULTURAL INFLUENCES ON PLAY

Ms. Sorcha enjoys sharing positive messages about the toddlers in her classroom. When 2-year-old Miranda's Aunt Nola brings her early on Monday, Ms. Sorcha says, "Buenos dias mi cariño, Miranda" (Good morning, my sweetie). To Nola, she says, "We love having Miranda with us. What can we do for her today?" Nola responds, "I'm so glad you asked. My sister is away this week. I know Miranda misses her mother and may need extra comfort at naptime."

Mrs. Ramirez, Miranda's mother, usually comes to the program on Fridays to help the children play with puppets. She crochets a new animal puppet each month and enjoys creating shows and singing songs for the children. She helps the children put their hands in the puppets and make them talk. Nola smiles at Ms. Sorcha and says, "With my sister gone this week, I'm going to come on Friday to do the puppets for her. I will come after naptime."

The teachers in this program consider families to be essential assets for teaching. Teachers ask families for their ideas and invite them to participate in practical ways. While some of the children speak Spanish at home and others only English, they know all the children will benefit from multilingual activities.

Miranda is excited when her mother or aunt comes to the classroom. They make the puppets talk in Spanish—and then in English—so all the children can learn. When Miranda's mother first came to lead puppet play, she thought the children would sit quietly to watch. But she learned quickly the children needed to be active. She now invites them to hold puppets and join in the songs. Some of the children play in other areas of the room, while others play with the puppets.

Families hold views about play that influence expectations, planning, and conversations about classroom activities. They may differ in the degree to which they promote play at home, how they provide materials and space, and whether they engage with their child. These ideas also impact their thinking about children's participation in the classroom (Hyun et al., 2022; Laforette & Mendez, 2017). Cultural differences are evident in the way adults talk with children about their emotions, thoughts, and preferences (Wang & Wang, 2019). For example, at first, Ms. Ramirez thought the puppet play would be teacher directed. But she changed her thinking as she saw how much the children enjoyed being active participants.

Teachers also hold views about play that impact their choices. For example, culture determines who takes the lead, the teacher or child; the extent of risk allowed and encouraged; and the level of control during play (Faircloth & Murray, 2015). Culturally determined aspects of play include the extent to which children and teachers collaborate during play and beliefs about how much play promotes learning (Wu, 2019). For example, one teacher may let children experiment with how a toy works, whereas another may feel it is important to show them the correct way to play. Western views about play place a high value on children's individuality, agency, and sense of self, and include an emphasis on self-expression and autonomy, whereas collectivist cultures place a high value on suppression of self, conformity, harmony, and group identity (Dai et al., 2020).

Children's ways of playing are also culturally determined. They imitate the behaviors and attitudes they see in adults, such as gender expectations, ways of showing affection, and expectations for engaging. In this way, children regulate their behaviors according to culture-specific roles, rules, and norms (Doebel & Lillard, 2023). In some cultures, infants are treated as conversational partners, whereas in others, adults speak for children (Cebioğlu et al., 2023). A child may be asked what they wish to play, or the parent may explain what the child wants. One approach draws attention to the child, whereas the other draws it away from the child.

Play "can vary significantly by social and cultural contexts as children use play as a means of interpreting and making sense of their experiences" (NAEYC, 2020, p. 6). Just as the neighborhood location (rural, urban), socioeconomic status, language, and cultural context offer meaning to a child's developing identity, their play reflects the unique contexts, values, and assets of their families. In this way, play experiences are firmly anchored within the cultural frameworks of each child's contexts, including the learning goals that are prioritized (Loizou & Loizou, 2022).

OVERCOMING PRACTICAL CHALLENGES: IMPLICATIONS OF PLAY VALUES AND BELIEFS

Consider how values and goals impact practical teaching decisions. A teacher may correct the way a toddler uses blocks, thinking the child's noisy attempts to make them be rockets would better be channeled into a quiet building activity. A teacher may not feel comfortable with a child's level of energy or misinterpret their intentions. This is an area that calls for sensitivity and awareness, as research shows teachers attach persistent negative attributions to boys, and particularly to Black boys' behaviors (Owens, 2016, 2022). Beliefs and expectations about the level of activity, types of play, and ways of behaving during play are often deeply held, remain unexamined, and are linked to hidden cultural ideas.

There are many subtle daily interactions that may embody bias. Personal values may play out many times during a typical day. In each of the following scenarios, teachers may respond more positively to children whose traits fit with their own beliefs and norms.

Teachers who value individuality may interact more often with toddlers who express their emotions, thoughts, and preferences than with those who are quiet. A teacher who values initiative may view timid or quiet behaviors as less advanced. Quiet children may be overlooked and simply experience fewer one-on-one interactions with their teachers and therefore, have less opportunity for learning. Children who show initiative by asking questions or "jumping right into an activity" may be seen as leaders or more intelligent.

In contrast, teachers with a collectivist perspective may value the behavior of children who wait quietly, interpreting this as respect. They may judge a child who interrupts, answers questions, or takes initiative as being disrespectful. Children who reach for materials or express their wants directly (e.g., take food without being served, say they are hungry while food is being prepared, or ask to go first) may be perceived as rude or pushy. Teachers with a collectivist mindset may focus more on children's physical cues and talk about events rather than making children the focus of a conversation. They may view play through a more directive lens where adults impart knowledge to children without valuing a child who plays in divergent ways.

The first step toward understanding and affirming children begins with reflection on one's own cultural contexts. What insights do you have when considering the teacher perspectives above? Do you recognize your own ways of thinking or responding? Families are also valued resources for providing information about culturally affirming practices (Santamaría & Santamaría, 2015). What values do they hold? What differences do your colleagues notice about their own or your ways of thinking and responding to children and families? These insights can help you be more intentional about learning from and understanding the perspectives of others.

Strategy Toolbox: Enriching Doll Play

Making program experiences feel like home is the starting point for nurturing infants and toddlers. All children reenact familiar routines during housekeeping play through cooking, cleaning, caregiving, and comforting play.

Doll play is a mirror, reflecting children's cultural experiences. Tucking a doll under the arm, holding a bottle, and rocking a doll connect children to the positive emotions they feel with their families. Doll play reflects compassion, empathy, caring, and kindness for self and others. Dolls with diverse hair colors and textures, facial features, skin tones, and eye colors allow children to interact with babies that look like they do—as well as care for and learn about those who are different.

Take time daily to dress the dolls and arrange them in a bassinette or basket. This effort demonstrates that babies are always treated with respect and gentle caring. It also reflects specific cultural ways of caring, such as swaddling or covering dolls with a crocheted blanket or dressing them in clothing used by families. Provide knitwear, clothing, wraps, and blankets that reflect those the children use at home. Dressing the dolls as part of cleanup routines is a powerful way to model responsibility, empathy, and respect. When children see you gently dressing a doll, they recognize this as an important value.

Include a basket of picture board books near the dolls so children can "read" to their babies. Toddlers love to "go to the market," So include hooks with fabric bags for children to take shopping. As doll play is a high-value activity, invest in an adequate number of strollers or buggies so children who want to can participate. Laminate family photos and affix child-safe mirrors at children's eye level on the wall near the pretend kitchen, so the space feels like home to the children. Personal touches enrich doll play and affirm children's connection with their families.

LEARNING ABOUT CHILDREN THROUGH OBSERVATION, DOCUMENTATION, AND ASSESSMENT

Ms. Mira sits on the floor next to 15-month-old Avery and 17-month-old Jack and watches them carefully. Avery puts three baby bunnies into a felt basket and then shakes the bunnies out. Jack holds a wooden bead and pushes a stiff cord through the large opening. He grunts, keeps trying, and finally a bead slips on the cord. Jack takes both ends of the bead cord, shakes it vigorously, and places it on top of his head. "Hat," he says to Ms. Mira. "You did it. You made a bead hat," she responds. Jack smiles. "Bead hat."

Avery reaches into the container and puts three beads into the felt basket. Ms. Mira says, "Are the bunnies hungry? Are you feeding them lettuce?" "Neh. Neh," Avery says. Ms. Mira pauses for a minute, thinking Avery is saying "no." But then she realizes Avery means. "Nest. You are feeding lettuce to the bunnies in the nest!"

During play, the children are unaware that Ms. Mira takes photos and digital videos of their interactions. She holds the iPad low in her lap so she doesn't distract them. She sees they play close to each other, showing they feel comfortable and safe. She is pleased that after several weeks of trying, Jack is successful stringing the beads. At first, Jack struggled to hold a bead steady while aiming the cord through the hole. Now this is his favorite activity.

Ms. Mira understands Avery's first use of the word "nest." They have been reading books about animal homes and making nests with blankets and boxes. During the children's naptime, Ms. Mira uploads videos to the children's portfolios and adds developmental notes. She shares videos on the digital portfolio app, where the families can access them.

Documentation captures objective data—what you saw, heard, and the contexts surrounding the observation. During planned and spontaneous observation, use a clipboard, camera, video camera, and note cards to record the child's name, time, situation, interactions, and play details. The goal is to capture a full picture of children's development and learning and create meaningful documentation, like sequential portfolios, wall displays, photo boards, and books that invite children and families to celebrate learning.

You may use physical or digital daily sheets to record information about breakfast/snacks, diapering/toileting times, napping routines, play activities, and other details of each child's day, or you may use a commercial developmental tracker. Whatever your approach, it is critical to use intentional observation and documentation daily over time to establish an accurate picture of children's progress. The following are important approaches for ensuring bias-free observation, documentation, and assessment.

- **Use objective language.** The U.S. Department of Health and Human Services Early Childhood Learning and Knowledge Center (2023) suggests avoiding generalizations like stating a child is upset or is having a hard time. Use objective language by describing specific actions, vocalizations, quotes of children's language, facial expressions and gestures, and behaviors. For example, rather than, "Rachel cried for *a long time*," be sure to record the actual time and duration of behaviors. "Rachel cried at 2:30 for 4 minutes after her nap, but then became absorbed in playing peek-a-book with the toy bunny and Ms. Claire."
- **Reframe deficit language.** Replace the words "weaknesses" and "challenges" with the words "areas for support" or "areas of opportunity." Instead of "Olivia doesn't like to read," state "Olivia enjoyed reading for 2 minutes. She will benefit from daily focused reading. She enjoys farm books and making animal sounds."
- **Record emerging skills.** "Marabel transferred the block back and forth from hand to hand and flipped a puzzle piece upside down for

the first time." "Marabel put all the horses into the bucket by herself." Include special and funny moments that reflect social and emotional development. For example, "Marabel laughed when the ball rolled down the tube." "Marabel held the blanket over her own head and initiated peek-a-boo."

- **Create individualized portfolios.** Evidence for infant and toddler development and learning is collected through portfolios. Information includes observation (anecdotal) notes; written records; checklists; photographs; videos; notes from conversations with children; children's artifacts, like artwork and drawings; and the results of informal and formal assessments. Portfolios also include family information, like language and family surveys and other documentation of children's lives outside the program.
- **Know ethical considerations and limitations.** Because of rapid development, variability day to day, and a range of personal factors (the child's sleep, illness, changing patterns), teachers should gather multiple sources of information and evidence and use a combination of sources for evaluation of children's progress.

While there are a range of developmental assessments that measure communication, language, cognitive, motor, and social–emotional skills, these may only be used by staff with professional training and credentials that meet the requirements of each particular tool. A commercial assessment must be research-based to show it measures what it was designed to measure; that the use of the tool provides accurate results; that it serves children from a range of backgrounds accurately and without bias; and that it assesses and provides results consistently across settings. To ensure cultural and linguistic equity, a child must be familiar with the adult conducting the assessment, and when possible, share the home language, race, and culture of the child. The New York State Department of Health provides a list of developmental screening and assessment instruments frequently used with infants and toddlers that may be administered by trained professionals and included in a child's portfolio: https://www.health.ny.gov/community/infants_children/early_intervention/docs/2025-01_list_developmental_assessment_instruments.pdf.

DAILY OBSERVATION CHECKLIST

Use the following observation checklist to help you understand children more deeply. You may want to focus on answers to specific questions or use the list to develop an overall understanding of children's progress.

- ❑ What activities and materials does this child enjoy?
- ❑ What new activities and interactions result in joy or laughter?
- ❑ What behaviors demonstrate new skills or interests?
- ❑ What do you notice about communication and first and second language development?
- ❑ What knowledge, skills, concepts, and vocabulary are emerging?
- ❑ What do verbal and nonverbal cues tell you about a child's interest in the materials?
- ❑ What emerging skills are present that should be challenged?
- ❑ How does this child show they are delighted, lonely, or hungry?
- ❑ What signs indicate a child is tired, bored, or needs a change of pace?
- ❑ What schedule or routine patterns are working well or changing?
- ❑ How does this child respond to other children? With whom do they prefer to play?
- ❑ During what activities or circumstances does this child seek attention?
- ❑ What materials, activities, and interactions will strengthen specific skills?
- ❑ What specific books, songs, stories, and games engage this child best?
- ❑ What ways of comforting and encouraging work best for this child?
- ❑ What experiences are frustrating or require additional support?
- ❑ What changes to the setting reduce frustration and increase positive success?
- ❑ What strengths and unique traits can be encouraged?
- ❑ What social skills and approaches to learning do you observe (listening, helping, self- and other-awareness, initiative, curiosity, persistence, problem solving)?
- ❑ How does this child respond to your ways of support?
- ❑ What special interests are present that should be encouraged?
- ❑ What follow-up steps do you need to take (e.g., select additional materials, adjust spaces or timing)?
- ❑ What ways of comforting and supporting work best for each child?
- ❑ In what area does this child need additional support and encouragement?
- ❑ What new materials can be introduced to provide higher levels of challenge?
- ❑ What barriers are present that can be removed to encourage more active engagement?
- ❑ What do you notice about your own responses to this child?
- ❑ What can you do to better understand, interact with, and encourage this child?
- ❑ If you have a required digital assessment, what authentic documentation can you add to capture a fair, unbiased, and complete perspective about children's developmental progress and learning?

In addition to daily observations, you may want to conduct a more extensive evaluation of a child's skills. Figure 3.1 is an example of completed Child Observation Chart. Scan the QR code below and go to the "Download" tab on that page for a blank, printable version of Figure 3.1.

You can also create a similar form to conduct an ongoing or extended evaluation for each child. The bottom area of the Child Observation Chart is designed for planning activities, books, and individualized supports to strengthen specific skills. Consider the skills that are independent (already present and consistent), skills that are emerging (the child demonstrates inconsistently or with assistance), and next-step skills (those soon to emerge).

Figure 3.1. Example of Completed Child Observation Chart

Child: *Mandy* 14 months	Dates: *May 1–15*	Independent skills	Emerging skills	Next-step skills
Speech, language, communication		Points in response to "Which one do you want?" Answers, "What does the animal say." Sings along to "Old MacDonald." Sings to self during play.	Asks "What's that?" "Wanna' that." (I want to have that.) Says "Come here." "I have it." "Bubbles pop." Uses simple signs for drink, and want more.	Extend partial words: *Ba—bottle* *Ru—run* *Ma—Mandy* Fill in rhymes: "Old MacDonald had a ___." Encourage two- and three-word sentences.
Shared book reading		Enjoys turning pages of "Every Little Thing." Points to objects in pictures.	Pulls book from shelf. Turns pages and babbles to "pretend read."	Fill in words to repetitive books: *Brown Bear* and *Jesse Bear, What Will You Wear?*
Cognitive and reasoning		Holds a block to her ear and "talks" on her "cell phone."	Puts blocks on top of each other. Places rings in tower. Fits shape in box, with advanced fine motor skill.	Introduce shape-sorter bin and stacking blocks with support.

(*continued*)

Figure 3.1. (*continued*)

Child: *Mandy* 14 months	Dates: *May 1–15*	Independent skills	Emerging skills	Next-step skills
Social and emotional		Crawls over and pats teacher's leg for help. Blows kisses.	Shows empathy. Pats Jose's back when crying. Nurtures baby dolls. Says "happy day."	Point to images in *Little Faces, Big Feelings* and *Baby's Feelings* and name feelings.
Fine motor		Pincer grip—Mandy uses a spoon very well. She grabs crayons and scribbles.	Moves beads across the activity cube. Opens and closes knob doors on toys.	Introduce stringing large beads, geoboard, and knob puzzles.
Gross motor		Takes eight steps while holding to furniture. Stands.	Rolls on the mat, crawls up ramp. Uses push cart to walk.	Balance on the stepping blocks holding hands with teacher.
Creativity and problem solving		Enjoys pulling her laces out of the bow and taking off her shoes.	Points to objects she wants, including a drink (cup). Got pushcart unstuck by backing up.	Offer flower peg stack game and stuff beanbags in container. Use words *in* and *out, pull* and *push.*
Self-identity and personal traits		Feeds the doll with the baby bottle and holds the stroller to walk her "baby." Mandy is very confident and enjoys laughing.	Shows empathy to peers—pats Andrew when crying. Enjoys the book *My Hands Were Made for Helping.* Helps "feed the dog" (put beads in a dish) with support.	Focus on families: *Babies Around the World. The Color of Us, Whose Toes Are Those,* and *Chicago Baby.* Discuss family and friends that are special to Mandy.
Other emerging skills		Mandy is very expressive, moves to music, makes funny faces in the mirror. She likes using the large brushes on the easel.		
Areas of opportunity		Expect Mandy to be walking independently within a few weeks. This will expand gross motor play options.		
Notes for lesson planning		Select and introduce new materials as listed. Focus on paired words: *in-out, up-down, pull-push, over-under, open-shut, top-bottom.* Ask Mandy's family for photo and names of family friends.		

APPLYING FAMILY COMMUNICATION TO LESSON PLANNING

Thirteen-month-old Amir's father has been ill, and Amir has been dropped off and picked up over the last few weeks by his Aunt Khadija. Today, Ms. Sania meets to touch base with Amir's mother, Yasmin, to talk about Amir's individualized play plan. Ms. Sania learns that Amir's father is better and that the family has strong support. Yasmin says, "My sisters help, and Amir plays with his cousins and siblings every day."

Ms. Sania responds, "I can see how confident Amir is. Look how he crawls up the ramp and goes down the slide. And I can also tell you read with him at home. He loves books." Ms. Sania responds, "Yes, we read a lot."

Amir crawls over to the sensory box. He tries to turn the knob on a small door, but it sticks. His mother shows him. "Twist the knob this way." He twists the knob and pulls it open. Ms. Sania says, "Amir is a good problem-solver! What does he enjoy most at home?"

Amir's mother explains that Amir spends most of the time pushing a cart to take a baby doll or stuffed animal for a walk. He enjoys pulling out plastic containers from the cupboard and playing with kitchen tools. They review Amir's favorite books and discuss the nap schedule. Yasmin hugs Ms. Sania as she prepares to leave. "Thanks for spending time with us. It makes going to work every day much easier."

During the family meeting, Ms. Sania notices the way Yasmin interacts with Amir—showing him how to use the toy and giving him a chance to try new skills for himself. She identifies what is important to the family, like reading, spending time with family, music and movement, and supporting Amir's verbal development. She looks for meaningful ways to include Arabic into interactions, even though she and the other teachers speak only English.

Ms. Sania knows other teachers use a laptop to enter notes, but she prefers to use a clipboard to record what Yasmin and she discuss during the family meeting. Ms. Sania and the program staff include the experiences and stories of families in their planning. They use a family meeting chart to record information from families and ensure cultural congruence between home and the program. See Figure 3.2 for a completed example of Yasmin's family meeting chart. Scan the QR code below and go to the "Download" tab on that page for a blank, printable version of Figure 3.2.

Figure 3.2 includes notes Ms. Sania created to share with Amir's family and to use in lesson planning. As the information comes from shared conversations and through active observation, it is a current record of Amir's progress. A copy of the family meeting chart is placed in Amir's portfolio. Ms. Sania uses the notes as she creates lesson plans and individualized play plans.

Figure 3.2. Family Meeting Chart

<table>
<tr><th colspan="2">Amir Dawood, February 15 Meeting with Yasmin</th></tr>
<tr><th>Home Activities</th><th>Classroom Activity Goals</th></tr>
<tr><td>Physical play: Pushcart with baby dolls. Rolling, climbing, sliding.</td><td>Gross motor goals: (balance and walking) Pushcart, climbing ramp/slide, mat play/rolling, ball play, music/movement.</td></tr>
<tr><td>Favorite books: Amir learns Arabic and English at home. The family reads a set of Arabic board books with drawings of objects in his home. They read Eric Carl's Brown Bear, Brown Bear; My Very First Book of Words; and The Very Hungry Caterpillar using Arabic translations.</td><td>Reading goals: Amir enjoys the peek-a-boo books (Peekaboo Sun, Peekaboo Apple, and Peekaboo Baby) and Bath! Bath! Bath! by Douglas Florian. He likes Whose Toes Are Those? by Jabari Asim. Add English versions of Eric Carl books, including The Very Hungry Caterpillar; My Very First Book of Words; and Brown Bear, Brown Bear, What Do You See?</td></tr>
<tr><td>Fine motor activities: Amir frequently uses teething toys. In addition to chewing them, he puts them in and out of a basket and pushes them in his cart. He plays with pop-it toys, a multigrip teething spinner, and a set of rattle keys. He turns the keys in his ride-on car.</td><td>Fine motor goals: Assist with sipping water from a cup. Amir's favorite activity is pushing the pegs out of the pegboard with his fingers. Assist with rotating the board. Support in-and-out games: pushing beanbags into a tube and shaking them out, exploring music toys, and using the ball ramp. Provide support with shape sorter.</td></tr>
<tr><td>Language: Amir uses Arabic and English at home.

Finger family finger play: "Abu finger, ummi finger, akhi finger, ukhti finger, tifli finger." (Daddy finger, mommy finger, brother finger, sister finger, baby finger). Yasmin will record this in Arabic and English for the classroom.</td><td>Language goals: Aunt Khadija will stay to sing songs and read in Arabic on Wednesdays.

Finger play goals: Add "Finger Family," "Itsy-Bitsy Spider," "Wheels on the Bus," and "Five Little Ducks."</td></tr>
<tr><td>Social–emotional: Amir is carried frequently at home and has constant positive interaction with older brothers, sisters, and extended family.</td><td rowspan="2">Social–emotional goals: Use Arabic words during book reading and routines:

Happy—Saeid
Sad—Hazin Sleepy—Naesan
Milk—Laban
Daddy—Babi
Momma—Mommy

Amir likes stays in close proximity to Ms. Sania and likes to be held. He enjoys social interaction and playing games.
Will assist in moving morning nap forward in 15-minute increments.</td></tr>
<tr><td>Caregiving goals: Amir is held for bottle and preparation for sleep.

In process of moving morning nap in 15-minute increments, so he doesn't fall asleep until 11:30.</td></tr>
</table>

CREATING INDIVIDUALIZED LESSON PLANS

Lesson planning creates a roadmap for what you will do to promote learning, not just a list of activities children will do. As you prepare, consider the developmental progress of the group as a whole and the emerging skills and contexts of individual children.

Areas of Child Development. The format of a lesson plan typically is organized by areas of development. As you plan, remember that areas of development are interdependent. For example, social skills are dependent on communication and regulatory skills. As you plan, think about what and how the child will be learning. These include:

- Language, communication, and literacy skills
- Social and emotional development
- Physical development (gross motor, health, well-being)
- Fine motor skills
- Cognitive development
- Scientific inquiry and social studies knowledge
- Creative expression (art, music, movement)

In order to engage in activities, four other competency areas need to be considered. These include skills for successful engagement in activities and interactions:

1. *Approaches to learning* include initiative, curiosity, persistence, and problem-solving skills.
2. *Regulatory skills* include assisted emotion competence, cognitive and behavior skills, flexibility, and attention.
3. *Processing skills* include the way the brain coordinates body systems, like visual, hearing, haptic, and sensory processing skills. These integrate the ways children respond to stimulation; their spatial awareness; and their responses to touch, pressure, proximity to others, and texture.
4. *Cultural and linguistic contexts* include the activities, people, places, and experiences already familiar to children. This understanding is needed to create cohesion between new learning and what children already understand.

A competency-based lens can encourage a broader view of children's independent, emerging, and future skills. These are the capabilities that need to be evaluated when children have difficulty adjusting or express frustration. Children cannot analyze their current situation or modify their setting. They need the knowledgeable support of adults to make appropriate evaluations and adjustments that ensure security, engagement, and learning.

Teacher Planning. As you prepare, consider the ingredients of the classroom and interactions that can strengthen children's skills, including:

- Spaces, furniture, and room arrangement that will support learning
- Integration of children's identity, culture, language, and family contexts
- Materials and activities children will enjoy exploring and investigating
- Concepts and vocabulary you want to support
- Teacher interactions needed to facilitate specific types of play
- Schedule and timing to foster child engagement

Practical Considerations. As you prepare, create a materials list. How will materials be moved or transported, if needed? What items need to be organized, prepared, or set up ahead of time? How will you meet the needs of individual children while supervising and addressing the needs of the group? What tasks will be assigned and carried out by a coteacher or other staff?

Designing a Lesson Plan. The lesson plan in Figure 3.3 focuses on a group of young toddlers exploring the contexts of their families. Your lesson plans may be adapted to include additional notes, developmental areas, or details that work best for you and your program. You will not use all the information in this chapter at the same time, but awareness of these skills, categories, and considerations will allow you to plan experiences using a more complex and accurate lens.

Figure 3.3. Lesson Planning Chart

Week: March 15	**Skills to Support**	*General theme:* **Families, Caring, Helping, Belonging** **Age: Young Toddler**	
Language and communication multilingual development	Identifying familiar people, places, and events Noticing and listening to others	*Concepts and Questions:* • Who is in your family? • What do you do with your family? • Who takes care of you? • How do you help your family? • Where do you go with your family? • How does your family comfort you? • What makes you and your family special?	*Vocabulary:* • Tall, short, big, small (*alto, bajo, grande, pequeño*) • Activities at home and in the neighborhood (*actividades en case y en el barrio*) • Family members (*miembros de la familia*) • Grocery store, house, building, library, park, zoo (*la tienda, case, edificio, biblioteca, parque, zoológico*)

(*continued*)

Figure 3.3. (*continued*)

<table>
<tr><th>Week:
March 15</th><th>Skills to Support</th><th colspan="2">General theme: Families, Caring, Helping, Belonging
Age: Young Toddler</th></tr>
<tr><td>Early literacy and book reading</td><td>Engaging with stories and books
Listening and understanding
Speaking, communicating, responding</td><td colspan="2">Book List:
Littles: And How They Grow Board Book, by K. DiPucchio
Families Grow, by D. Saks
Who Takes Care of You? by H. Eliot
I Am a Baby Board Book, by K. Allen
Me and My Mama: Celebrate Black Joy and Family Love, by C. Weatherford
All Kinds of People, by S. Rotner
The Family Book/El libro de la familia, by T. Parr
Mama Do You Love Me? by B. Joosse
I Love Us! A Book About Family, by C. Books
I Belong/Yo pertenezco, by C. Meiners
Responding:
Puppets, finger puppets, and flannel board paired with reading</td></tr>
<tr><td>Social–emotional development</td><td>Personal and cultural identity and belonging
Awareness of self and others
Helping and caring</td><td>Concepts and questions:
Families help and care for one another. Families are unique and special. A family is where you belong.
• Your family keeps you safe.
• Your family comforts you.
• Your family loves you. How do you help your family?
What songs and activities does your family enjoy?</td><td>Materials:
Family activities: Laminated family photos for child conversations; "I'm Special" child books to create and read; comforting activities, individual blankets, rocking, personal talking time.
Caring activities: Stuffed animals, puppets, doll care, blankets, baby bottles, strollers, high chair.
Helping activities: Washing dishes, folding clothes, feeding a pet, taking a bath.
Water play: Giving animals/pets a bath</td></tr>
<tr><td>Gross motor, physical development, health, and well-being</td><td>Rolling, catching, kicking, balancing, crawling, rolling, running</td><td colspan="2">Materials and activities:
• Ramp activity—partner ball rolling (with teacher)
• Balancing steps
• Ride-on bike and wiggle scooter
• Crawling and rolling on mat
• Stuffed animal buddy run with hoops and cones</td></tr>
</table>

(*continued*)

Figure 3.3. (*continued*)

Week: March 15	Skills to Support	*General theme:* **Families, Caring, Helping, Belonging** **Age: Young Toddler**
Fine motor	Fine motor, sequencing, comparing, cause and effect Persistence, making choices	*Materials and activities:* • Knob puzzles with families • Markers and stickers for the cardboard box house • Crumpling and throwing paper into the basket • Play dough "cooking" • Sorting cups and shape sorters • Matryoshka dolls
Cognitive development	Nature-science exploration	*Outdoor play:* Treasure bags for collecting nature objects. Nature tools: Magnifying glasses, tweezers *Nature books: Animals in My Backyard,* by Baby Professor and *Whose House Is This?* by E. Gregoire
Creative expression: Music and movement	Listening and responding, fine motor, language	*Song list:* • "Daddy Finger, Mommy Finger" • "Big and Small": "Some families are big, some families are small, I love my family, best of all." • "Grandma's Glasses": These are Grandma's glasses. This is Grandma's hat. This is the way she folds her hands and lays them in her lap. These are Grandpa's glasses. This is Grandpa's hat. This is the way he folds his arms, and takes a little nap."
Creative expression: Art	Listening and responding, fine motor	*Activities:* • Tissue collage on large print of individual families • Ms. Sanchez volunteers Monday and Wednesday • Easel painting with smocks, with laminated family photo clipped to easel and mirror for self-exploration • Mural drawing with family photos • Hand and foot tracing
Materials list: Tissue paper, glue sticks, books, colored paper, markers, stickers, laminated family photos, family books, puppets, finger puppets, flannel board		
Notes: Coordinate family support for creating "I am Special" books for new children (Noah and Kendra). Order tissue paper and glue sticks.		

CREATING INDIVIDUALIZED PLAY PLANS

Ms. Ella plays Peek-a-Boo with 10-month-old Oliver. She puts the blanket over her face and pops out with a laugh, "A boo!" Oliver giggles and wiggles. Ms. Ella hands Oliver the soft blanket and places a sock snowman underneath. "Where is the snowman? Where is he hiding?" She pulls the blanket off. "There is Mr. Snowman." Oliver laughs so hard, he topples onto Luis, who laughs, too.

Eleven-month-old Rio and 12-month-old Triana lean on a soft basket filled with cotton snowballs. They reach in and swirl the snowballs with their hands and arms. Ms. Maria says, "The snowballs are soft."

Ms. Ella (who speaks only English) and Ms. Maria (who is bilingual Spanish) have organized the spaces, prepared the materials ahead of time, and reflected together about the cultural and linguistic frameworks of the children. They carefully delegate tasks between them so they can focus their attention on the children's play.

Ms. Ella and Ms. Maria have worked with the city librarian to select winter books for the infants. The books include *I See Winter* by Charles Ghigna; *The Snowy Day* (*Un día de nieve*) by Ezra Jack Keats; *My Snow Day: Mi día nevado*, by Ally Nathaniel; *Winter Babies* by Kathryn Galbraith; *Hello Winter* by Shelly Rotner; *Snow Globe Wishes* by Erin Dealey; *Winter Walk in the City* by Cathy Goldberg Fishman; *Estamos en invierno* (*It's Winter*) by Joyce Jeffries; and *The Mitten* (*El mitón*) by Jan Brett.

Families receive the book list, and the books are sent home over the weekends in plastic zip bags with activities for the children. Materials include felt mittens that fit on the paws of a small bear, a scarf and hat to dress a sock snowman, finger puppets, and felt and laminated animals for children to hold that match the book characters.

In addition to lesson planning for the group, the teachers create an *individualized play plan* for each child. The plan describes specific ways they adapt teaching to a specific child during book reading, physical and sensory play, games and activities, and songs/finger plays. They use information from family meeting charts, observations, and goals defined in an IFSP, when available, to personalize the plan.

As you complete an individualized play plan, think about the child's emerging skills. What materials fit with their particular interests and development? What ways can you adjust the timing or presentation of materials to enhance playful engagement? How can you adjust the setting to ensure minimal frustration and an appropriate level of stimulation?

Figure 3.4 is an individualized play plan for an 11-month-old infant. Consider the learning goals, book lists, vocabulary and concepts, materials, activities, modifications, and adaptations. The individual play plan is shared with the family, the program director, substitute teachers, and other classroom teachers, so that daily interactions support the child's skills. You may add other areas of focus that make sense for the children in your care and your specific program.

Figure 3.4. Individualized Play Plan

Rowena B. 11-months	Skills	Spanish and English Vocabulary
Activity Roll the ball. *Rodar la pelota.*	• Eye–hand coordination • Coordinated attention • Attaching word labels	*Roll* the ball to me. *Throw* the ball into the basket. *Lanzar la pelota a la canasta.*
Book *Rosa Plays Ball. A Rosa le encanta jugar a la pelota,* by Jessica Spanyol	• Listening and language • Spanish and English vocabulary	Rosa can *kick* the ball. Kick the ball *into* the *net. Rosa patea la pelota. Patear el la pelota en la neto.*
Sorting/Sensory Sensory ball bin	• Sensory words • Understanding objects through tactile exploration • Coordinated attention	The balls are *squishy, round, soft,* and *smooth. La bola es blanda, redonda, suave y tersa.*
Game Peek-A-Boo with balls and blanket	• Attention and memory • Position vocabulary • Coordinated attention	Peek-a-boo, I see you. *Where* are you? You are *under* the *blanket. Peek-a-boo, te veo. ¿Dónde estás? Estás debajo de la manta.*
Song "Here's a Ball for Baby." Aquí tienes una pelota para bebé.	• Listening • Imitating • Assisted hand motions	"Here's a ball for baby, *big* and *soft* and *round." Aquí tienes una pelota para bebé, grande, suave y redonda.*

PROVIDING SUPERVISION FOR PLAY

"Good morning, Ms. Naomi." Ms. Patel, 2-year-old Ramon's mother, hangs his jacket, washes his hands, and comes with him to the carpeted area. There is a basket of folded clothes with shirts, shorts, and socks in sizes large enough to fit over the children's clothing. Ms. Patel says, "Want to play?" Ramon looks in the basket and pulls out a hand mirror and looks at himself. His mother helps him pull out a red shirt and socks. Ramon works hard to pull on the socks and kisses his mother goodbye. He climbs on Ms. Naomi's lap. She says, "Teddy bear has a zipper on his jacket. Can you pull it?" He zips the zipper up and down. She reads, I Can Do It Too! *by Karen Baicker. They point to the pictures and talk about what Ramon does at home.*

When Tyr and Hannah arrive, they read Brown Sugar Baby Board Book *by Kevin Lewis with Ms. Kait. They giggle and cover themselves up with the blanket on her lap. She reads, "Brown sugar baby, I'll keep you toasty warm." Then she asks, "What keeps you warm at home? Is your food warm? Is your bath warm? Is momma's hug warm?" Tyr says, "Blankey warm." Ms. Kait says, "Yes, your blanket is warm."*

Mr. Naomi and Ms. Kait have a busy day with 10 toddlers. They need to keep the children engaged, look out for safety, redirect busy bodies and hands, and encourage meaningful play. To extend the "I can do it" theme and match the activities in *Brown Sugar Baby*, the water table has pitchers and cups. The baby dolls have new caps, crocheted by Tyr's grandmother. The kitchen table has bright place mats with bowls and cups to feed the dolls and pots with spoons for cooking. Hannah's father comes in the afternoon to play the guitar, and Kayden's mother comes to read. This morning, the teachers are extra busy with snack and bathroom needs. They work together to make sure all the children are supported.

Figure 3.5. Responsive Supervision Checklist

As you consider your play spaces from the view of your infants and toddlers, try sitting on the floor just inside your classroom or play areas. Where would you go first if you were a child? What would be appealing to you that you could not wait to touch and explore? In what ways can you supervise the group as a whole yet still give focused time to individual children? What needs to be planned with your coteacher to coordinate supervision? The following questions can help you reflect on supervision, spaces, individual needs, and materials.

Supervision

- ❑ Do you have visual access to all children? The changing table and other furniture should not block visual supervision.
- ❑ Do you stay in close physical proximity, listening and watching with the goal of intervening early to minimize frustrations?
- ❑ Do you conduct a daily safety check of all materials and spaces? Shelving and heavy items should be secured to the wall. Cupboards with cleaning supplies should be secured, out of reach of children at all times. Monitor spaces and changing circumstances to ensure safety throughout the day.
- ❑ Do teachers monitor different areas of the room and supervise a specific group of children to coordinate support?
- ❑ Do you anticipate the ways children may need assistance with peer interactions?

Spaces

- ❑ Do children use all the spaces in the room, or do they congregate in just one area? What can you do to engage them in new areas?
- ❑ Are spaces for active play large/open enough for vigorous dancing and movement?
- ❑ Are spaces large enough for children to play without interruption or frustration? Monitor crowding, as infants and toddlers congregating in small spaces can introduce frustration.

Individual Children

- ❑ Do children have the skills to manage and enjoy the spaces, activities, and experiences?
- ❑ Are children's sensory needs met, such that they are not over- or understimulated by peers, activity and noise level, and duration of activities?

(*continued*)

Figure 3.5. (*continued*)

- ❑ Are children comforted and soothed? Is there a soft, inviting area of the classroom for them to take a protected break from the activity of other children?
- ❑ Do activities offer range of challenge levels that match individual children's skills?
- ❑ Do activities offer choices about how to engage? Are children free to disengage as they choose?

Materials

- ❑ Are materials waiting for children that are fresh and interesting daily?
- ❑ Do activities meet children's energy needs, including more intense activity and rest?
- ❑ What new or rotated materials, activities, or special projects are available?
- ❑ Are materials organized by theme and type to invite meaningful play?
- ❑ Are containers easy for children to retrieve, lift, and open?
- ❑ Do open-ended play materials encourage a wide range of play and sensory experiences?
- ❑ Are there enough high-value toys and props for multiple children to play?
- ❑ Are books and interesting materials displayed on the children's eye level and around the room in accessible containers and on open shelves?
- ❑ Are blankets and caring props (bottles, diapers, carriers, strollers) available for dolls?
- ❑ Are toys stored near appropriate play spaces, like a smooth surface available cars and block play?
- ❑ Do furniture and props engage range of skills across all areas of development (e.g., sand, water, light table, housekeeping and accessories, active play equipment)?
- ❑ Do younger infants have access to play gyms and portable cubes?

Q&As FROM THE FIELD: GETTING ORGANIZED AND STAYING FLEXIBLE

Question 1: May I reuse lesson plans from year to year?

Answer: Yes. File digital copies of lesson plans. Label lesson plans by date and theme. While lesson plan themes can be carried over year to year, specific application and selection of activities and materials will change, depending on the individual children you teach. Save reflection notes that indicate what you would plan or do differently next time. Individual play plans connected to specific lesson plans should be saved as part of the children's portfolio, with notes that record children's progress toward goals. Lesson plans and play plans are wonderful resources for communication with families and for ensuring accurate documentation of children's progress over time.

Question 2: *When I am working with one or two children, how can the other children be adequately supervised?*

Answer: Try using a large whiteboard for the daily schedule to indicate when it will be best for you and your coteacher to divide supervision. You will need to stay flexible, recognizing that what you plan for one child may result in a spontaneous small-group activity. You also will need to be responsive to the attention span and stimulation needs of the children. Over time, you will get to know individual differences and be able to plan accordingly.

FOR YOUR INFORMATION: RESOURCES FOR SOCIAL–EMOTIONAL AND REGULATION SKILLS

To learn more about the developmental processes and contributions to children's emerging social–emotional and regulatory skills, check out the following resources:

- The Center on the Developing Child at Harvard University offers information about brain building through play: https://developingchild.harvard.edu/resources/brainbuildingthroughplay/
- The Center for Early Childhood Mental Health Consultation at Georgetown University provides strategies for social and emotional development: https://www.ecmhc.org/tutorials/social-emotional/mod2_3.html
- The Center on the Developing Child at Harvard University presents information about executive function: https://developingchild.harvard.edu/resources

REFLECTION QUESTIONS

1. What are the most difficult challenges you have experienced or observed when teaching infants or toddlers at play? What specific factors contribute to these issues?
2. What action steps will improve play experiences for the infants and toddlers you teach?
3. What steps will help you be more intentional in observing and documenting children's play? How can you apply what you learn from observing children to lesson planning?
4. How can families be more involved in creating culturally relevant play experiences?

CHAPTER 4

Creating Consistent Routines and Transitions

This chapter presents the role of caring routines and rituals, such as arrival and departure procedures, mealtimes, diapering and toileting, and sleeping transitions in creating patterns for lifelong health and well-being. It offers a range of strategies for aligning home and program practices, with tips and ideas for planning, coordinating care with coteachers, and individualizing teaching to enhance learning and development throughout the day.

Learning Goal 1: Understand the roles of attunement, intersubjectivity, and culture sharing that are sustained by relationships that honor development and cultural differences and establish continuity between the home and the program.

Learning Goal 2: Identify the impact of respect for and affirmation of children's bodies, emotions, and perceptions during caregiving routines with the goal of establishing lifelong habits of self-identity, self-awareness, self-agency, and self-care.

Learning Goal 3: Describe teachers' active roles in strengthening children's skill development, language, and learning during caring routines, using consistent staffing patterns and schedules to coordinate planning and supervision.

MAKING MEANING THROUGH ROUTINES AND RITUALS

Ms. Lennon notices 2-year-old Lilly needs to blow her nose. Lilly is lying on her tummy, playing with a small doll, fitting it carefully into a small purse. "Hi, Lilly. Are you taking your doll to the store?" Lilly nods. Ms. Lennon continues. "I see your nose needs blowing. Does dolly need her nose blown, too?" Lilly stands up, takes Ms. Lennon's hand, and walks with her to the tissue box.

Ms. Lennon says, "Look Lilly. I'm going to wear a glove. Do you want to wear a glove to blow your doll's nose?" Lilly nods. She helps Lilly put on a glove. Lilly counts to three and blows the doll's nose. Ms. Lennon says, "Lilly, your nose looks sore. I will be very gentle." She counts to three and helps Lilly blow her nose. When they are finished, they drop the gloves in the garbage can and wash their hands, singing, "This is the way we wash our hands. . . . Now we wash the germs away."

Nearby, Ms. Jordyn helps Thomas change his wet shirt. He pushes his left arm into the sleeve. Ms. Jordyn says, "Next goes your right arm." After tucking in the shirt, she smiles and gives Jordyn a hug. "You are learning to get dressed by yourself." Ms. Jordyn notices Bailey, who is trying to spread a small blanket on the floor. "You take this end. Thomas and I will take that end." She offers one corner of the blanket to Thomas, and the three stretch the blanket on the floor.

It may seem the main goal of routines is to clean a runny nose or change a wet shirt. But these teachers focus on the primary goal—to create meaningful learning experiences for the children. They are playful, show affection, and ensure children are able to have choices and feel secure. The children join in willingly and enjoy personal time with the teachers.

The intentional awareness of children's experiences is called *attunement*, which involves a two-way transaction, as both the teacher and child contribute (Walbam, 2023). Teachers must be able to interpret children's cues correctly and recognize their thoughts, preferences, and feelings, also called *mind-mindedness* (Regueiro et al., 2022). Teachers are mindful of children's thoughts and intentions and attribute meaning and agency to their behaviors (Meins, 2013). These understandings, in turn, allow teachers to respond appropriately and engage children in meaningful learning and relational experiences.

While ways of responding differ within and between cultures, the use of *contingent responding* is universal (Lansford, 2022). Adults respond in timely and relevant ways to children's needs, even when ways of emotion expression, verbal interaction, or physical ways of comforting embody cultural differences. This sensitive ability to "synchronize in attunement" is demonstrated universally across cultures (Salih et al., 2023).

These interactions also reflect *intersubjectivity*, with shared awareness of an experience and of each other, when the adult is aware of the child's feelings, focus, and thinking (Gitz-Johansen, 2022). "The subjective states (e.g., excitement, sadness, joy, enthusiasm, discomfort, frustration, and confusion) that are shared by child and caregiver become parts of the child's personal experience that are shareable with the outer world" (p. 114). The teacher understands and "to some extent enters the feeling-state together with the child" (p. 115). Earlier work of Trevarthen (1992) explains intersubjectivity as a way of engagement, including *culture sharing* that happens actively, as infants are innate companions and cooperators. Culture sharing always takes place but may be unexamined or invisible. It must become a visible and intentional priority for practice.

Creating this physical and psychological space for belonging and caring about others is an important social justice issue that anchors children's sense of responsibility for self and others (Fleer, 2018). During routines, teachers serve as important role models for empathy, caring, and respect. They communicate affirmation for the unique contexts, perceptions, and ways of being of each child. As a result, children learn to observe, listen, and understand the feelings and needs of others, making sure all are included. The critical transactions of attunement, mind-mindedness, and intersubjectivity transform routines into sacred spaces for meaning-making and learning about the self and others.

Strategy Toolbox: Tips for Creating Positive Routines

Be affirming. Get to know and affirm each child's individual patterns, ways of responding, preferences, likes and dislikes, sense of humor, sensory responses, and unique or special traits.

Reflect family practices. Use familiar (family) vocabulary for diapering and comforting routines.

Create emotionally safe spaces. Give reassurance through phrases like "You can do it." "You're figuring it out." "You are making progress."

Make learning multidimensional. For example, show a child how you will change a diaper or use the toilet by demonstrating first with a plush animal or doll. Talk about how the diaper wipe feels on the bottom by demonstrating first on the arm.

See from the child's point of view. Sensitivity includes "the caregiver's ability to perceive and interpret accurately the signals and communications of the children's behavior, and to respond to them appropriately and promptly," a definition that comes from the work of Ainsworth et al., 1978, in Ramos et al., 2023, p. 2. Sensitive responding helps children learn how to manage their emotions, cope with stress, and over time develop the ability to self-regulate.

TEACHING CHILDREN ABOUT THEMSELVES

After using the bathroom, 2½-year-old Malek grunts as he tries to pull his pants up. He loses his balance and tips over onto Ms. Ellie's arm. "I have you. You are steady. Hold onto me," she encourages. "Let's pull together. You hold the front. Got it? I'll hold the back. One, two, three, pull!" Malek grins as the waistband slides into place. "Malik—you did it," says Ms. Ellie. You pushed your thumbs inside the front of your pants and pulled hard."

Routines are intimate and personal because they relate to care for the body and the associated emotions and sense of security connected with physical functions and self-awareness. The words adults say become the words children feel about themselves. Positive words include "You're okay. I will wait for you." "You can do it. You are a good helper." "It's okay. We'll clean it together." Words that may promote anxiety include "Hurry up." "I told you not to do that." "Look out. Stop doing that." "What's wrong with you?"

Kathy Reschke (2019) notes that children internalize perceptions about their physical selves and develop growing awareness of their abilities (i.e., what they can do) from the way they are treated during daily experiences. Children learn whether they are worthy of gentle care, personal attention, and support and kindness, especially when they need help, feel frustrated, or are upset. They define themselves by the experiences related to their physical selves, by what they can do, and by who others say they are (Garner & Yogman, 2021; Reschke, 2019, 2020). Affirming narratives may strengthen the positive messages or replace the negative messages children hear outside the program. Safe, stable, nurturing relationships cushion childhood adversity and strengthen skills for resilience (Garner & Yogman, 2021).

The words spoken during daily routines become the "words of life" that follow children as inner scripts for years to come. When they are older and feel upset, how will they soothe themselves? When they are hungry, will they have a healthy relationship with food? When their stomach hurts or it takes time to brush their teeth or use the toilet, will their inner dialog communicate self-kindness and patience? The way adults speak to, touch, and respond to children's physical needs teaches them self-compassion.

During self-care, a soiled diaper, fatigue, or frustration places children in a position of vulnerability, just at the time they are dependent on an adult to respond to them. Children may feel lonely for their family. They may worry an experience will be painful. Over time, they learn the sequence of events, timing, and rituals that feel comforting. Self-care interactions are a primary mechanism to establish trust and soothe stress.

The presence and awareness of a caring teacher strengthens the child's self-identity. During routines, children learn the patterns and joys of shared communication. They feel affirmed as worthy and important. This is the way their inner world of sensations connects with the shared world of interactions and learning. Teachers affirm children's sense of self.

Research Revisited: Checking In With Families

The contexts of the family, culture, language, and community set the priorities for interactions. The National Academies of Sciences, Engineering, and Medicine (NASEM) (2016) consensus report *Parenting Matters: Supporting Parents of Children Ages 0–8* explains that families are the most important factor for children's social, emotional, physical, and cognitive development and general well-being.

Families are also an important source of knowledge about their children's contexts and how to best nurture them (APA, 2023). The National Association for the Education of Young Children Position Statement on Developmentally Appropriate Practice (2020) also articulates the importance of families as children's first teachers and the source of children's identity and worth.

Yet cultural differences—unless actively explored—can be overlooked. "We can learn from each other across cultural boundaries, and . . . what we learn can be put to work for supporting the care and education of young children everywhere" (Harkness & Super, 2020, p. 10). Key cultural values are pointed out by Joan Test (2006/2015).

- Teachers in the United States often respond to children's disagreements about toys by asking, "Who had it first?" In contrast, children in Sweden are asked to consider offering the toy to the child who has not played with it as much.
- In the United States, teachers tend to assist children during meals, and children are encouraged to pay attention to their own experiences. "What does it taste like?" "Do you need anything?" In contrast, children in Italy are taught to notice the needs of other children during meals and to help them. "Can you see if Jacob needs help?"
- In the United States, children "transition" from one classroom to another alone. In Japan, children stay with a specific group over time.
- In the United States, children are encouraged to learn and discover in individual exploration, while in China, teachers focus on discipline, harmony, and responsibility.

Test notes that by 9 months, children begin to understand cultural values communicated by adults and internalize their meanings. By the ages of 9 to 14 months, children are active partners in creating cultural meaning. What values come to mind when you consider your ideas about sharing toys and supporting children during meals? What benefits do you see as important when a child transitions to a new teacher alone or in a group? Differences in cultural values lead to different experiences for children.

ANCHORING ROUTINES WITH PREDICTABILITY

Brynn is 9 months old and has not yet begun to crawl. She enjoys watching the antics of others and laughs heartily at funny sounds and games. Brynn's grandmother wakes her up on a strict schedule to dress and feed her. Brynn's mouth is wiped carefully, and the high chair tray is kept clean during feeding. Grandmother takes Brynn out of the high chair, wipes her hands, and dresses her in a sweater. Within 5 minutes, Brynn is tucked into the stroller for a brisk walk to the program.

After a morning of happy play, Ms. Diedie changes Brynn's diaper and puts on her pajamas and a sleep sack. She lays Brynn in the crib at 11:30 and pats her back for just a minute. "Night, night. Sleep tight, sweet Brynn. Have a happy sleeping time." Ms. Diedie normally rocks the infants before sleeping, but she is careful to follow the families' instructions.

The ritual of changing from clothing to pajamas, the warmth of the sleep sack, the back patting, and quiet words mirror the home routine and are signals to Brynn that it is sleeping time. Ms. Diedie knows Brynn's family is highly attuned to her needs, even adjusting her arms and legs so they are straight, once she falls asleep. She and the other teachers value this level of care and structure and see these practices as reflecting the family's strengths.

This classroom offers many connections to home. The arrival and departure routines, morning feedings, diaper changing, and naptimes are comfortably structured by familiar greetings, cues, and interactions. The teachers have a system for who will do what and keep the routines consistent.

Depending on consistent people, places, and routines is essential for children's emotional development, mental health, and well-being (Gee & Cohodes, 2021, 2023). The external predictability influences internal emotion regulation. Through consistent ways of adult responding, daily songs and cues, and the familiar patterns of play and routines, children learn what is expected. Predictability is especially critical during the rapid brain development of the infant and toddler years. Children internalize external patterns as being normal and depend on stable and responsive relationships to decrease stress and promote resilience (Cantor et al., 2018).

Research Revisited: Primary Caregiving and Continuity of Care

Practicing relationship-based caring and teaching approaches provides important relational connectedness and continuity for teachers, as well as for families and children. Families seek trustworthy and coordinated care, and children benefit from individualized care.

Notably, infant and toddler teachers experience the highest turnover rate in the field. **Forty-nine percent leave their centers or the field each year (Bassok et al., 2021).** Unfortunately, the turnover rate is higher (50%) for programs serving children birth to 3 receiving subsidies; yet only 26–27% turnover is present when serving families without subsidies (Amadon et al., 2023). With children's critical needed for stability, focusing on the importance of predictable relationships can make a difference.

Predictability for infants and toddlers can be supported through specific staffing patterns, including a co-caring model, primary caregiving, and continuity of care. Each approach contributes to developing rich and meaningful knowledge of and relationships with the family and children.

- ***Co-caring models of care*** are provided when caregiving decisions are shared by families and teachers. Teachers know a family's ways of nurturing and ensure consistency between home and program. Children feel secure, and families feel included in the decisions that relate to children's development and learning (Lang et al., 2016).
- In ***primary caregiving,*** one teacher takes the main responsibility for a small group of children. They facilitate caring routines, individualize teaching, maintain records, and take the lead role in communication with families. This ensures children experience security and that teachers establish deep and rich bonds with families (Lee et al., 2016).
- ***Continuity of care*** means that young children and their teachers stay together as a group for 2 to 3 years, with the goal of ensuring stability through the 3rd year (Benson McMullen, 2017; Polk & Bogard, 2016). Continuity of care results in more secure attachment and fewer behavior and emotional adjustments for children (Ruprecht et al., 2016; Sosinsky et al., 2016). Children feel secure and connected (Horm et al., 2018). A consistent teacher is more likely to affirm a child's identity and context and provide personalized and responsive care (Ebbeck et al., 2022).

While space, staffing, and enrollment instability may impact implementation, programs are encouraged to consider adaptive ways to incorporate continuity of care. For example:

- A teacher may go with the children as they move to a new classroom.
- A teacher may remain with the children in the same classroom over time by revising spaces and materials to meet the needs of advancing development.
- A teacher may work in a multi-age classroom where children range from infancy to age 3. Children transition to a preschool classroom (age 3–5) when developmentally ready.

The way children are assigned to teachers depends on the decision-making processes of the program. Teachers must demonstrate professional insight about their own characteristics and approaches to teaching to ensure a good fit with the temperament, cultural background, language, and specific strengths and needs of each child. Care should be taken to connect families and children with teachers who may best provide support for second-language acquisition. While racial and ethnic matches between teacher and children are encouraged, all teachers can promote and protect children's identity and family practices (DeMeo Cook et al., 2023).

FACILITATING ARRIVAL AND DEPARTURE RITUALS

Nine-month-old Anna's mother, Dr. Nowak, reaches out to hug her and makes loud kissing sounds onto her daughter's neck. "Kochanie, Kochanie kotku, kocham, cię!" (This means "Darling, darling kitten, I love you," in Polish.) Dr. Nowak greets her the same way every afternoon. Anna always laughs. Ms. Halina laughs, as well. "Dr. Nowak, you have to see what Anna did today. Can you stay for a few minutes?" Dr. Nowak agrees.

After saying goodbye to Gavin and Kiri, Ms. Halina sits by the crawling tunnel. "Look, Anna." Ms. Halina makes a squeaking sound with a stuffed parrot at the opening of the tunnel and says, "Come see the parrot!" Anna crawls inside the other end of the tunnel, stopping to shriek and smile back at her mother. She heads toward the parrot but then turns and crawls back to her mother. "I love how she comes to you and laughs," says Ms. Halina. "I love to see the way she hugs you when she crawls onto your lap."

This infant classroom has welcoming arrival and departure routines. Families who need to leave for work know they can visit later in the day. Ms. Halina wants Dr. Nowak to experience the joy of watching Anna in the tunnel, rather than just hearing about her progress. The shared observation time builds trust between the teacher and family. The infants also benefit from the warm relationships they see between their teacher and family.

Strategy Toolbox: Creating Reassuring Coming and Going Routines

Ask families to share special rituals they enjoy with their children when coming to and leaving the program. Below are some strategies you can adapt for your program.

Welcome and Goodbye Routines

- Encourage families to have a special ritual daily, with hello and goodbye words, a whispered pet name, a song, or finger play.
- Offer a sincere greeting. "I can't wait to play with you." "I have a kitten waiting for you." "I've been waiting for you to come." "You are so special to me."
- Laminate and display family photos by the door, so families and children can point to the images during rituals. "Say goodbye to Daddy. Say goodbye to Nana."
- Make a welcoming space with a counter, shelves, and bulletin board where families pick up daily information and leave written communication, even when the program uses a digital app for family communication.

- Locate cubbies by the entrance wall, so families don't have to walk across the room to tuck in children's belongings.
- Ensure a direct and meaningful exchange of children from families to teachers in each classroom, even when your program uses a technology-based sign-in/out process (computer or iPad) at the entrance of the building.
- Remove children from car seats or safety carriers before transferring care to the teacher. Review your state licensing restrictions for physical care and supervision related to the use of car seats, swings, walkers, bouncy chairs, and high chairs.
- Prepare a special transition from afternoon play to family pickup. For example, play soft music, read a book, and sing a special goodbye song.
- Carry out a consistent ritual for leaving the program, including blowing kisses goodbye or giving a high five. Use children's names and say, "I'll be thinking of you. See you tomorrow!" "Have fun with Momma!"

Preparing Inviting Spaces and Activities

- Prepare arrival activities for calming and soothing with quiet meditation music, soft scarves, stuffed animals, and care materials for dolls like blankets and bottles.
- Introduce busy boards, construction materials, puzzles, and other fine motor activities. Support with one-on-one interaction and focus.
- Design soft cozy spaces for comforting and quiet time with teachers.
- Group thematic materials, like books about animals, tucked in a basket with soft plush animals that are easily visible and accessible.
- Interact with finger play, rocking, and singing. A soft container of rattles, rain sticks, shakers, drums, castanets, and bells invite listening and responding.
- Engage the senses. Use low tables to offer open-ended sensory play, including play dough, fabric and scarf play, with soft, interactive touch books.
- Provide cups, tubes, and water toys for squeezing, filling, and pouring during water play. Sand tables should include a child-sized broom, smocks, and many types of scooping and molding materials.

CREATING CONTINUITY IN FEEDING ROUTINES

Ms. Karim brings a padded lunch container with a cold pack around baby bottles filled with milk. She hands the container to Ms. JoAnn and explains that Alvina's milk can be warmed as usual in the bottle warmer. Ms. JoAnn asks, "Is this your normal formula for Alvina?" Ms. Karim says, "No, we are treating her for allergies and have switched to camel's milk. It heats and is fed the same way."

While Ms. JoAnn thanks Ms. Karim politely, she has never heard of feeding a child camel's milk. Later in the day, she conducts a quick Internet search and finds that camel milk is rich in antioxidants and provides a wide variety of health benefits. She also sees that it is used widely by families from the Middle East and Russia and is gaining in popularity in the United States.

Cultural practices are often visible through ways of feeding. Some infants are fed on demand, while others are kept on a strict time schedule. Some families allow children to self-select food and don't make them finish what is given to them. Other families may value neatness and be concerned when children play with food, make a mess, or waste food. Understanding differences can help you be sensitive and supportive to children.

Adjusting to a high chair or family-style eating may be a new experience. Older infants and toddlers may have been hand-fed and never managed food independently. Other children may come to the table to receive a bite of food when they are ready and then return to playing. Sensitivity, support, and patience will be needed as they gradually adjust to eating with other children.

Families may request the use of alternative formulas like camel and goat milk, along with breast milk, which needs to be handled following family instructions. Other food allergies need to be taken into consideration, such as dairy, gluten, and nut restrictions. Families may request gripe water, tea, and other supplements. Many ways of feeding are part of religious or cultural practices, and teachers may need to support children in new ways.

State and professional standards provide guidelines for safe feeding that may require sensitive conversations with families. To be as responsive and inclusive as possible about family feeding requests, consult with your local licensing representative, as well as a cultural broker. You will likely be able to incorporate family requests, including ways of preparing formula and inclusion of familiar foods.

Your program should provide guidelines in the family handbook when feeding practices are required as part of licensing regulations. For example, bottles and blankets are not allowed in cribs with infants. It's okay to explain licensing regulations clearly: "I am happy to adjust Daria's schedule and feed her in the rocking chair, but we don't give bottles in the crib due to licensing regulations."

Collaborate with families to create an individualized feeding plan for each child. What are the specific feeding instructions, type of foods, amounts, and schedule? Instructions must be updated regularly to stay current with each child's development. The individualized feeding plan and instructions should be signed by the family and you. One copy is kept and used by the program, and the other copy is given to the family.

PROMOTING AUTONOMY, CHOICE, AND SELF-AGENCY

Ms. Marie sees that 13-month-old Luke turns his head when offered a drink. She puts the cup down and asks, "Luke, do you want more sweet potatoes?" Luke leans over the side of the high chair and reaches for the floor. "More banana?" Luke shakes his head. "Okay, sweetie. Let's get your hands clean so you can play." Ms. Marie adds, "Want to play with the pop beads?" Soon they are laughing at the funny sounds the beads make when pulled apart.

Ms. Marie watches carefully for children's responses, always honoring cues that indicate they are hungry for more or are finished. Creating a safe space for autonomy, choice, and self-agency during feeding is important for child well-being. Coercive eating practices often create an ongoing unhealthy relationship with food, including emotional overeating, disordered eating, and obesity (Patel et al., 2018).

Telling a child to finish a food item before receiving more of another, suggesting what a child should eat, or telling a child to eat everything on the plate are examples of coercive practices. Being made to sit at the table (or high chair) until finished and spoon-feeding to make them eat more rob children of control and self-agency, with detrimental impacts to eating patterns and health that can last a lifetime. Children need teachers to ensure eating experiences are positive and comfortable, without control or conflict (Johnson et al., 2024).

Children should be encouraged to eat at their own pace, without being asked to finish or to hurry eating. Comments like "Take another bite," "Don't eat too fast," and "You can't play until you finish" remove autonomy and choice. Adults are never to urge children to eat more, use food to control or reward behavior, or make children finish what they have taken, no matter whether the teacher or child serves the food (Blaine et al., 2015). Ongoing adult spoon-feeding also increases dependence on the adult to determine how much and what should be eaten and increases the risk of overfeeding (Markham Risica et al., 2022).

Children should be encouraged to serve themselves, allowing them control over what and the amount they eat (AAP, 2024b). When body cues are respected, children learn to recognize and honor their own cues for hunger and satiation. When food is restricted or used as a threat or bribe, children's biologically wired ability to balance energy and food needs becomes impaired. Adults may have been raised with strong messages ingrained: "You've had enough." "If you don't clean up, you can't have a treat." When these patterns continue, children listen to the external coercive messages given by others instead of noticing and responding to their own balanced, internal cues for hunger.

In addition, food should not be used to soothe or comfort emotions (e.g., "Let's give you a hug and get you a snack to feel better"). This practice leads to children using food to comfort themselves rather than learning to recognize, label, and express their emotions. The goal is to model healthy ways to satisfy emotional needs through positive relationships.

For similar reasons, the American Academy of Pediatrics (AAP) asks families and programs to avoid the use of media at all times during meals (AAP, 2023a). The AAP guidelines note that when watching or interacting with media, children may eat beyond feeling full and will miss out on important conversations, and watching TV while eating is directly linked to obesity. One in five children in the United States are obese, disproportionately impacting racial, ethnic, and lower socioeconomic communities (CDC, 2024a; Kim et al., 2023).

A good phrase to remember is "The adult provides, the child decides" (Riley et al., 2018). Toddlers should have access to fresh and minimally processed foods with little or no added sugar (e.g., fruits, vegetables, lean protein, seeds, whole grains). Children will begin to try new foods as they see teachers eating a variety of foods themselves and enjoying them, and when healthy foods are made available as choices. Positive modeling affirms children's developing awareness of their physical needs and the ability to express their needs to others.

Research Revisited: Talking During Meals

Responsive feeding means teachers offer "timely, developmentally appropriate, and contingent responses to children's cues and includes providing clear mealtime structure and a warm emotional tone to the feeding environment" (Barrett et al., 2023, p. 1297). This approach is incredibly important to children's long-term well-being. "Beyond their nutritional aspect, meals are so central in the very young child's daily life that the quality of the feeding and eating experience affects the child's sense of security and basic trust, inner sense of self, mastery, autonomy, and initiative" (Keren, 2019, p. 393).

Research shows that during meals, teachers are less likely to be warm and sensitive and have fewer stimulating conversations compared to during free play interactions (Guedes et al., 2020). Teachers interact less frequently and have lower-quality conversations during meals than during other parts of the day, even in high-quality programs (Degotardi et al., 2016; Hallam et al., 2016). Teachers need to take care of tasks early so they can focus on the children and provide personal and positive eating experiences daily.

Children quickly progress from being nursed or bottle-fed to eating finger foods in a high chair, learning to use utensils, and finally sitting at a low table. For this reason, teachers need to stay in touch with families on a regular basis—updating information frequently. Below are steps to help you make mealtimes meaningful.

Strategy Toolbox: Making Meal and Snack Times Responsive

Talking

- ❑ Sit with the children and talk with them, making sure mealtime is happy and relaxed.
- ❑ Model table manners, like saying please and thank you, and show enjoyment of the children and the time together.
- ❑ Provide assisted support and encouragement as children sit at the table, manage the food, take care of spills, and interact with peers.

Planning

- ❑ Gather materials and foodstuffs ahead of time so transitions to and from meals are brief. Use a cart to transport materials to facilitate table setting and serving.
- ❑ Place food on the table when ready to assist with serving and feeding so children don't wait for an extended time.
- ❑ Prepare snacks prior to the start of the program day to minimize transitions.
- ❑ Indicate task assignments for snacks and meals on a whiteboard. Maintain a system for cleanup; include a freshly lined trash container, spray bottle and paper towels for spills, and broom and dustpan.
- ❑ Include food choices suggested by families that reflect what children eat at home.
- ❑ Seek online resources from your state Child Care Resource and Referral (CCR&R) agency, department of health, and state extension program for additional information about nutrition and feeding practices for infants and toddlers.

OVERCOMING PRACTICAL CHALLENGES: CAUTIONS AND INFORMATION ABOUT FOOD SAFETY

Programs must keep up-to-date health records, including a detailed food plan for children with allergies. Program staff need training to prevent, recognize, and treat allergic reactions to food. The most frequent allergies for infants and toddlers include eggs, cow's milk, peanuts, soy, fish, and shellfish (Johns Hopkins Medicine, 2024). Program staff must be able to manage food allergies, preventing access to allergy-inducing foods, and posting food allergies prominently in the child care facility, the food preparation areas, and classrooms.

All foods that present choking risks must be avoided, including hot dogs, nut/seed butters (unless spread thinly), cherries, hard candy and jelly beans, gum, whole grapes and cherry tomatoes, marshmallows, raw carrots and beans, celery, popcorn, seeds, and large chunks of any food such as meat, potatoes, and raw vegetables and fruits (AAP, 2024a). Infants should never be propped up with bottles or given cereal in the bottle. These practices present a choking hazard, prevent children from removing the bottle when finished, and deprive them of important physical and social connections during feeding.

Explore the following resources to learn more about feeding and food safety requirements for infants and toddlers:

- Centers for Disease Control and Prevention, Advancing Early Child Nutrition in Early Care and Education: https://www.cdc.gov/early-care-education/php/early-child-nutrition/
- The USDA Feeding Infants in the Child and Adult Care Food Program (2021) national guidelines for infants: https://www.fns.usda.gov/tn/feeding-infants-child-and-adult-care-food-program
- The USDA Food and Nutrition Service: Nutrition Standards for CACFP Meals and Snacks (Updated 2016, with additional policy memos) guidelines for infants and toddlers: https://www.fns.usda.gov/cacfp/meals-and-snacks

INTERACTING DURING DIAPERING AND TOILETING

Kendra, at 2 and a half, is just beginning potty training. Ms. Hannah usually takes Kendra to the potty every 2 hours as planned with Kendra's mother. But at 10:30, Kendra pulls on Ms. Hannah's hand. Ms. Hannah responds, "Oooh, my girl. Ready to go?" Kendra nods. They walk together to the bathroom. "Whoo hoo! You came to get me! Let's pull your pants down. Can you get on the potty by yourself" "Do it," says Kendra. Ms. Hannah hands Kendra toilet paper. When Kendra is finished, she wipes. "Your momma will be proud of you." She gives a silent cheer with her hands in the air. "Okay. Cover your ears!" Kendra places her hands on both sides of her head and nods. Ms. Kendra flushes.

Ms. Hannah helps Kendra get her pants back up, which is harder than pulling them down. She helps Kendra wash her hands and says, "You want to play with the panda bears?" Kendra nods, and Ms. Hannah gives her a hug.

Easton is deeply focused on playing. Ms. Hannah goes to him and says, "Time for a potty break. You can come back to the pegboards afterward. I'll go with you to the bathroom." Easton takes her hand but wets his pants just as he gets inside the bathroom. Ms. Hannah says, "Don't worry. You are making progress. Do you need to go more?" Easton nods yes. Ms. Hannah helps him get his clothing off, and he sits on the toilet. "Good. You went some more. I'll help you wipe." Because Easton has a bowel movement, Ms. Hannah helps him and finishes cleaning him with a wet wipe on his bottom. "Here are dry underwear and pants." Easton holds onto Ms. Hannah's shoulder while pushing one leg and then another into the dry pants. "We are a good potty team," says Ms. Hannah. "I am glad we can do it together."

Ms. Hannah is reassuring and sensitive to the children. She knows Kendra doesn't like the flushing sound. She knows Easton often is so focused on play that he doesn't notice the signals that he needs to go to the bathroom. She is very careful to be gentle and encouraging, knowing that going to the bathroom involves alignment with home practices, readiness, and a lot of practice.

The bathroom has bright, colorful pictures displayed on the bathroom wall at the children's eye level with the steps as a reminder to the children and the teachers. Pull pants down. Get on potty. Wipe with toilet paper. Pull up pants. Wash hands. The teachers point to the pictures as they talk with the children. The teachers keep a whiteboard on the wall next to the bathroom door, where they schedule times to take individual children, with a column to note the time the children actually go to the bathroom.

This classroom has a potty song and a basket of books about going to the potty. The children like *Toilet Time* by Janet Hall, *Suho Goes to Poop, It's Potty Time: A Toddler Prep Book,* and *Let's Go to the Potty!* by Allison Jandu, which show photos and realistic pictures. Books are available in Spanish, such as *El libro de basinica del pequeñito* (*The Toddler's Potty Book* by Alida Allison). The teachers use animal puppets to read the books and act out the steps, which the children enjoy. They use words each family uses for body parts, urine, and bowel movements. There is a pretend potty, and the children play with stuffed animals and dolls to help them go to the pretend potty.

What seems like simple tasks actually involve a range of complex cultural, social, physical, and emotional factors. Teachers must consider variations in physical readiness, monitor anxiety and sensory issues, understand professional standards, view routines as times for meaningful connection and learning, and understand cultural and family variations for diapering and potty training,

- **Physical readiness.** Going to the bathroom starts sooner than what happens in the bathroom, as children learn to recognize their body's signals and respond soon enough to make it to the bathroom in time. "They need to be able to sense the urge to go, be able to understand what the feeling means, and then be able to verbalize that they need your help to make it to the toilet and actually go" (American Academy of Pediatrics, 2022, p. 1). When accidents happen, the teachers are gentle, kind, and supportive.

  Importantly, the teachers know that between 12 and 18 months, children have very little control, and that generally children begin to toilet train between 27 and 36 months of age (Johns Hopkins Medicine, 2024). They honor individual differences and respect family requests related to timing. While some toddlers will be ready to sleep at naptime with regular underwear, others will use a pull-up or diaper.

- **Anxiety and sensory issues.** Children may have anxiety about using the potty or being diapered away from home. At times, they have a diaper rash and may associate getting wiped with having a sore bottom. They may feel uncomfortable with the texture or temperature of clothing, wipes, ointments, and diapers. Toddlers may fear disappointing an adult or having an adult become angry with them. For these reasons, consistency, encouragement, and gentle support are always used.
- **Professional standards.** The Caring for Our Children Basics: Health and Safety Foundations for Early Care and Education (ACF USDHHS, 2015) explicitly prohibits toilet learning and training methods that punish, demean, or humiliate a child, and forbid any sarcastic language or derogatory remarks about the child or child's family, along with threats about physical punishment. Diapering and toileting must be respectful.
- **Meaningful learning.** Caring routines are a prime time for building relationships and having personal conversation. However, research shows that "diapering is completed quickly, on average in less than 2 minutes" (Lauren, 2018, p. 11). This fast pace does not allow time for high-quality interactions, nor does it accommodate the slower pace infants and toddlers require for absorbing and processing information and communication. Diapering and toileting are perfect times for spending meaningful time with children.
- **Cultural variations.** Cultural approaches to diapering and toileting differ widely, from adult regimented to completely child initiated (Howard, 2017). Over the decades, toilet training approaches have varied widely and have been dictated by the culture, societal contexts, and parenting trends. Families may begin to train children as infants, which requires conscientious monitoring of children's subtle cues. In contrast, they may use late training, allowing children to wear diapers into the third year of life.
- **Family variations.** In addition to cultural variation in diapering approaches, families use different terms, sequences, and styles of diapering. The ways families talk with children during diapering and toileting, sensitivity to physical needs, and relational interactions during caring routines can differ widely (Sundnes, 2018). Physical support differs, including the positioning of the child (standing up, laying down, squatting) and types of diapers (wool, cotton cloth, disposable) and clothing styles. For each of these differences, teachers will need to have sensitive communication with families and stay in communication with the licensing representative.

Strategy Toolbox: Tips for Diapering and Toileting

Check and change diapers at specific times so children expect the routine and rituals. For example, after breakfast (or feeding), after coming inside, and after nap, routines become part of the daily pattern. Licensing regulations require that diapers are checked for wetness and soiling at least hourly, with visual inspection at least every 2 hours, or when children indicate discomfort or give other cues they are wet or soiled. Diapers should be checked immediately after children wake up from a nap. Check your state licensing regulations for details.

Be scrupulous about health and safety. When changing a diaper, follow sanitary procedures for removing and disposing of soiled materials. Wash both your hands and the baby's hands after diaper changing and toileting, following licensing requirements. Also follow rules for routine cleaning, sanitizing, and disinfecting of all diapering and bathroom areas.

Create a daily report for families. The family report should include the time of the diaper change, any details about the process, and a description of the diaper content. Ask families what words they want you to use to describe wetness or soiling. For toddlers learning to use a toilet, provide a daily schedule of trying times and eliminating times, along with details about accidents and successes. Use strengths-based language and focus on positive progress.

Honor children's focus and engagement. When changing diapers or taking a child to the bathroom during play, provide verbal reassurance that they can return to the same play. This helps them feel safe leaving play for a few minutes.

Supervise constantly. *At all times*, stay in immediate, direct contact with infants or toddlers while diapering or assisting with toileting. Visual supervision is not enough. You must be in immediate proximity to the child, meaning you are able to touch the child. For this reason, all diapering materials and clothing should be gathered together ahead of time. Sinks and supplies should be convenient. Diapering tables should not block visual supervision of other children.

Communicate with your coteachers. Even with the use of a whiteboard and schedule, ongoing verbal and visual communication with your colleagues can ensure you each understands the other's intentions and plans. When it comes to safety, constant double-checking and confirming of supervision is required.

PROVIDING CONSISTENCY FOR SLEEPING ROUTINES

Mr. Novak enters the infant classroom to pick up 4-month-old Cooper. When he arrives, Cooper is sleeping. When Ms. Sarah gets Cooper from the crib, Mr. Novak sees he is not sleeping with the teddy bear the family provided. He asks, "Where is Cooper's teddy bear?" Ms. Sarah smiles and says, "The teddy bear is so beautiful. Can you tell me about it?" Mr. Novak explains. "Yes, my wife Ciarra's mother made it for Cooper. It means a lot to us that Cooper has it while sleeping. It is what helps him sleep at home."

Sarah responds, "Oh, I can tell it was made specially for him. The colors and patterns are so pretty. I let Ms. Novak know that we aren't able to let Cooper keep the bear in the crib. Our program licensing requirements require infants to be alone in the crib without soft items. We do let him play with it for comforting when he is awake. Today, Cooper played with it for a few minutes after his feeding, and he had no trouble going to sleep."

"I really appreciate that you talked with me about it." Mr. Novak responds, "Thank you for explaining. I am glad that you talked about it with Ciarra, too."

There are many daily issues that may seem insignificant to a teacher but that provide important reassurance to families. The Novaks' first child was cared for at home by Ciarra's mother, so this is the family's first experience leaving one of their children in the care of others. Rather than simply stating the rules, Ms. Sarah thoughtfully asks Mr. Cooper about the bear. By asking first, she learns more about the family and the relationship Cooper has with his grandmother. She uses the bear as a way to connect and build understanding.

Through this interaction, Sarah reassures the family that Cooper is able to spend time with the bear and use it as a comfort item outside of the crib. Because Sarah asks for more information and shows personal care and interest, the conversation feels reassuring to Mr. Novak. Approach all questions related to comfort items, sleeping procedures, clothing, pacifiers, and rituals for naptime as a way to learn and connect. Responding with thoughtful care and sensitivity can help families feel heard, understood, and included.

Sleeping routines can raise many issues for teachers. Families may request binding or swaddling past the age a teacher believes is appropriate. They may request that infants wear clothing with long ties or buttons that are considered a strangling or choking hazard. Like Ms. Sarah, teachers may admire the clothing and explain that the program requires that knitted caps be slip-on, without ties. These are issues that should be discussed fully when the family first enrolls in the program.

Napping procedures can raise questions, as well. Teachers may be used to settling children by rocking and holding them facing inward. They will need to know when a family positions a child outward to comfort her (Keller et al., 2018). A family may wish to have a child placed in the crib on a very strict schedule that is followed at home, when the teacher is used to following children's cues for sleepiness, low energy, or fussiness. A teacher may want to soothe an infant when she fusses, when the family wants the child to be placed in the crib, even when fussing. To transition a child to sleep, families may ask teachers to rock the child to sleep or to stand by the crib to comfort. Teachers also may interact with infants and toddlers that have never slept in a crib because they co-sleep with families at home.

While napping routines are always individualized for infants and toddlers, older infants and toddlers may be consolidating two naps into one. Families may request children sleep only in the early afternoon. Over time, with a consistent schedule and routines, toddlers conform to a regular napping schedule. You may hear family members say that they are surprised to see the consistency of sleep patterns in the classroom—and thank you for helping get the child onto a regular schedule.

Making decisions that are culturally appropriate for a child requires teachers to invite families to show them how they put children to sleep. How quickly adults anticipate needs, step in, styles of touching, ways of holding, approaches to co-regulation, and strategies for soothing contribute to the predictable pattern of naptime. Teachers learn from observing sleeping routines, as well as discussing them. Because many ways of carrying out routines should not be assumed, teachers must take active steps to learn from families about what is done in the home. Understanding the ways families provide emotional support and comforting are part of napping success.

Strategy Toolbox: Learning About Sleeping Patterns

During nap transitions, children seek the comfort of their families. What do you need to know about facilitating sleeping routines? How do you know what families do at home? How do you assume children will respond? You will need to ask families the following questions.

- ❑ Does the child co-sleep or sleep alone?
- ❑ Does the child sleep in a crib, in the parent's bed, on the floor, or in another location?
- ❑ What is the sleep schedule at home? What happens before and after sleep?
- ❑ What happens during sleep? Does the child sleep with the light on? Do they listen to white noise or music? Are they accustomed to household noise?
- ❑ What does the child wear for napping? Do they wear their regular clothing, pajamas, and/or a sleep sack?

- ❑ Does the child use a pacifier, lovey, or snuggle blanket (the small plush blankets with a stuffed animal head attached), teething toys, or a plush animal?
- ❑ What routines like book reading, singing, rocking, walking, or back patting are used at home?
- ❑ Is the child fed a bottle or nursed at home before napping or bedtime sleeping?
- ❑ How is the child laid in the crib? Are they adjusted in any way after falling asleep?
- ❑ How does the child typically wake up? What greeting and comforting rituals are used?
- ❑ How long does the child typically transition after napping before going on to play activities? What do they typically prefer after waking up?

The use of pacifiers during napping is a decision that families should make in collaboration with their pediatrician. For both infants and toddlers, pacifiers used during naptime are sanitized and kept in cubbies until naptime and then sanitized and stored after napping.

PLANNING THE DAILY SCHEDULE

Planning an effective schedule depends on a variety of factors. While the schedule provides a basic framework for the day, the needs of the children also are considered on a daily basis. The goal is to design the schedule for your specific context so families, staff, and children have a consistent and practical pattern to follow. The following are some considerations:

- The schedule will be adjusted over time to align with the ages and abilities of children.
- Opening and closing times and enrollment patterns will set the boundaries for your particular planning.
- Families in one program may drop off and pick up children consistently at stated hours, whereas other programs may have a more flexible arrival and departure policy.
- Outdoor play space scheduling may need to be coordinated with other classroom groups.
- Teachers may take children outdoors to play or for a walk to accommodate the weather patterns or the stimulation needs of the children.
- For infants and young toddlers, naptime may take place in the morning prior to lunch rather than after. For example, naptime may take place from 11:00 to 12:30, with lunch and outdoor time to follow.

Once you create a written schedule, test it over a 2-week period, making adjustments until the actual schedule is congruent with the printed schedule. Figure 4.1 shows a sample schedule for your reference.

Figure 4.1. Sample Daily Schedule

7:00–8:30 a.m.

- ❑ Welcome rituals
- ❑ Comfort and individualized playtime
- ❑ Bottles, breakfast
- ❑ Handwashing, diapering, and toileting

8:30–10:30 a.m.

- ❑ Individualized teacher–child interactions
- ❑ Free play
- ❑ Handwashing, diapering, and toileting
- ❑ Snack

10:30–11:30 a.m.

- ❑ Outdoor play: When weather does not permit, alternative indoor gross motor play
- ❑ Handwashing, diapering, and toileting

11:30 a.m.–12:30 p.m.

- ❑ Lunch
- ❑ Handwashing, diapering, and toileting
- ❑ Quiet play and book reading

12:30–1:00 p.m.

- ❑ Transition to napping

1:00-2:30 p.m.

- ❑ Naptime
- ❑ Handwashing, diapering, and toileting
- ❑ Play

3:00–3:30 p.m.

- ❑ Outdoor play
- ❑ Handwashing, diapering, and toileting

3:30—5:30 p.m.

- ❑ Snack
- ❑ Play—indoor and outdoor
- ❑ Handwashing, diapering, and toileting
- ❑ Departure routines

COMMUNICATING WITH COLLEAGUES

In addition to working out the timing of the schedule, you will need to create some infrastructure around carrying out the schedule. The following tips can help you coordinate scheduling with your coteacher.

Task Board Planning. In addition to using a clipboard or printed schedule, use a large whiteboard to write the daily schedule, including who is responsible for specific tasks. In this way, anyone who comes into the classroom can understand what is needed. For example, if a director or educational staff comes to provide bathroom breaks, they can look at the board and know exactly which children you are teaching and what responsibilities are to be assumed. The schedule remains stable, but specific activities, tasks, and staff assignments should be clearly written. You may take a photo and store this as a digital record, as needed.

Preparation. In order to ensure personal interaction is consistent, other tasks of the classroom—getting materials ready, preparing snacks and meals, storing the children's items, stocking and cleaning routine areas (diapering, drinks, sinks, tissues, bathrooms, feeding areas)—are tasks that may need procedures of their own. When you use the schedule as a planning map for coordinating teacher tasks, ask the following questions:

- Do teachers take primary caregiving responsibilities for specific children?
- Is an adequate and accurate amount of time planned for handwashing, diapering, and toileting?
- Does the schedule allow you to synchronize one teacher's caregiving tasks (diapering, etc.) with the other teacher's teaching time? For example, while one teacher is diapering, the other is playing on the floor with children.
- Are transitions minimized so that children don't need to wait? For example, is food for older infants and toddlers prepared ahead of time, so that toddlers are not sitting for extended time in high chairs?

Teacher Communication. Schedule a 5-minute touch-base meeting before children arrive and/or at the end of the day. Ask, "What went well?" "What needs to be adjusted?" Update the visual task board and discuss any out-of-the-ordinary factors that will impact the functioning of the classroom and any specific requests of families for children.

Q&As FROM THE FIELD: COORDINATING WITH COLLEAGUES

Question 1: *I'm not sure how to coordinate diapering. We check diapers throughout the day, but it seems like a full-time job, leaving little time for teaching. Some days, it feels like the entire day is an assembly line of diaper changes or cleaning up spit-up.*

Answer: First, use diaper changing to connect individually, so it feels like an important teaching time. Second, visually maintain supervision of the other children, communicating with your coteacher ahead of time and during the routine. Finally, use a planning sheet (clipboard) or whiteboard to create chunks of time for planned diaper changes. Being proactive in planning for and recording diaper changes can help keep the routine from becoming overwhelming.

Question 2: *I'd like to use a schedule board, but how do I get my coteacher to agree with using one?*

Answer: Plan daily "one-plus-one" conversations. Each teacher states one positive success. Then each presents a question or concern. Use neutral "I" statements. "I feel like diapering is constant. I would like to use a whiteboard to help me better plan for and carry out the routine. What do you think?" Neutral communication leads to practical solutions and positive collaboration.

FOR YOUR INFORMATION: RESOURCES FOR LICENSING REGULATIONS

- Child Care Aware offers an interactive map linked to your local licensing resources: https://www.childcareaware.org/resources/map/
- Specific information about licensing in each state and Canadian territories can be found through the Child Care Technical Assistance Network: https://licensingregulations.acf.hhs.gov/
- Child care licensing and regulations information can be found at a single source database provided by the Administration for Children and Families: https://childcare.gov/consumer-education/child-care-licensing-and-regulations
- Zero to Three provides state-based resources related to the care and teaching of infants and toddlers: https://www.zerotothree.org/resources/states/
- You'll want to know and maintain the teacher-child ratios established by your state or accrediting group: https://childcare.gov/consumer-education/ratios-and-group-sizes

REFLECTION QUESTIONS

1. How has your understanding about the purpose of routines and rituals changed after reading this chapter? What did you learn about the perspectives and experiences of children?
2. What can you do during routines to recognize, honor, and respect children's sense of identity and developing self-perceptions? Why are children particularly vulnerable during caring routines to the words and actions of adults?
3. What new strategies would you like to use with infants and toddlers during caring routines and rituals? How will those strategies impact children's learning and development?
4. What interdependent skills are strengthened through predictable routines and caring interactions?

CHAPTER 5

Nurturing Identity Through Creativity and Self-Expression

This chapter presents the role of the creative arts, creativity, and self-expression in infant and toddler development. Through playful, creative exploration, children learn about themselves and the world around them. Daily creative arts experiences—music, movement, visual arts, and the dramatic arts—provide opportunities for creative thinking, communication, and collaboration with others. The creative arts create meaningful connections to cultural, linguistic, and family contexts as children enjoy joyful discovery and practice persistence, risk-taking, problem solving, inventiveness, playfulness, and self-agency.

Learning Goal 1: Examine the remarkable impact of arts experiences on all areas of child development and content learning, including creativity and creative thinking.

Learning Goal 2: Identify practical skills to strengthen language and literacy learning with music, movement, finger plays, art engagement, puppets, and creative play.

Learning Goal 3: Establish the role of the creative arts in promoting self-identity and well-being, incorporating and expanding on the rich cultural and linguistic contexts of children's lives.

ENHANCING TEACHING WITH CREATIVE THINKING

Ms. Paula gently bounces 8-month-old Kienya on her knees in time to the beat of the Irish jig. One-year-olds Nia and Timmy sit together, kicking their feet on the carpet. Ms. Catherine makes soft beats with a mallet on a small drum. Nia and Timmy lean on each other and then roll over onto the floor, laughing. Ms. Paula helps them get untangled.

Ten-month-old Ewan grabs Ms. Catherine's pant leg with two hands and pulls himself up to a standing position. Holding tight to stay steady, he jiggles his body and rocks back and forth to the music, wiggling one hand side to side in front of him. Ms. Catherine hands the mallet to Ewen and offers small cage bells and egg shakers to Kienya and Marlin, who reach for them.

Ms. Paula replaces the Smokey Mountain Band Irish Dance *CD with the* Putumayo Celtic Dreamland *CD. The soft sounds are a cue for more quiet play. Ms. Catherine reads* Babies Around the World Dancing *by Tamara Barker to Kienya and Marlin. They sit, one on each leg, facing toward her. They are captivated by Ms. Paula's smiling face, the dancing babies in the illustrations, and the quiet music.*

While the soft music plays for just a few minutes, it is used to transition the children from interactive dance to quieter play and reading. The teachers have selected books that engage the children: *Babies Around the World* by Puck and *What I Like About Me: A Book Celebrating Differences* by Allia Zobel Nolan. They coordinate book selections with Putumayo Kids recordings that represent many kinds of music: Latin, African, Brazilian, French, Celtic, and Asian. They enjoy seeing the joy on the infants' faces and watching each one respond in unique ways. They share their own passion for the arts with simple music, gentle dancing, and stories and illustrations rich in cultural meaning.

The program works with community arts groups, the library, and families to incorporate creative experiences. Asiana's mother brings a silk sari for the children to explore. The children enjoy touching the buttery soft folds and peeking through the sheer fabric. Zoe's mother brings colorful swatches of fabric designed with wax print patterns that are part of the Ghanian tradition. The fabrics' textures, colors, and sensory experiences are beautiful and engaging.

In this program, aesthetic development is as much a part of children's learning as social–emotional or cognitive development. In classrooms, "natural light, elements of nature, color and beauty, mirrors, and a homelike seating for small-group interaction are some examples of ways that the classroom environment contributes to the children's aesthetic development" (Jacobi, 2019, p. 4). Aesthetic learning includes the interdisciplinary arts: music, visual arts, textiles, dance and movement, puppetry, and drama and theater arts.

Infants and toddlers are curious about sights, sounds, movement, textures, and colors. Teachers respond by encouraging them to carry out their ideas (Guedes et al., 2020). Watch as an infant listens to the sounds a block or bell makes when it drops to the floor. The child repeats the action to listen again. Consider a toddler who holds a fine motor busy board steady with her feet to manipulate the zippers and snaps with her fingers. Infants and toddlers try different options, without limiting themselves to conventions or expected ways of behaving. They are excellent problem-solvers because they are curious, inventive, and experimental.

Creativity is an inborn trait, but it can be nurtured intentionally, just as children develop other cognitive and learning skills (Leggett, 2017). A child is "born with the spirit of an inquisitive and creative human being, seeking understanding of what to do with body and mind in a world of invented possibilities" (Trevarthen & Delafield-Butt, 2014, p. 1). Creativity doesn't happen alone, as it is driven by social interaction. Infants make meaning through observation and playful, coordinated interactions with significant others.

What people and experiences influenced your own creative traits? What experiences do you remember that helped you understand yourself as a creative person? Were you doing something special, or did someone recognize and affirm your creativity? Researchers have found that children can adopt adults' exploration styles, such as using objects in different ways, demonstrating creativity in solving problems, and using innovative solutions (Hoicka et al., 2016). During creative activities, children coordinate their actions and intentions with others, an important part of joint interaction and action (Fantasia & Delafield-Butt, 2023). In this way, creativity is not a set or fixed trait. It can be greatly influenced by early experiences and by role models who value creative thinking and exploration.

OVERCOMING PRACTICAL CHALLENGES: FOSTERING CREATIVITY AS A HIGH-IMPACT SKILL

Creativity may not seem like a top priority for younger children, but this is exactly the time that early patterns for self-identity, creative expression, and love of the creative arts take root. Playful engagement in the arts helps infants and toddlers see things in unique ways, notice details, explore patterns, make connections, and try out innovative ways to solve problems. Creativity and creative thinking have a positive impact on cognitive development and learning (Yildirim & Yilmaz, 2023).

The NAEYC Early Learning Program Accreditation Standards and Assessment Items (2019) require teachers to offer children opportunities to appreciate culturally diverse visual arts and dramatic arts in their programs. Through arts experiences, children develop awareness of themselves as a creative people who both contribute and respond to aesthetic experiences. Creative thinking strengthens companion traits like persistence, risk-taking, problem solving, inventiveness, and playfulness (Fielding et al., 2023). Because of these connections, the arts are integrated together in science, technology, engineering, arts, and math (STEAM) education.

Creativity fits perfectly with the principles of universal design for learning (UDL). UDL requires teachers to offer children a variety of ways to learn new skills and information. Children are encouraged to engage using many kinds of expression. They are given opportunities to demonstrate their capabilities in flexible ways—ensuring equitable access to information, concepts, and understanding (US DHHS, 2024). Teachers offer ways of connecting to learning that are uniquely designed to fit the needs and strengths of each child.

UDL also aligns with NAEYC developmentally appropriate practice (2020), as

> educators arrange firsthand, meaningful experiences that are cognitively and creatively stimulating, invite exploration and investigation, and engage children's active, sustained involvement. They do this by providing a rich variety of materials, challenges, and ideas that are worthy of children's attention and that reflect the funds of knowledge each child brings to the setting. (p. 22)

Teachers "learn from close observation and from the family about the individual child's interests, skills, and abilities and about practices of importance to the family" (p. 12). In this way, engagement in creative experiences is dynamic and responsive—and fuels joyful learning for infants and toddlers.

Strategy Toolbox: Jump-Starting Creativity in the Classroom

Invite family creativity. Family contributions—like introducing scarves, fabrics, tapestries, woven mats, baskets, or clothing—may be wonderfully diverse. They may offer to play the guitar and sing, juggle, read a book, or design a playhouse.

Get moving. Music and movement are fun for infants and toddlers but also provide exercise in your day. Singing and dancing have benefits for personal well-being and health that are unsurpassed by other activities (Sheppard & Broughton, 2020).

Share your skills. What are creative activities you enjoyed as a child? How can you infuse your own creative ideas in teaching? Whether sharing a song or book from your childhood, making a puppet talk in different voices, sewing a sock doll, reciting a poem, or playing the flute, your classroom can reflect your own creativity.

Introduce choices in materials and processes. When children use toys or tools in divergent ways, like making patterns in paint with their fingers or using two or three markers at once to create scribbles, watch and observe without restraining their actions or adapting their thinking into one "correct way."

Learn from children. What materials and experiences do children most enjoy? Do they eagerly engage in painting at the easel, using puppets, or dancing? Then consider expanding their interests by offering painting on a mural, outdoor painting, using nature materials to make prints, creating puppets using open-ended materials, or adding dance costumes. Introduce materials that invite children to engage in new and diverse ways.

CREATIVITY, WONDER, AND IDENTITY—EXPERIENCES THAT CONNECT THE SELF

In the morning, Jasmine, Sebastian's babysitter, places him on the floor of the young toddler classroom with his blanket. Sebastian runs to his teacher, Ms. LeeAnn, and snuggles with his blanket next to her. Ms. LeeAnn helps Sebastian push the bird song buttons in Andrea Pinnington and Caz Buckingham's Little Book of Backyard Bird Songs. *With each picture and song, she leans close to his ear and whistles or chirps the birdcall. Her breath tickles in Sebastian's ear, and he laughs.*

Sebastian reaches for Birdsongs, *a book by Betsy Franco, that is in the basket next to Ms. LeeAnn. She points to the cover and calls, "Chicka dee dee dee." Twelve-month-old Natasha crawls over, and 14-month-old William joins them. Ms. LeeAnn makes the "tat, tat, tat" and "coo, coo, coo" and "chip, chip, chip" sounds as she points to the bright pictures. She rocks her body side to side, and the children rock with her—copying her sounds. They draw out the long "coo" sounds and make their voices high for the "tat, tat, tat" sounds. After a few minutes, Sebastian heads over to play with a toy telephone. Natasha and William stay with Ms. LeeAnn.*

Seventeen-month-old Sebastian has experienced multiple child care arrangements. Living with his father and brother, he sees his mother on weekends. Two babysitters bring him to the program during the week. In this small, community center–based program, Sebastian finds comfort and consistency with Miss LeeAnn and Ms. Mindy.

Ms. LeeAnn uses her voice and body in intentional ways, drawing the children into each activity and sustaining their engagement until they are ready to move on. She connects the children's enjoyment of the birdsongs into other integrated activities. She provides cardboard boxes large enough for the children to crawl inside. She lays large strips of soft cotton flannel in the bottom and places plush birds inside. The children are free to explore these materials in their own way and time.

Ms. LeeAnn plays Elizabeth Mitchell's "Little Bird, Little Bird" song. The children use the soft flannel fabric strips for wings and "fly" around the room. They run to look at themselves in the plexiglass mirror and laugh at the fabric strips on their heads. They turn upside down to peer at each other between their legs. While the activities are brief, children imagine, imitate, play, and discover. In the afternoon, the teachers lift the feeders down, so the children can fill them with birdseed.

The families also are partners in a neighborhood "I spy" activity. They help children point to the birds they see while walking to the program. These creative and connected activities give each child many ways to learn about birds around them. But they also require advanced planning and supervision.

The activities engage all the senses and inspire children's engagement. The funny noises and sounds introduce new birdcalls, folk music, and ways of moving. While the teachers remain attentive to daily changes and are responsive to the moment-by-moment focus of the children, these activities are part of a purposefully planned curriculum.

The teachers also understand they are meeting the children's emotional need for soothing and attachment. Sebastian knows Ms. LeeAnn has a safe lap to enjoy. He takes pride in navigating the classroom spaces and shows confidence in making choices about play. The classroom feels predictable, with welcoming faces, hugs, and snuggles, with teachers who talk with him and make him feel special.

From My Experience: *I think teachers consider art and music something used to entertain children. They don't realize how essential creative experiences are in connecting children with their developing sense of identity—and the way creativity is the heart of infant and toddler teaching.*

Strategy Toolbox: Understanding the Child's Perspective

Art experiences allow teachers to listen and learn from children about who they are, about their creativity, and about the identities they represent. Art experiences allow infants and toddlers to explore and express themselves with freedom and confidence. The following strategies help you learn from children.

Self-monitor. When you are changing a diaper and chanting, "This Little Piggy," pay attention to your body position, eye contact, and facial expressions. Are you smiling? What does the child see and hear? What is the child's response? When you sing a familiar song to an infant as she wakes up, how does she respond? How do you make the routines feel safe and personal?

Look for cultural connections. When you first walk into your teaching space, what clues does the room give about the children who play there? What might the children notice that looks like and feels like the people, places, and experiences they know and love? How can they see themselves reflected in the spaces? Do specific songs, lullabies, doll clothing, decorations, illustrations, books, finger plays, or poems hold meaning or significance to particular children? How do you know? What experiences relate to their personal lives?

Evaluate engagement. What materials are interesting to the children you teach? Maybe the mobile in the window catches their attention. Is the light dancing on the carpet, or are the flowers in the window captivating? Follow an infant's eye gaze, gestures, and vocalizations. How do toddlers show their interest differently? What kinds of activities capture attention? What shows you children are involved and engaged?

Review access. What spaces and room arrangements make sense to children? Are mirrors, artwork, and photographs at children's eye level? Do plexiglass display boards allow children to see and enjoy photographs and artwork? Do they have easy access to plush animals, books, and toys? Are these arranged in thematic and inviting ways?

Notice children. What personal traits do you notice about children as they engage in creative experiences? Careful observation will reveal their perspectives, sense of humor, and personal traits that are unique and special. How are children's responses unique?

EXPRESSING FAMILY AND CULTURAL TRADITIONS

"Buenos días, Milora y Tía Sofia," says Ms. Nancy. Sofia gives Milora a kiss goodbye on the forehead and a kiss on each hand. Then she blows a kiss twice before patting Milora's arm and saying, "Nos vemos." (See you later.)

Ms. Nancy takes Milora and sings, "Hola, ¿Cómo estás? ¡Estoy muy bien! Hola, ¿Cómo estás? ¡Estoy contenta! ¡Hola! ¿Cómo estáis? ¡Estamos emocionados!" (Hello, how are you? I am very good. Hello, how are you? I am happy! Hello, how are you both? We are excited.) Ms. Nancy and Aunt Sofia keep this routine the same every morning. Eight-month-old Milora smiles and reaches for Ms. Nancy.

In the rocking chair, Nancy reads the book How Are You? ¿Cómo estás? *by Angela Dominguez. She says, "Welcome! ¡Bienvenida! ¿Cómo estás? How are you? Are you shy? ¿Eres tímida? No." She goes on to ask, "Are you hungry? Are you tired?" Ms. Nancy has gathered bilingual versions of other books, including* Are You My mother? *by P. D. Eastman and* The Rainbow Fish *by Marcus Pfister. But after the first book, Milora is ready to get down. She crawls to the basket of toys and reaches for a wooden block shaker.*

The teachers encourage each family to share a good-bye ritual with a consistent activity to follow. Milora enjoys a few minutes of snuggling and reading, and then likes to explore. She is an early crawler but still likes to scoot and can make it across the room quickly. Ms. Nancy has introduced new instruments, with a large whistle, shakers, bells, and spin drums. Milora loves the spin drum but needs assistance turning it to make it ring.

Music is an instinctive part of childrearing across cultures, including singing to infants, swaying, and dancing. Children's first exposure to music is in utero, where researchers have found that after birth, infants recognize their mother's voices and the music played or sung to them before birth (Poćwierz-Marciniak & Harciarek, 2021). Infants learn the specific rhythms and music structures they hear during the first year of life. Over time, they learn culture-specific pitch, melody, and rhythm patterns that are incorporated during planned and impromptu activities (Buren et al., 2021).

As children grow, they develop aesthetic awareness. They participate in movement and dance, songs and music activities, and dramatic stories. These individual and group experiences and dramatic reenactments reflect and express who they are in the context of their families and cultures. The ability to tell personal stories and to represent experiences in creative ways develops children's identities and perceptions of themselves in relationship to the world around them (Hamilton et al., 2019).

An essential focus of child development and teaching includes the recognition, representation, and expression of culture. Artistic and creative expression invites children to see themselves as valued and capable participants in the classroom community. This happens as teachers embrace cultural diversity as a developmental asset and integrate cultural knowledge in teaching (Bennett et al., 2018).

The arts serve as windows and mirrors both reflecting the personal context of children as they make meaning about their own lives and introducing them to the cultural experience and values of others (NAEYC, 2022). Creative play invites children to express family culture while learning about and experiencing the expression of others. The arts strengthen personal identity, promote self-expression, and offer empowerment for each child as they experience self-agency as creators through naturalistic learning opportunities (Ajodhia & Cohen Miller, 2024).

Cultural identity is linked to sensory experiences that are familiar, including the smells of essential oils and food; gentle touch for healing, visual, and tactile experiences with artifacts and art pieces; and the kinds of music used to soothe, energize, and communicate. In the same way, children naturally interact with the world through each of their senses and internalize patterns that are familiar. The language used, the way phrases and expressions communicate emotions, and the daily sensory experiences of the home become part of children's identity, the way they relate to others, and the ways they learn.

Each of these ways of processing the sensory world are related to the ways children experience and manage emotions and create memories (Rodriguez & Kross, 2023). These are the ways through which children make meaning about themselves and their relationship to others. Connecting the cultural practices of the home and the early childhood program can help them develop a strong sense of themselves (Rameka et al., 2017). This is especially true during the multisensory experiences of the arts.

In infant and toddler classrooms, sound can be used to evoke pleasure and to soothe stress. Listening to music can moderate heart rate, blood pressure, and cortisol levels, as well as bring pleasure (De Witte et al., 2020). Children learn the syntax and rhythmic structures they hear, internalizing melody and rhythm in culturally specific ways (Politimou et al., 2019). In the same way, smell and touch are associated with children's connections to their family experiences and memories. Each of these has roots in the cultural norms and the ways children experience sensory inputs at home. Through musical experiences, they develop a sense of identity in relationship with others.

Infants are innately musical, listening to the patterns and inflection of voices and hearing the rhythm and melody of music in their environment. An in-depth report from Carnegie Hall (Palmer Wolf, 2020), "Why Making Music Matters," shows that infants can distinguish between music and speaking and internalize the unique inflections and patterns of Western or non-Western speech and music. Children with musical experiences develop better language processing and listening skills (Pino et al., 2023). During singing and movement, they coordinate their interactions and share a face-to-face coordination, aligning breathing and reducing stress (Lense et al., 2022). Importantly, these benefits are universal across cultures.

> In this complex world, sound play and music can create a kind of third space where young children can knit together new identities that combine their first languages, traditions, and culture with contemporary, English-speaking, and U.S.-anchored identities. In this sense, music can provide the raw materials for an evolving sense of identity. When day-care and preschools feature the music of multiple cultures and homelands, they model an inclusive and connected world. (Palmer Wolf, 2020, p. 19)

Through aesthetic experiences, infants and toddlers engage with and respond to artistic experiences and develop a sense of belonging. Kurt Vonnegut (2006) said that interacting with art, music, singing, dancing, acting, drawing, painting, sculpture, poetry, and stories about life is "to experience becoming, to find out what's inside you, and to make your soul grow" (para. 2). In the same way, Jamal Cole (2023) explains that music and art help children express themselves. As children see themselves as part of their community, their cultural ways of being become part of their creative development and expression.

Strategy Toolbox: Engaging in Inclusive Planning With Families

There are many ways to promote cultural cohesion as foundational for teaching beyond including objects in the classroom that reflect children's homes, families, and communities. Below are approaches to use as a springboard for other ideas that fit best for the context of your own program.

Update communication. Include a statement in the program handbook that prioritizes collaboration with families to introduce creative arts experiences that focus on cultural belonging and expression. Promote a caring and connected community of families and children who learn together.

Identify rituals and traditions valued at home. Seek multigenerational stories, rituals, and songs, understanding that families are multicultural and multilingual. Seek to identify and understand the stories, values, and cultural priorities and practices that are connected to family history. For example, a family member can write a brief story about an event in their childhood or talk about special events at home.

Make a family book for each child. A family book can include photos, words, and messages from the family members and special friends, with pictures of the daily life of the child outside the home. Families can text or email the photos for teachers to print and compile books. Bookmaking can also become the focus of a family event. A personal storybook reinforces pride in family life.

Display a family quilt, tree, mural, or mobile. Represent the lives, cultures, and languages of families. Ask families to provide photographs, poems, a collage, handprints, or a drawing for each quilt square. Create a mobile with laminated photos representing children's daily lives. Create a wall mural to document special family members and events. These artifacts will become storyboards to interact with children and communicate with families.

Create a "Where in the World" board. Connect strings to geographical places of origin on a map linked to note cards with a brief story that represents families. "My grandma and grandpa are from China." "My dad is Assyrian and was born and raised in Iran." "My mom is from the Dominican Republic and lives in New York City." "My mom is from San Francisco, and my gram is from New Orleans." This beautiful visual provides opportunities for families to find commonalities and develop appreciation for the rich contexts represented in a program.

Prepare nap buddies. Laminate a family photo. Offer the photo as a way for children to "hug their family" when napping.

Post an arts dream board. Ask families what traits and kinds of creative goals they hope for their children. Display on a dream board. Use a prompt like "I want my child to . . . (dance like no one is watching; think like an artist; develop pride in themselves as a creative person)." Messages may be created separately and hung together or may be created as part of a paper or fabric mural.

Compile a songbook for families and by families. Include favorite lullabies, finger plays, and other chants or songs that are meaningful to families. When families are multilingual and provide a contribution in the home language, include the words in English and in the home language. Invite extended family members and family friends of the children to be contributors.

Expand the ways children can interact with diverse materials. Introduce new music styles, art displays, and artifacts that represent families. Include scarves, costumes, a dance mirror, lullabies, and finger plays that reflect home culture and language. Select open-ended cultural materials: instruments, fabrics, ethnic and multiracial dolls that reflect the community. Consider creating a sound wall on the playground, where children can listen to wind chimes, tip rain sticks, and strike pots, buckets, or gongs.

Observe, document, and share. Look for unique and special creativity in individual children. Video capture a sense of humor, dance moves, interests and curiosities, and ways of being to share with families. Use your observations to create a learning story (Escamilla et al., 2021), which captures the strengths of children, what they are doing, and what their communication or actions show you about the child. This reflective process captured in a written journal or in photos on a storyboard can deepen your relationship with children and their families.

Practice reflection with colleagues. During creative projects, you have the opportunity to observe families interacting with children. You will see unique contributions, ideas, stories, designs, and artifacts that reflect their lives. How do infants respond to music, movement, and beautiful objects? How do older infants and toddlers interact with new materials, music, and experiences? What have you learned about children, families, and yourself in the process?

BUILDING SKILLS THROUGH CREATIVE INTERACTIONS

Ms. Anna and Mr. Henry are putting the children's jackets on to go outside. They make the routine fun and meaningful by using puppets. Darling Dog (the spotted Dalmatian puppet) says, "Woof, woof! I'm going outside." Laughy Lion shakes his body and says, "Brrr! It's cold. I want to stay inside. My hands are cold. My fingers are cold." The children laugh when Laughy Lion talks in a high, squeaky voice.

Darling Dog says, "I can put on my own hat and mittens. Mr. Henry, can you help Laughy Lion?" Mr. Henry helps Ms. Anna's puppet put on a hat and mittens. Ms. Anna says to the children, "Mr. Henry helped Darling Dog put his mittens on. Let's put our mittens on. Darling Dog and Laughy Lion can help you."

Ms. Anna and Mr. Henry invite the children to explore ways for getting dressed. They prepare a box of shoes—dress shoes, sneakers, Crocs, and sandals. The children enjoy marching around in the big shoes and wearing hats. There is a bin with socks and a container of dress-up clothing, including sweaters, shirts, scarves, and purses. The teachers have added a safe wall mirror for dressing. There are picture books about getting dressed, including *Let's Get Dressed!* by Caroline Church, *What We Wear: Dressing Up Around the World* by Maya Ajmera, *What Riley Wore* by Elana Arnold, and *Happy in Our Skin* by Fran Manushkin.

There are two ways to make creative teaching intentional. First, planned experiences give children sequential and immersive experiences to express themselves. Second, daily moments of responsive teaching weave music, art, and creativity into activities in ways that connect children to each other and to their setting. The use of puppets makes book reading—and getting dressed to go outside—engaging and multidimensional.

During play, teachers collaborate with infants and toddlers by involving them in decisions and shared tasks. This relies on a "You do this, I'll do that" pattern. "You put the baby on the blanket. I'll wrap the blanket around the baby." "I'll put the elephant in the cart. You push the cart." This is a way of teaching by doing things together.

Strategy Toolbox: Infusing Creativity in Language and Literacy Activities

Below are strategies to incorporate creativity in teaching.

Let children initiate. Reflect back infant sounds. For example, when an infant coos, mimic the sound in return. Then wait for the child's response. This kind of turn-taking happens as early as 8 weeks. Turn-taking exchanges increase vocalization and benefit language processing and acquisition (Nguyen et al., 2023).

When reading, use creative voices. Read books using voices and animated expressions to represent the personality of characters. Use props or costumes to bring the story to life, like wearing a hat or shawl.

Enjoy traditional nursery rhymes. "The slow, rising and falling rhythm of nursery rhymes like Humpty Dumpty, much like the relaxed sing-song speech parents use with young infants, helps babies to identify the individual words within sentences, evidence suggests" (Allen, 2023, para. 2). Invite children to fill in the end rhymes. "Twinkle, twinkle, little star. How I wonder what you ___."

Draw attention to indoor and outdoor sensations, textures, movement, and colors by using prompts and questions. "Feel the wind. Does it tickle your hair when it blows?" "The blanket is warm. Does it feel soft?" "The ribbons are dangling. See them wiggle?"

Inspire descriptive language with sensory materials. Use rich, specific vocabulary to describe objects. Words like *silky, scratchy, smooth,* and *bumpy* describe textures.

Play with words and substitute words. For example, "Do you know the muffin man" becomes "Do you know the pancake man?" when you serve pancakes for breakfast.

Sing lullabies in home languages. A lullaby sung in an infant's home language reduces stress, increases oxygen saturation, offers pain relief, and improves language and other developmental milestones (Standley & Gutierrez, 2020). Comforting is powerful!

Modify songs. Use silly word variations, like "The cows on the bus go moo, moo, moo."

Make up songs for daily activities. Use a familiar tune with your own words. "This is the way we put on a coat, so we can go out and play."

Tell stories. Children enjoy listening to puppets and felt board characters. Retell or make up stories about taking a nap or helping others.

Enjoy finger plays. Children benefit from daily repetition, silly rhythms and tunes, and the personal interaction.

Keep learning. Make use of translations in Spanish, for example, for nursery rhymes and songs you already know in English. Use finger plays families recommend. The connection to home promotes multilingual strengths.

Infant and toddler teachers can build on the individual contexts of families by learning about and introducing culturally valued forms of creativity. Through the creative arts, teachers and children communicate who they are and learn by observing the special and unique ways others express themselves. Creative and collaborative experiences nurture awareness of self and others.

Research Revisited: Cross-Cultural Expression and Well-Being

The diverse forms of expressive learning aim to "support development of children's musical, visual as well as verbal and physical expression in a goal-oriented manner as well as to familiarize them with their cultural heritage and different forms of art" (FNAE, 2018, p. 42).

Children's need for self-expression plays an important role in developing self-identity. Cultural norms that promote creativity include openness to new experiences, encouraging expression rather than conformity, psychological safety, autonomy, and confidence to explore divergent ways of thinking (Pugsley & Acar, 2018). "Although clear differences in creative expression are evident between and within cultures, we contend that an embodied creativity perspective may be applied cross-culturally" (Frith et al., 2019, p. 1075).

Arts experiences incorporate cultural differences, unique ways of being, and individual creative processes. In this way, creative thinking, creativity, and authenticity are universal connections across cultures (Runco, 2019). Arts activities provide the foundation for a lifetime of enjoyment of arts participation, self-identity, and self-expression.

> Early childhood care and preschools are a key intersection of immigration and education, since they are an immigrant family's first experience at the intersection of home, outside care, and education. It is in these settings that children learn some of their earliest lessons about who "belongs," who is "an outsider," and which languages are for learning and which can only be whispered. (Palmer Wolf, 2020, p. 19)

For families experiencing displacement, trauma, and chronic change, infant and toddler classrooms that provide artistic experiences can make a difference. When programs reflect the multiple cultures of families, this inclusive approach supports stability. The arts play a critical role in mental health and well-being, as well as in stress management, trauma informed care, and resilience.

ENJOYING MUSIC AND MOVEMENT

Aila Rose pushes the yellow bus back and forth in front of her. At 11 months, she's sitting but not yet crawling. Mr. Griffin asks, "See all the children inside the bus?" He sings "The Wheels on the Bus," alternating verses from Spanish to English. "Las ruedas del bus girando van . . . por toda la ciudad." He takes Aila Rose's hands gently, helps her make the motions for "round and round," and sings again, "The wheels on the bus go round and round . . . all through the ___." He leaves off the last word. Thirteen-month-old Thalia fills in the pause with, "town."

Mr. Griffin sings, "Las puertas del bus se abren ye cierran . . . por toda la ciudad." He makes his hands come together, and his arms open wide. The children copy him, and he sings, "The doors on the bus go open and shut . . . all through the town." Mr. Griffin bobs his head and emphasizes the word "town" loudly. Aila Rose bobs her head and makes the motions, too. This is a song the children know well, even though they don't yet clearly pronounce all the words.

Across the room, Ms. Jenny finishes changing Omar's diaper. Omar turns his head to watch Mr. Griffin singing, so Ms. Jenny joins in. She washes Omar's hands, still singing along.

The teachers understand the natural ways children are drawn to music, including the fun, the motions, the happy tunes, and the beat. They know the children will use their voices and bodies responsively. During singing, the teachers establish an intimate connection. They are aware of the children and of each other, making eye contact, using physical touch, and responding with movement. The teachers sing throughout the day during play activities and caregiving routines.

From birth, music, movement, and rhythm patterns are part of brain development, where all parts of the body are integrated. Sailer and Guilmartin (2019) explain that music activities impact the brain in a holistic way, including the auditory cortex, visual cortex, sensory cortex, motor cortex, amygdala (emotions), cerebellum (motor and emotion control), hippocampus (memories), and corpus callosum (synchronizing sides of the brain).

Music is the perfect serve-and-return activity for the teacher and infant or toddler (Kells, 2019). "Science supports what parents have instinctively known for centuries: music can calm, express love, and foster closeness" (p. 40). Music is an instinctive part of childrearing across cultures, as mothers carry children during daily routines at home, sing while completing chores, and use songs and musical styles learned from their families.

Music by its nature is collaborative. The child and adult synchronize their sounds and body movements. "Children enter into a musical culture where their innate communicative musicality can be encouraged and strengthened through sensitive, respectful, playful, culturally informed teaching in companionship" (Malloch & Trevarthen, 2018, para. 1). Music infused in routines and daily activities contributes to transferrable skills, including listening, turn-taking, matching sounds, and joyful engagement. Shared musical experiences are a rich source of positive memories and contribute to children's feelings of belonging and self-identity.

Music involves much more than singing, playing a song, or letting children explore musical instruments. Music can be used to gain attention, soothe and calm, facilitate routines, regulate emotions, strengthen social bonds, teach language, and support learning and communication (Evans et al., 2022). In addition, music requires a balance of independence and collaboration, with listening, shared attention, and self-regulation as children guide their bodies to participate. This coordinated engagement results in remarkable benefits across every area of development.

Research Revisited: The Remarkable Impacts of Music and Movement

Music has many long-term impacts on learning and development. The evidence below offers profound reasons why music activities for infants and toddlers should be planned, purposeful, and sustained.

Benefits to development and learning

- Music impacts brain development positively across all brain functions, including cognitive functions, memory, attention span, and social behaviors (Toader et al., 2023).
- Musical engagement supports young children's development, including health and physical and psychological well-being (Welch, 2020).
- Daily musical experiences that are brief, random, purposeful, or sustained strengthen linguistic, motor, visual, and social interactions, engaging multiple developmental processes (Mendoza & Fausey, 2022). All kinds of music experiences are beneficial.
- Music listening makes children happier and more content (Roukonen et al., 2021).
- Music and dance positively impact social well-being and learning (Savage et al., 2015; Steinberg et al., 2021).
- Music promotes social–emotional skills, including emotion understanding, cooperation, and relationship skills (Zero to Three, 2016c).
- Music promotes sensory–motor coordination and creativity (Penalba et al., 2020).

Benefits to communication and language

- Music strengthens expressive and receptive language, sound recognition and reproduction, phonological awareness, auditory processing, and sound discrimination (Hooper, 2023).
- Music boosts social communication and language development (Oesch, 2019).
- Music increases children's gestural communication, word comprehension, and language (Franco et al., 2021; Papadimitriou et al., 2021).
- Music listening and participation increase auditory pattern detection and understanding of rhythmic patterns in speech (Zhao & Kuhl, 2016).
- Early music engagement boosts literacy, numeracy, social skills, attention, and emotion regulation at the age of 5 (Williams et al., 2015).

Strategy Toolbox: Music Tips for Daily Engagement

Music and movement foster closeness and belonging, as well as learning. Below are strategies for singing, playing with rhythm, dancing, and movement.

Singing

- **Make singing personal.** Sing with individual infants and toddlers. Encourage verbal infants and toddlers to choose songs and finger plays. Let their responses guide your choices and repeat songs they enjoy.
- **Listen, observe, and respond.** For example, when you sing a pitch or make a sound, wait for the infant or toddler to respond. Also respond by repeating infants' verbal pitches and singing songs toddlers request.
- **Invite participation.** Pause before the last word in repetitive songs. For example, say, "Hickory, dickory dock, the mouse went up the___." (Wait for "clock.") "Old MacDonald Had a Farm_____." (Wait for the E I E I O.)
- **Include multisensory experiences.** For example, sing and rock a child, dance and shake bells, or use a puppet to sing a song. Sensory experiences include auditory (sound), kinesthetic (touch), visual (seeing), physical response (actions and movement) and interacting with real objects to anchor learning.
- **Make up songs for daily routines.** For example, sing to the tune of "London Bridge": "Everybody gets a plate, gets a plate, gets a plate. Everybody gets a plate. I'm a helper."
- **Use ritual songs.** During handwashing, meal preparation, diapering, transitioning outdoors, and napping, use finger plays, poems, nursery rhymes, and songs individualized for each child.
- **Sing key songs in home languages and in English.** Use song recordings and translations online and family recordings to incorporate new songs if you do not speak the home language of the children. Interact with both languages.
- **Introduce a range of music genres.** Include traditional nursery rhymes, folk songs, new music folk songs, repetition songs ("Wheels on the Bus," "Muffin Man"), and traditional children's songs and lullabies, as well as classical music, light jazz, and cultural folk songs.

Playing with rhythm

- **Introduce traditional instruments.** Introduce the African djembe, Chinese sheng (bamboo pipe), and rain stick, along with rhythm and pitch instruments.
- **Use gentle rhythmic touch.** Help infants clap their hands, tap feet gently together, or pat rhythmic patterns on their back or arms.
- **Use actions to emphasize the beat.** Include clapping, waving, tapping, marching, wiggling, and jumping.
- **Make creative sounds.** Introduce a variety of timbres (sound qualities), including shaking a maraca, ringing a bell, rubbing or tapping rhythm sticks, rolling a rain

stick, shaking a rattle or gourd, tapping a drum, ringing handbells, and tapping a tambourine. Experiment with humming, clicking, popping, and making up songs and rhythms.

- **Make drums from simple household items.** Use pots, oatmeal boxes, or containers to strike with mallets, sticks, or the hands.

Dancing and movement

- **Model interpretive dancing.** Demonstrate ways for children to move, and encourage their own movements. Crawl like a turtle, stomp like an elephant, flutter like a butterfly, swim like a fish, and grow like a flower.
- **Use repetitive body patterns.** Model gentle swaying, rocking, rolling, patting, or waving a scarf. Carry or hold infants to let them experience rocking and swaying.
- **Enjoy movement without music.** Incorporate infant or toddler yoga and play follow-the-leader.
- **Dance with props.** Offer scarves, streamers, hoops, hats, costumes, puppets, or plush animals.
- **Be expressive.** Use hand gestures and facial expression along with body movements to communicate emotions, experiences, and ideas. Use hand and body motions during finger plays, dancing, movement, and singing.

PLANNING AHEAD: USING A SONG AND FINGER PLAY GUIDE

Music activities serve multiple purposes. Music should be incorporated in lesson planning, as well as spontaneously introduced throughout the day. Request napping and calming songs from families. Create a program-specific song and finger play guide that supports the daily rituals, routines, and music activities of your particular setting. Figure 5.1 includes favorite choices from the United States. However, it is important to include songs that reflect your unique program context. Lists should be printed for families, substitute staff, volunteers, and others who support teaching.

Figure 5.1. Finger Plays and Songs

<table>
<tr><th>Classics</th><th>Fun and Energy</th></tr>
<tr><td>Bumblebee
Where Is Thumbkin
Diddle Dumpling
Here Are Baby's Fingers
Hickelty Pickelty Bumblebee
Inch Worm
Itsy Bitsy Spider
Open Shut Them
Peek-a-Boo
Pat-a-Cake
Round and Round the Cornfield
This Little Piggy—Este Cochinito
Twinkle Twinkle, Little Star
One Little Finger Tap-Tap-Tap (Con Tu Dedito)
Chants and Sing-Songs
A Tisket a Tasket
Here are Grandma's Glasses
Hey Diddle Diddle
How Big Is Baby? (So Big!)
It's Raining, It's Pouring
Frere Jacque
Little Robin Redbreast
Obwisana
Peas Porridge Hot
Pop! Goes the Weasel
Rain, Rain, Go Away
Row, Row, Row Your Boat
Rub-a-Dub-Dub
Willoughby Wallaby Woo
Gentle Lap Bounces
Hickory Dickory Dock
Home Again, Home Again Jiggety Jig
Mary Had a Little Lamb
Ride a Cock Horse to Banbury Cross
To Market, to Market
Jack and Jill
Little Jack Horner
Jack Be Nimble</td><td>A Sailor Went to Sea, Sea, Sea, to See What He Could See, See, See
Old MacDonald Had a Farm
Baa Baa Black Sheep
Do You Know the Muffin Man?
Variation: Do you know the pancake man who lives on (name your street)?
Row, Row, Row Your Boat
Farmer in the Dell
Five Green and Speckled Frogs
Five Little Monkeys
Five Little Ducks
Go in and out the Window
Gray Squirrel, Gray Squirrel
Mulberry Bush
Oh, Mr. Sun, Sun, Mr. Golden Sun
Sally Go Round the Sun
Shoo Fly Don't Bother Me
Six Little Ducks
Old MacDonald Had a Farm
Skinnamarinky Dinky Dink (I Love You)
Wheels on the Bus
You Are My Sunshine
You're My Honey Bunch Sugar Plum
Quiet and Calming
Hush a-Bye, Don't You Cry (Go to Sleep, Little Baby)
Hush Little Baby, Don't Say a Word
Rock-a-Bye Baby
You Are My Sunshine
Lullaby (Cradle Song)
Good Night, My Angel
World Music
A number of world lullabies, classical music, and folk songs from around the world for infants are available digitally or on CD.
• Include a variety of genres, such as light classical, jazz, and traditional children's songs.
• Try Elizabeth Mitchell, including Songs for Children in Spanish
• Adopt choices from Putumayo Kids, like World Playground for Latin and African children's songs and Dreamland: World Lullabies.</td></tr>
</table>

INCORPORATING THE VISUAL ARTS

Two-year-olds Vonya and Jacob are painting with big strokes on the wall mural, using large brushes. Jacob's mother holds the paint container steady. Vonya makes big splashes of yellow, rolling her brush against the paper canvas in circular motions. She exclaims, "Look at me. I'm a painter!"

These toddlers have had many experiences with paintbrushes and water. The children are using brushes loaded in trays and are making wide swipes of colors on a canvas made of a paint drop cloth, suspended on the wall. They also paint on large easels, use plain water to create designs on the sidewalk, and use large flat beach rocks to roll paint patterns on paper. They are learning through experience that paint makes a surface change color and that objects like sponges, feathers, pine cones, truck wheels, and pieces of rope and string make shapes, lines, and textures in the paint.

Arts engagement includes enjoying and responding as much as active participation. The teachers provide books, along with posters and prints. Their collection includes: *ABCs of Art* by Sabrina Hahn, *The Artist Who Painted a Blue Horse* by Eric Carle, *This Little Artist* by Mudpuppy, *Artists* by Maria Isabel Sánchez Vegara, and the *Mini Masters Set* (Picasso, Seurat, Degas, Monet, Matisse, and Van Gogh) by Suzanne Bober and Julie Merberg. Below are guidelines the teachers use to design projects:

- **Safe and nontoxic materials.** Many materials (paint dabbers, dot-a-dot paints, and markers with caps) are okay for preschool children but are *not safe* for infants and toddlers.
- **No food items.** Food and grains like rice, beans, and pasta are not used in art projects to show respect for food as nutrition. In addition, these are choking hazards.
- **Self-selected.** Infants and toddlers should engage by their own choice, work as long as is comfortable for them, and be allowed to use materials in their own way—not restricted to adult expectations.
- **Open-ended.** Materials should represent a range of mediums, such as collage, printing, coloring, and constructing three-dimensional objects. To collage, children may use fabric, a range of ripped papers, leaves, felt, decorative binding, and ribbon.
- **Varied tools.** Tools for painting should fit the hands and developmental abilities of children. Options for painting include brushes with easy-grip knobs, round- or chubby-handled paint rollers, textured sponges, and wide and stubby bristle and foam brushes.
- **Novel materials.** For older toddlers, combs, toothbrushes, feathers, and loofah sponges can be used to create designs in paint. Prints (dipping an object into paint and pressing on a surface) can be created with shells, pine cones, leaves, bark, and rubber stamps.

- **Accommodations.** Teachers must understand which materials feel okay to children. Some children feel uncomfortable in plastic smocks, so alternative cotton or thick flannel smocks should be available. They may not like the feel of wet or sticky materials, so offer non-latex gloves. Model how to put on the gloves, and let the children try them on before attempting to work with materials.

Families may expect "cookie-cutter" craft-type projects. Communicating with families about the use of open-ended materials can help them understand the benefits, like creativity, motivation, self-agency, and art appreciation. Fine motor skills are not advanced enough for children to complete craft-type projects alone, so these are not considered appropriate. Children should enjoy and take pride in their own creations.

You may have access to craft sticks, large pom-poms, plastic craft papers, tissue paper, and pipe cleaners. While these are appropriate at times, encourage engagement with natural and open-ended materials like tubes, containers, boxes, fabric, and a variety of papers and textures that inspire imagination and creative use (see Figure 5.2).

Figure 5.2. Arts Activities List

What projects do toddlers enjoy? Those below may be adapted to older infants as they begin showing interest in materials and processes. Children enjoy making choices about participation, materials, and processes.

- **Body drawing, self-portraits, and hand and feet drawing.** Body art requires an adult to outline the child or the foot or hand on a large sheet of paper. Children may scribble, paint, or color on the image. Provide child-safe mirrors and laminated photos for inspiration.
- **Easel painting.** Older infants and toddlers love easel play. Paint cups and large paper are affixed to the easel. Offer a range of brushes and alternative materials for making patterns.
- **Cardboard boxes.** Toddlers and older infants enjoy sitting in and coloring on or using markers inside the walls. Cut a doorway so they can easily come in and out.
- **Tape, stickers, and craft tape.** Toddlers like to pull tape from surfaces when one corner is available for them to grasp. They like sticking tape and stickers on surfaces, including boxes, paper, other three-dimensional cartons—and on themselves. Brightly colored craft tape is available in many colors and in nontoxic versions.
- **Sidewalk chalk.** Chalk is available in easy-to-grip disks, sticks, and shapes. Older infants and toddlers enjoy chalking outdoors on hard surfaces or indoors on black paper affixed to the floor or wall.
- **Wall murals.** Children, as described in the vignette, enjoy painting on large surfaces with wide strokes and easy-to-handle brushes. Create a three-dimensional mural with recyclable tubes, containers, small boxes—and invite toddlers to paint the materials and the backdrop. When affixed at the children's eye level, toddlers enjoy working with paint, comfortable brushes, large chalks, and other easy-to-grasp coloring materials. Invite families to participate and add their own designs and objects.

(continued)

Figure 5.2. (*continued*)

- **Coloring and painting.** Large paper affixed to a low table surface provides opportunity to roll cars in paint and "make tracks," paint with natural objects, finger paint, or make prints. Provide a variety of markers and palm-grasp crayons.
- **Collage.** Toddlers enjoy the processes of collaging. They energetically rip colorful papers. With nontoxic glue sticks, children press a variety of objects to paper or containers, such as paper, bits of fabric and yarn, felt, and other flexible materials.
- **Molding materials.** Introduce play dough and other molding materials like kinetic sand. Add a range of tools (scoops, bowls, child-safe scissors, extruders, and molds) in low-sided tubs on a low table. Add plastic animals or natural objects to make patterns.
- **Open-ended construction.** Offer cardboard boxes, empty containers, paper rolls, and other recyclables to invite experimentation. Feathers glued to tubes become birds, and ripped papers attached to containers become puppets or robots. Children decide what to make and how to use the materials.
- **Playing with light.** Older infants and toddlers enjoy manipulating translucent objects like blocks, child-safe clear tiles, rods, colored geodes, opaque shapes, and sensory bottles to explore colors at a light table. The light illuminates their artwork and other objects.
- **Mobiles.** Simple mobiles can be made by suspending collected objects from wire or a stick with yarn or string. Hang by the window for children to enjoy the gentle movement.
- **Patterns.** Introduce patterns with stamps, large beads, play dough, and pegs. Cut cardboard tubes in various lengths to paint and compare by height or thread the loops on pipe cleaners.
- **Inspirations.** Provide lovely flowers in a stable, unbreakable vase. Fill a wooden bowl with child-safe seedpods and pine cones. Hang examples of beautiful art. Inspirational visual models inspire creativity.

Art projects invite children to engage. A mobile with photos or objects collected on a walk can be used to talk about their experiences. Art books, posters, or prints hung near play areas or a diapering table become part of daily conversations. The classroom setting, activities, and materials invite children to share in the wonder of creativity and joyful learning.

Multisensory arts experiences impact the developing self in profound ways. During arts-infused play, children learn from positive role models about creative ways to collaborate and cooperate with others. They are encouraged to make choices and discoveries on their own, which promotes self-agency and a sense of belonging. Above all, children grow roots of trust and confidence in themselves, within safe, protected spaces to explore and learn.

Q&As FROM THE FIELD: EXPANDING OPPORTUNITIES FOR CREATIVITY

Question 1: How do we engage infants and toddlers in art activities that aren't crafts? In the past, we have used items like paper plates and craft sticks, and all the results look the same.

Answer: Expand the tools and materials children use. Offer many options. For example, instead of a giving a single paper plate with bits of orange construction paper to create all-alike pumpkins, offer a range of surfaces like boxes, tubes, papers, and a variety of collaging materials, like fabric, tissue, and ripped paper. Let the children decide.

Question 2. The toddlers really enjoy the art materials, especially using stamps. We branched out to press leaves into paint and then push them onto paper, leaving the leaf patterns. We used pods and feathers to paint on large papers, and the children had fun. What other projects can we consider?

Answer. Just like the *Learn from Children* strategies in this chapter, respond to and build on the activities children enjoy most by providing additional tools and materials. Consider expanding to group creativity experiences that are fun and active like outdoor group painting on a tarp or mural, a large mobile that features smaller objects children create, or a group collage activity to encourage the social processes of art. Take photos of children and invite them to color or paint on their own photo prints for a wall display. When they participate in collaborative projects, take photos and videos of the process. These can be shared with families and included in portfolios. Invite families to brainstorm and participate in communal creative projects that reflect family interests.

FOR YOUR INFORMATION: RESOURCES FOR ARTS EXPLORATION

- Carnegie Hall presents *Why Making Music Matters*: https://wolfbrown.com/wp-content/uploads/Why-Music-Matters.pdf
- The Children's Museum of Southern Minnesota offers the benefits of the arts: https://www.cmsouthernmn.org/2023/04/10/art-and-the-young-brain-engaging-children-in-the-arts/
- Raising Children Australia presents creative activities for toddlers: https://raisingchildren.net.au/toddlers/development/creative-development/toddler-creative-activities

REFLECTION QUESTIONS

1. What experience in your own childhood encouraged your creativity? What kinds of creativity do you bring to teaching that are important to you?
2. How are culture and identity represented in children's creative processes, dramatic expressions, musical engagement, ways of thinking,

artistic approaches, innovative thinking, and ideas? How do you see these processes in children, and what do they reveal about children?

3. What strategies from this chapter do you want to facilitate, document, and display? Why is important for children to see themselves represented in the displays of the setting?

CHAPTER 6

Building Competence Through Skill-Affirming Behavior Guidance

This chapter focuses on the role of responsive relationships, meaningful curriculum, culturally and linguistically responsive teaching, and a prepared setting to minimize frustration and maximize children's successful engagement. It introduces steps for strengthening children's emerging social skills across all domains of development through co-regulation, strengths-based encouragement, and consistency over time.

Learning Goal 1: Prepare the foundations for positive guidance, including conditions for behavior success through arrangement of spaces, selection and preparation of materials, responsive relationships, and effective supervision.

Learning Goal 2: Eliminate bias and disproportionate practices of punitive discipline methods, shame, and isolation, and replace with respectful and empowering guidance that fosters honor for individual difference and respect for children's developing skills.

Learning Goal 3: Understand and use a range of strengths-based strategies including emotion coaching, stress mediation, trauma-informed care, and effective redirection to strengthen children's developmental, behavioral, regulatory, language, and social skills.

DEFINING POSITIVE GUIDANCE

Ms. Lavanya sits next to 11-month-old Samay and 14-month-old Nyiah. The children pull colorful, soft scarves from the top of sensory boxes made from clean wet wipe containers. Samay pushes a scarf into the hole with her fingers. Nyiah slides a scarf over her head. Ms. Lavanya smiles. "Are you hiding under the scarf, Nyiah? Where did you go?" Nyiah peeks out. Samay laughs. Ms. Lavanya helps him tuck the scarf back into the box.

Ms. Lavanya whispers in Samay's ear, "Let's go change your diaper." Samay reaches up to put his arms around her neck and touches her braid. Ms. Lavanya notices and says, "I like to put my hair in a braid. It looks different today, doesn't it?" She walks with Samay to the changing table and says, "It's cooler today. Your momma dressed you in long sleeves to keep you warm." She tugs gently on the soft cotton sleeves and says, "See how your sleeves come down to your hands? Long sleeves keep you warm."

As Samay lies down, he raises one foot to Ms. Lavanya's face. She laughs. "Thanks for helping me. Let's pull your pants off—one foot, two feet." While removing the diaper, she says, "Ooops, the tape is stuck." Samay giggles when she says, "stuck" with a grunt of emphasis. "Stuck, stuck, stuck," she repeats in a silly voice. Samay laughs aloud.

It takes Ms. Lavanya just a few minutes to change the diaper. She cleans Samay, applies cream, and places on a new diaper—keeping him engaged in conversation. "This morning, your momma told me you scooped dog food all by yourself. Did you help momma feed your puppy? She uses the Urdu words for a puppy, "kutte ka bachcha." "Does Botan go on a walk with you and momma?"

While she snaps the pants, Ms. Lavanya says, "Let's read the puppy book after we wash hands, okay?" She helps Samay with handwashing and then sits on the soft mat next to him. They read The Babies and Doggies Book *by John Schindel and Molly Woodward. Niyah and Jameal join them. The children like the pictures of the puppies licking milk out of a dish and chasing the ball.*

What seems like a simple diaper change involves a complex set of interactions, where teacher and child coordinate their emotions, efforts, and actions to accomplish a task. Ms. Lavanya exemplifies what successful guidance looks like with young children. The transition and routine run successfully, as the children understand what is needed and take pleasure in cooperating.

When play activities, routines, and procedures are consistent over time, children know what to expect. Adults and children become synchronized within daily patterns of activity and interaction. Children develop confidence that their experiences today will be similar to the ways adults talked, acted, and responded in the past. In turn, adults are attuned to the patterns of the children and adjust their level of support to fit the rhythms of their behavior.

These interactions are deeply connected to children's emotional security and sense of belonging. Their emerging sense of self is formed by the quality of the interactions and the positive feelings of being in close proximity to others. Children internalize the values and ways of behaving that are modeled by those around them.

Behavior guidance simply means to teach and train (Kersey & Masterson, 2013). It is proactive—nurturing and supporting emerging skills across all domains of development through co-regulation, strengths-based encouragement, and consistency over time. Infants and toddlers do not yet have the skills to regulate behavior independently and depend on a caring teacher for co-regulation (Rosanbalm & Murray, 2017).

Co-regulation, or assisted regulation, means that teachers provide external support, scaffolding, and assistance for children's emotional and physical regulation to foster emerging competence (Paley & Hajal, 2022). Assisted regulation is one of an "extensive repertoire of skills and teaching strategies" that are part of developmentally appropriate practice (NAEYC, 2020, p. 21).

Behavior guidance is fundamentally preventative. Teachers create the optimal conditions for children to be nurtured, learn, grow, and participate. Teachers tend to children's basic need for belonging, for physical and emotional safety, and for meaningful relationships. They also pay meticulous attention to the effectiveness of the setting and supervision.

Once those foundations are set, effective behavior guidance depends on understanding the developmental skills children need to manage an activity. Toddlers, especially, need an abundance of active play to support neurological development and contribute to the coordination and regulation of the body (Parkarinen et al., 2020). In addition, when a child is upset, struggling, frustrated, or angry, their amygdala is active, and they need assistance to calm arousal—and over time to be able to recognize, understand, label, and manage emotions, which are elements of emotion competence (Housman, 2017).

Behavior guidance requires teachers to model, support, and encourage physical and social–emotional skills consistently. With these prerequisites in place, children develop the ability to navigate the social and learning environments, and challenging behavior patterns are minimized. When frustrations do occur, they are brief, and children are soothed and supported in moving forward.

SETTING GOALS FOR GUIDANCE

Duri hits a pot with a wooden spoon. Yu-jin hits a pipe chime with a small mallet. Hana shakes the wooden jingle bell bracelet. The toddlers sing, "I'm a Little Tea Pot," marching with Ms. Chloe. When they sing "pot," they yell it loudly. Hana bumps into Yu-Jin, and the two fall to the ground, laughing and wrapping their arms around each other. Duri comes next and falls on top of them. Ms. Chloe understands they are having fun but needs to be sure they are safe.

Ms. Chloe quickly offers a basket to collect the instruments and reaches for a handful of washcloths and spray bottles. She uses a sing-song voice to the tune of "Tea Pot" to keep the children's attention. "All the little teddy bears are coming for tea. Let's wash the table, it's time to eat." The children roll away from each other and drop the bells, chimes, and mallets into the basket. They like using the spray bottles and jump up to use them. While they spray and wipe the play table, Ms. Chloe brings over the tea set.

Ms. Chloe has worked in the program for 8 months. During this time, she learns about the families, many of whom are Korean. She knows the families expect the children to be well-mannered. They also hold high expectations for what toddlers should be able to do. Ms. Chloe wants the children to enjoy working and playing together. She intervenes before the children's play becomes too rambunctious by offering them a sensory activity that quickly absorbs their focus and cooperation. Rather than scolding them for typical toddler behavior, she simply moves them forward to a new activity.

Ms. Chloe has particular goals in mind for behavior guidance. She wants to strengthen children's emerging social skills and help them develop awareness and empathy for others. She also ensures that they have a safe space to play freely and manage day-to-day routines and challenges in increasingly flexible and effective ways. She knows the families will be pleased to hear about the parade and tea party and the children's cooperation.

As Ms. Chloe plans and supervises activities, she considers the following:

- What do the children need to understand about the physical setting, the experiences of others, and the expectations of an activity?
- What skills do children need to manage activities and upcoming tasks?
- Are children dependent on adults to participate in and guide an activity, or can they manage it independently with little intervention?
- Can children make their own choices and independent decisions about participation?
- What thematic materials and activities provide quick options for distraction and redirection?
- What materials can be prepared ahead of time to minimize wait time?

The teachers in this classroom understand the goals of guidance and have created a list of values they share with families. In the same way, you and your colleagues can create a list of priorities that are valued and practiced in your program and include these in your family handbook (see Figure 6.1).

Figure 6.1 Example Positive Guidance Statement

Thank you for entrusting your children to us. We use positive behavior guidance as part of a curriculum that supports learning across all areas of development. We are committed to:

- **Successful outcomes for children.** We support positive social–emotional development through encouragement, without the use of shame or punishment.
- **Assisted regulation.** We provide assisted support for emerging skills to strengthen children's emerging strengths and capabilities.
- **Strengths-based interactions.** We respect and value the unique experiences, skills, developmental pathways, and timeline of each child, viewing differences as assets.
- **A safe place for developing a positive sense of self.** We protect each child's sense of self, modeling gentleness, respect, consistency, and caring.

(*continued*)

Figure 6.1 (*continued*)

- **A prepared setting.** We evaluate spaces, materials, schedules, and routines to ensure the best possible adjustment for each child.
- **Culturally and linguistically relevant learning.** We promote pride in self-identity, self-agency, and support families, cultures, and communities through affirming words and messages.
- **Protection from stress.** We provide proactive intervention to help children manage a range of stresses and challenges, using nurturing strategies for comforting, calming, and promoting resilience.

Families are experts concerning their own children's behavior. Establishing close relationships and meeting on a regular basis invites conversations about issues before they become patterns. When teachers work closely with families, children's development thrives and there are fewer behavior problems (Žužek Lackovič & Pšunder, 2019). Regular meetings with families establish foundations for trust and offer a wealth of insights teachers can use to support children.

Strategy Toolbox: Learning From Families

To ensure communication is strengths-based, the following sequence can be used as a guide to talking with families about children's behaviors:

Pick up the phone and arrange an in-person meeting. Don't discuss learning or behavior progress by email or text. Reserve written communication for general information and scheduling.

Thank families for coming. To open a conversation, tell them about a special experience or something you enjoy about their child.

Invite family updates. The prompt "Tell me about Max" (using the child's name), is open-ended and invites families to talk about what is important to them. It is likely the family sees similar strengths and potential areas for support that you observe in the classroom.

Focus on home. When you want to ask families about a specific situation, focus on what happens at home. Ask, "When putting Jose to bed at home, if he doesn't fall asleep right away, what do you do?" "If Jose doesn't want to put on his coat when it is cold out, how do you encourage him?" By asking about a program issue in the context of the home, you place families in the position of the expert. When the family says the issue doesn't happen at home, ask how they would support this at home. This invites new ideas and insights.

Seek more information. "How would you like me to support Max (in this situation) in the classroom?" Listen. Take notes. Let the family know you will implement the strategies they recommend.

Family stories yield insights that are critical for understanding the full context of each child. These funds of identity are powerful resources that can be incorporated into informed, strengths-based support for children (Cebioğlu & Broesch, 2021). A reciprocal partnership provides insight and information that help you make positive and effective changes.

PREPARING SPACES TO MINIMIZE FRUSTRATION

Ms. Hallie is a new coteacher in Mr. Kilian's young toddler classroom. They have worked together for just 4 weeks. The two come in early with coffee and bagels to talk about the schedule and assignments for tasks and learning activities. They talk about what happened yesterday when Ayla took the busy board from Benjamin. Benjamin responded and pushed Ayla. Ayla grabbed Benjamin's arm, and both cried. An hour later, Lucas grabbed the mallet for the pounding game from Asher. Mr. Kilian, who was sitting with the boys at the time, intervened to offer Lucas the transport truck and cars. Mr. Kilian's intervention disrupted prolonged conflict.

After reflecting on the incidents, the teachers recognize that space is a problem and decide to reorganize the play area. They agree to separate high-interest toys by organizing them on shelves and to use soft baskets for easy access to portable items. They order additional high-interest items, including additional pounding boards. Finally, they push back the shelving unit to allow more room in the area. After trying out the changes, they are relieved to find the children no longer struggle to reach and access materials.

Like this toddler team, powerful observation allows you to reflect on the way children use materials and spaces. Small adjustments, like moving a shelf, reorganizing or adding to materials, and opening areas of access can minimize or remove frustrations. Children do not have the ability to evaluate a situation, determine what is not working, or make the needed changes. They depend on you to create conditions that lead to their adjustment and success.

Teachers may try to change the behavior of the children—rather than evaluate the factors that contribute to it—and end up dealing with the same situations over and over. Always evaluate the context first to find practical solutions. You may find that a minor change in supervision, timing, or furniture arrangement can help children navigate play successfully.

Behavior guidance is effective when teachers are proactive and intentional—preparing the setting, schedule, and activities; protecting children's physical and psychological safety; and providing individualized play experiences. The following six steps set children up for success:

1. **Ensure adequate space for the number of children.** Is there enough room for the children to play independently and to move freely? Shift furniture and equipment so the space suits the purpose of activities that take place.

2. **Protect children's play from interruptions.** When children use balls or bean bags on the floor while others are using connecting materials in the same space, frustrations will occur. While space use may be flexible, protect areas for specific types of play, such as quiet and active.
3. **Provide ample materials.** Many peer struggles happen when multiple high-interest materials are not available. When children are coloring, for example, be sure there are plenty of crayon choices for everyone. When children prefer dolls or trucks, there should be plenty for all to participate.
4. **Store materials for easy access.** Use containers with laminated picture labels, and store where children can easily reach and use them. When three mobile infants or toddlers are headed for the same container of trucks and cars, biting or aggressive behaviors are likely. Place high-interest materials where multiple children can easily reach them, such as in portable baskets organized by type.
5. **Offer a range of challenges.** Children are less likely to grab what others have when they are engaged with an appropriately challenging activity that works for them. Offer puzzles, for instance, that meet multiple cognitive and physical challenge levels. Provide palm grasp muffin or pebble crayons and chubby crayons along with other drawing materials.
6. **Be realistic about supervision.** Infants and toddlers need constant supervision. Even while encouraging independent exploration, your physical proximity to ensure safety and to monitor peer interactions is required at all times.

From My Experience: *Sometimes, I don't talk. I just sit next to the child. After a few minutes, they come to my lap. We might rock a little, but we just sit and are quiet together. That physical time together is calming and gives a reset for emotions.*

IDENTIFYING CULTURAL PRIORITIES

Mr. Cliff notices 14-month-old Ainsley heads to the beanbag chair to reach the large stuffed whale that Charlie is bouncing on his lap. Charlie is startled, as he is intensely focused. Mr. Cliff says, "It's okay, Charlie. You play here." To Ainsley, he says, "The sea lion and mermaid want to play. They can swim in the ocean." He offers the sea lion to Ainsley. She tucks it under her arm and goes with Mr. Cliff to the rug.

At the classroom door, Ms. Hazel greets Sian and her mother, Ms. Wors. Ms. Wors has bundled Sian in an extra shirt, heavy sweater, and knitted hat. Ms. Hazel says, "Good morning, Ms. Wors. I'm happy to see Sian. We are going to make leaf collections today. We'll see you later!" She helps Sian remove her sweater, hat, and extra shirt.

While Ms. Hazel smiles at Sian and offers her a drink of water, she wonders why Ms. Wors dresses Sian in so many clothes when it is warm outside. She wonders why her coteacher, Mr. Cliff, doesn't talk to Charlie and Ainsley about sharing. She thinks he should discuss Charlie's feelings instead of simply distracting the children.

Like Ms. Hazel, you may hold strong opinions as you watch other adults interacting with children. Their choices may be different from yours. Have you noticed when a child is frustrated, an adult may respond in frustration? When a child dumps food, refuses to go along with a request, or pushes another child, why do adults experience strong emotions? Unwinding these feelings is an important first step in making effective behavior guidance decisions.

Behavior guidance is deeply rooted in cultural beliefs and practices. Just as families are at home, teachers are socialization agents. Your interactions and choices related to guiding children's social–emotional development and learning are aligned with your culture and the culture of the program (Salminen et al., 2019). The way adults express, discuss, or respond to children's emotions may differ. The following examples illustrate variations in three key factors of guidance.

- **Responsibility.** In one study, Chinese educators prompted young children to think about the best way to do something. They addressed the child's view and held the child responsible by saying, "You forgot to do that." In contrast, Australian educators used joint perspective statements, such as "We forgot to do that, didn't we?" (Degotardi et al., 2022).
- **Praise.** Giner Torréns and Kartner (2017) noted that the use of praise in European American families is considered a positive strategy to build self-esteem and self-reliance, yet in Asian cultures, praise focuses on interdependence and obedience. In some Indian cultures, praise is considered a negative practice, as it is believed to spoil children or make them self-centered.
- **Obedience.** Cultural beliefs about obedience differ, with some cultures emphasizing respect and submission to parents and elders. Those with more strict and demanding parenting styles have higher expectation of compliance to requests (Zheng et al., 2021). Expectation of obedience is not necessarily grounded in control but can be focused on teaching empathy, respect, and gratitude.

The UK in the World Values Survey (2023) shows that family attitudes shift over time. For example, many who perceived obedience to be important in the past now prefer to reinforce independence, determination, and imagination as important qualities. Instead of obedience, families may reinforce the role of good manners, tolerance, and respect. While these differences may seem minor, they are deeply held and contribute to the ways expectations for children are formed and the ways adults respond to behaviors.

Consider your own cultural anchors. What beliefs about discipline were communicated in your family? Were you taught that children should obey immediately? Do you think adults should control children's behavior? Should adults promote self-agency and choice? What are the reasons for your emotional reactions when children cry, whine, or misbehave? The answers to these questions can offer insight about your beliefs and help you become more aware of your responses to children.

ENSURING BIAS-FREE BEHAVIOR GUIDANCE

Ms. Ayla encourages 22-month-old Ramona to hug her snuggle blanket at naptime. She sings the simple lullaby "Buenas noches" (Good Night) and pats Ramona's back. By the time Ms. Ayla gets to the last phrase, "ya se durmió" (already sleeping), Ramona is already asleep. Ms. Ayla has fond feelings for Ramona and her mother. During activities, Ramona waits until Ms. Ayla helps her. Ms. Ayla wants Ramona to enjoy singing and dancing with the other children. She also notices Ramona asks to be carried frequently and doesn't try to help take off her sweater or jacket. When Ramona refuses to come to the table or help when asked to join the other children, Ms. Ayla is unsure what to do.

Ms. Ayla understands that Ramona's family wants her to advance at her own pace. But she wants to encourage Ramona to be more active using words like hello, goodbye, and thank you—as first steps to join in more actively. After talking with Ms. Garcia, Ramona's mother, she feels more confident honoring Ramona's dependence. They also set action steps for areas of independence that both she and Ms. Garcia can use at home and in the program.

Like Ms. Ayla, you may know a family that you feel "babies" a child or "does for" the child what you think should be done independently. It may even feel that a family is working against the goals you have for children. Reciprocal communication can help you learn from family stories and experiences and help you set shared goals.

Behavior guidance cannot be considered in isolation. Without high-quality curriculum planning, teaching, and caregiving, the focus remains only on isolated behaviors, without considering the whole picture. Without an understanding of what children actually need, teachers may hold them responsible for expectations, schedules, spaces, and interactions they do not have the skills to manage. Misunderstanding about the importance of these foundational requirements can lead to hidden bias—and the belief that there is something amiss in the child causing the behavior.

Implicit biases can be seen through deficit-oriented language that conveys beliefs about what is normal, who is capable, and attitudes about families' economic status, mental health, and other lifestyle choices (Spence et al., 2022). Teachers may decide a behavior reflects a bad attitude. They may hold unrealistic expectations about children's ability to manage emotions and behaviors.

A focus on the child as the cause of behavior can lead to bias toward children of color. Black children are more likely to perceived as troublemakers, suspended or expelled, referred to special education, and less likely to be referred to gifted programs (NAEYC, 2016; Weir, 2016). Bias extends to beliefs about children's capability. Child Trends reports persistent racial and ethnic disparities in the referral of Black and American Indian children to special education (Harper, 2017). The expected low achievement and misbehavior attributed to children with disabilities keep teachers from identifying and removing barriers to children's positive growth and development (Beneke & Love, 2022).

The National Center for Learning Disabilities (2023) provides a critical report that details important insights for infant and toddler teachers. "Years of research point to inequities in education for students of color, students from low-income backgrounds, and students with disabilities. These inequities are particularly apparent when it comes to rates of discipline and special education enrollment" (p. 1).

Deeply held beliefs about the use of shame and punishment also persist. The American Psychological Association (2019) cautions that physical punishment can cause lasting harm to children, as it leads to increased behavioral and academic problems over time (Gershoff & Grogan-Kaylor, 2016; Glicksman, 2019). The American Academy of Pediatrics has called for the removal of corporal punishment from all early childhood programs and schools, citing ethical, legal, and psychological research that documents disproportionate practices for children who are Black and those with disabilities (APA, 2023b). Concern about inequitable discipline practices with infants and toddlers remains a pressing issue (Lieberman, 2023).

Exclusionary punishment—removing a child from the group, making a child sit with the teacher, forcing a child to play alone, or insisting a child sit out during recess or a game—has direct negative impacts on children's opportunities for learning (Perry & Morris, 2014). Time-outs are also a form of exclusionary punishment. This is a practice likely to reflect racial bias and is referred to as "soft" exclusion (Accavitti & Newland, 2023). Consistent research shows that very young children of color, including toddlers and infants, are removed from child care programs due to behavior issues. Children of color and those with disabilities are more likely to be excluded (Allen et al., 2022).

This book provides critical information to guide you in developing cultural knowledge and to recognize and remove bias in teaching, assessment, and behavior guidance practices. These serious issues require continual learning and reflective practice to ensure every child is respected, nurtured, and protected, and receives the highest quality of professional care and teaching. To do this, behavior guidance (teaching skills) must be grounded in respect for and protection of children's bodies, capabilities, self-identity, and well-being.

TEACHING THROUGH EMOTION COACHING

Ms. Teagan and 20-month-old Quinn play with shapes while sitting on the floor. He is upset with a block that won't fit into the shape sorter. Recognizing Quinn's intensive focus, Ms. Teagan suggests, "Try another block. See how I twist the shape to fit into the hole?" She hands the block to Quinn and pulls him onto her lap. She adds, "Let's breathe together." They both take a big breath. Ms. Teagan says, "When you feel frustrated, breathe a BIG breath and try again." He thinks the way she says breath is funny, and the conversation relaxes him. She adds, "Try again. You can do it." She holds Quinn as he works on the next two blocks. He claps his hands when the blocks push through the holes.

In the same classroom, Mr. Mark notices 2½-year-old Van needs help. His family wants him to wear cloth training pants. Mr. Mark notices Van is wet and says, "It's okay. You are learning. I'm proud you came for help. Let's get you dry." Mr. Mark talks quietly to Van and says, "I noticed you were so busy playing with the dogs and feeding them. When we are finished, let's play together."

Ms. Teagan's response to Quinn validates his feelings and reassures him that she will help him accomplish his goal. She often says to him, "I know that feels frustrating, but we can figure it out together." Mr. Mark helps Van develop a strong sense of confidence about his capability to be successful over time and to take pride in learning how to go to the bathroom independently. He knows there are different ways families approach diapering and potty training. He wants to support Van's family and build Van's confidence.

Importantly, Ms. Teagan and Mr. Mark use positive and encouraging approaches that help children manage their emotions. Ms. Teagan could have said, "Calm down. I told you not to throw blocks when you are frustrated. You could have hit someone." Mr. Mark could have said, "Why didn't you come and get me? Now we have to change you." For infants and toddlers, shaming sounds like "I told you not to do that," "You know better," or "Oooh, you are driving me crazy." Asking "Why did you do that?" is also a shaming comment because infants and toddlers don't have the capability to evaluate and explain their feelings.

Shame is always ineffective in changing behavior (Perry, 2019). Shaming makes children feel unworthy and powerless, lowers self-esteem, causes anger and embarrassment, and disrespects their dignity and right to protection (Goodman & Cook, 2019). A child may feel shamed when a teacher scolds for using too much toilet paper, tells a child to hurry up when eating, or simply responds with a frustrated facial expression or body language. Instead, with safe and encouraging adult support, toddlers can begin to identify and talk about their feelings. When caregivers talk about emotions, children also are better able to talk about their emotions (Cooper et al., 2023). Emotion coaching is a powerful way to help children develop competence in managing and talking about emotions.

Shaming may be used when it is part of an unexamined pattern from a teacher's own childhood or past experiences. It also may be used when adults hold unrealistic expectations for infants and toddlers, including expecting them to be able to self-regulate, share what they feel verbally, or control their emotions—long before they have the developmental capability. The Zero to Three (2016a) parent survey shows that 56% of parents mistakenly believe children have self-control before age 3, and 43% believe children can share and take turns before age 2, when these skills do not develop until preschool.

The following strategies and goals are part of proactive emotion coaching so that children develop awareness of their own needs and the needs of others and the ability to communicate these to others.

Strategy Toolbox: Providing Emotion Coaching, Calming, and Co-Regulation

As you focus on the child and attend to a specific need or circumstance (e.g., comfort a child when the parent leaves, calm a child after a minor fall, or support a child who is sad or upset), the following techniques are effective:

Connect. Give the child sensitive focus, observing and evaluating the contributions leading up to the event and being attuned to the child's attempts to manage it. Notice signs of stress, such as a change in behavior, crying, prolonged quietness, or anxiety.

Calm. Begin with yourself. Take a deep breath to calm and soothe yourself. Teach calming techniques like deep breathing, snuggling with a blanket, and seeking help.

Comfort. Validate, soothe, hug, be near, give calming touch, wrap child in a blanket, or give gentle pressure if needed. Play soothing music or sing softly and offer gentle rocking and patting. Offer lap time, sitting together, a lovey, blanket, or pacifier (when part of the family's guidance). Stuffed animals, puppets, and doll activities may promote vicarious soothing.

Contain. To help children manage the intensity of their feelings, confine the event within limits, reassure, and explain. Help them put boundaries around the experience—making the sensations manageable, as opposed to escalating them. Children don't know mom will be back. They don't know they will get what they need. They don't know how you will help them. These are patterns they need to internalize over time. Containing validates and then deescalates the emotions of fear, anxiety, sadness, or frustration children often experience.

Understanding the child's need for containment and soothing can help you take a deep breath, let go of any reactive feelings, and help you attend to the situation effectively. This proactive approach reduces your own—and children's—stress.

- **Use soothing touch.** There are many safe and soothing ways to comfort young children. Gently touch a child's fingers, pat their back, or rub their arm. Notice an infant's response, and respect their physical cues for more or less touch. Ask permission from older toddlers. "May I pat your back?" Watch younger children's faces and observe their responses to be sure they are comfortable with the touch. Offering a blanket or to wrap a child in a blanket can also feel soothing to a particular child. Create a calming space and monitor stimulation from bright lighting, noise, and activity.
- **Validate feelings.** Give words to experiences. "I know you miss momma. Let's read until she comes." "I know you are disappointed. It's okay to feel sad."
- **Promote empathy.** Nurture awareness of others. "Sara needs help with her straw." "Lela looks tired." "Jasmine is alone. Let's ask her to play." Your understanding helps children notice the needs of others.
- **Teach how to get help.** Model how to say, "No thank you" or "Please stop." When a toddler asks for help, say, "Thanks for taking my hand and saying, 'Help me.' I can help you."
- **Encourage children.** Be quick to reassure. "I will stay with you. I will help you." "You are making progress. Let's do this together."
- **Foster helping skills.** Children love to water plants, fold small towels, wipe the table, pour water, throw out paper, and carry toys. They want to do these with you.
- **Build body awareness.** For infants, say, "Where are your hands? Are these your hands (fingers, toes)?" For toddlers, say, "Are you tired/hungry/thirsty?" "Can you feel your breathing?"
- **Introduce puppets and social stories.** Use puppets to act out the challenges toddlers experience. Ask children what can the puppet do to solve the problem? Infants will giggle when you kiss a puppet and put it down for a nap. They enjoy seeing their own routines come to life.

UNDERSTANDING AND MEDIATING STRESS

Ms. Lambert holds 12-month-old Emilie tight on her hip and enters the vestibule of the child care center. Next to her, other families bring infants, toddlers, and preschoolers. They sign in using iPads located on the counter, say good morning to each other, and are greeted by the program director. Emilie is quiet, watching the other children. Ms. Lambert hopes this will be an easy transition day.

At 7:30 a.m., Emilie's mother places Emilie on the floor inside the classroom with a basket of stuffed bears. She plays for a few moments and then says goodbye. She sees Emilie's face bunch up, ready to cry. "Emilie, you will be okay. Mommy will be back later. We will go to the park." Emilie screams in protest, and with the shrieks, she begins to cry.

Ms. Paige picks up Emile and holds her. "Let's wave bye-bye to momma. She will be back after your nap. Let's get Mr. Bear and read to him. Mr. Bear misses his momma. Do you want to give Mr. Bear a bottle?" Ms. Page reaches for Mr. Bear, the blanket, and the bottle, and sits with Emilie on her lap in a soft, upholstered chair. She sings, "Mr. Bear, Mr. Bear, how are you today? Mr. Bear, Mr. Bear will you play with me?" Emilie stops crying and reaches for the bottle. She holds it up to the bear's mouth. "Drink, drink, drink," says Emilie. "Mr. Bear likes the drink," encourages Ms. Paige. She knows that soothing the bear helps Emilie feel soothed, as well.

When Emilie is upset at home, her grandmother provides full-body contact during comforting. Her mother, grandmother, and Aunt Stella often snuggle with her in a rocking chair and talk with her. Emilie's mother carries her in a sling, where she experiences comfort from the familiar scent, heartbeat, and movement. Before bedtime, her mother nurses Emilie. These calming routines happen in a space that is much quieter than the Sunshine infant room.

Helping children adjust into the routines of the group setting is one of the most important priorities of teaching. For infants and toddlers, soothing and addressing stress should be considered a daily activity. A structured yet individualized schedule helps children feel physically and emotionally safe, as adults help them understand, express, and manage their feelings and behaviors (Murray et al., 2015).

Families of very young children may be experiencing chronic stress, impacting the consistency of care at home (Lerner, 2017). Traumatic stress already can be present between birth and 6 months. The child's well-being and recovery depend on the presence of caregivers who provide safety, security, and emotional processing of the life events (Berg, 2005). Prolonged stress increases cortisol levels in the brain and may impact children's sense of security, mental health, and behavior, disrupting development and requiring sensitive intervention (Jones Harden, 2015). When teachers are sensitive to the transition from home to the program, they recognize and respond to children's need for a daily calming transition.

Families experiencing homelessness, frequent moves, changes in the family structure like divorce or death, persistent parenting stress, prolonged illness or medical treatment of a family member or the child, maternal depression, emotional abuse, physical punishment, child neglect, and neighborhood violence are just some factors that affect children and families (Administration for Children and Families, 2023; Hamby et al., 2021). The good news is that high-quality early childhood programs can serve as protective experiences for children and families that experience adverse experiences (Center on the Developing Child, 2021; Mendez Smith, 2020).

Teachers who demonstrate social and emotional competence and well-being respond with social and emotional support and effective behavior guidance (Kwon et al., 2019). Yet up to 36% of early childhood teachers may experience depression, which results in greater irritability, less positive affect, less flexibility, and negative perceptions of children's behavior. Because of the complete dependence of infants and toddlers, teachers also need to be mindful of their own well-being, including rest, mental health, and physiological health.

Almost half the teachers in the United States report high daily stress levels, and the younger the children, the greater are teacher stress and fatigue (Faulkner et al., 2016). In addition, emotional exhaustion can interfere with teachers' well-being and their ability to respond warmly and positively during individualized care with infants and toddlers (Brophy-Herb et al., 2023). Making a conscious connection between one's own mental health, well-being, physical care, and emotional stability is essential for responding adaptively and responsively to children.

New and current teachers of infants and toddlers can learn to manage their own stress by recognizing the causes, signs, and remedies, so that they are able, in turn, to manage the physical, emotional, and psychological demands of caring for young children. They "have a unique opportunity to cultivate tender ministrations that serve as protective and powerful guardians for the children in their care" (Silver Williams & Mulrooney, 2021, p. 11). Of course, there are many rewards in teaching infant and toddler, along with teachers' dedication and commitment to children and families, that may provide some protection for stress (Kwon et al., 2021). Place a priority on your own well-being and physical health so that you have the energy and stamina to guide young children.

Research Revisited: Responding to Adverse Childhood Experiences (ACEs)

Adverse childhood experiences (ACEs) are potentially traumatic events that occur in childhood; undermine children's sense of safety, stability, and bonding; and have lasting effects on health and well-being (CDC, 2023). These include stressful events in a child's life that can affect development and future health.

The risk to development increases as the number of ACEs accumulate, and children living in low-income communities are more likely to be exposed to early adverse experiences. All infants and toddlers experience a manageable degree of stress during daily life challenges. However, other critical factors may shift stress from the tolerable level to one that is persistent and toxic—meaning that there are adverse impacts on children's development.

Zero to Three finds that 18.6% of infants and toddlers in the United States experienced at least one ACE and 7.2% have experienced two or more ACEs (Cole et al., 2023). Key factors that impact mental health include parents' emotional well-being and the level of adverse events they experience, with increased risk for Black, Native American, and Hispanic infants and toddlers in families living in low-income communities.

Research for Child Trends points out the critical disparities. Children of different races and ethnicities do not experience ACEs equally. Nationally, 61% of black non-Hispanic children and 51% of Hispanic children have experienced at least one ACE, compared with 40% of white non-Hispanic children and only 23% of Asian non-Hispanic children (Sacks & Murphey, 2018, p. 4).

Toxic stress in infancy is linked to lifelong effects of stress reaction, anxiety, depression, and behavior issues (Newton, 2020). Early traumatic stress can be present between birth and 3 years old, and children's well-being and recovery depend on the presence of caregivers who provide safety, security, and emotional processing of the life events (Dym Bartlett & Smith, 2019).

How can you respond? Trauma-informed teaching practices are healing, safe, warm, and welcoming and help children feel safe and secure (Child Care State Capacity Building Center, 2022). Trauma-informed teaching is "a profound paradigm shift in knowledge, perspective, attitudes, and skills that continue to deepen and unfold over time" (The Pyramid Model Consortium, 2021, para. 2).

For children who are impacted by early traumatic stress, teachers will need to work closely with families and other professionals to help them manage stress, handle emotional reactions, and experience security and safety. Teachers can focus on the well-being of children and their families and provide a network of support, including connecting families to professional and therapeutic resources in the community. Intentional and informed intervention to mediate stress in early childhood programs can be a key ingredient in the development of resiliency.

Recommended practices include nurturing responsive relationships; safe learning environments; calm, predictable transitions; helping children regulate their emotions and express feelings appropriately; and providing intervention that responds to each child's unique experiences in and outside the program (Morris et al., 2021). For infants and toddlers, emotion regulation only takes place in the context of co-regulation with the teacher, so teachers need to be sensitive to emotional changes and be ready to comfort, soothe, and encourage.

Teachers can learn from families about children's experiences outside the program. They can assist infants and toddlers with coping and stress management. Predictable routines and schedules, along with calming routines, can make a difference. Importantly, remain sensitive to children during times of stress, being intentional about providing reassurance and stability. Remain sensitive and supportive during specific times of stress, helping children cope.

SETTING THE FOUNDATION FOR POSITIVE GUIDANCE

After washing hands with Ms. Taylor, 2-year-old Malik runs to play. Ali pushes a lawn mower. Zayn pulls a wagon. Malik reaches for a dog-shaped pull toy, but the cord is wrapped around the wheels, and it sticks. Ms. Taylor says, "You are a good problem-solver. What can you do to fix it?" Malik turns the phone upside down and shakes it. The cord drops down. Ms. Taylor says, "Awesome, Malik. Shaking the dog was a good idea. It made the cord fall down." Malik smiles and goes around the room with Ali and Zayn.

Ms. Taylor wanted to fix the dog for Malek. She knows the young toddlers are challenged in many ways—learning to balance, manipulating clothing, and handling the many frustrations of play. They need encouragement to figure things out and try. She wants the children to feel she is a trusted partner, nearby to encourage and support their efforts. She wants them to internalize the idea that they are capable of solving problems, persisting, and reaching goals.

Guidance begins with the close relationship of attunement that allows you to know and be sensitive to a child's schedule, preferences, strengths, needs, and interests. You will know their tolerance for frustration and learn when to step in or hold back as they figure out problems. This relational foundation, in turn, allows children to feel safe tuning into you, knowing you are ready to help as needed.

Infants and toddlers are completely dependent on caregivers to take care of them and to provide guidelines and limits for safety and well-being. Children follow what is expected, supported, and taught. They imitate what they see consistently in the behaviors of adults, including attention, kindness, and encouragement. In this way, expectations, life patterns, character traits, and values are communicated through daily life.

The following practices are essential prerequisites to guiding behavior and establishing a calm and happy setting.

- **Model the behaviors you want children to use.** Infants are soothed as they feel your relaxed muscles and hear your reassuring voice. They notice your gentle tone and actions when you change their diaper. Your patience, encouragement, quiet personal conversation, and attention help children regulate their own bodies and emotions. When you say, "Please may I sit with you?" and "May I help you?" and "May I share my doll?" children learn social norms of cooperation and caring. They learn how to be kind, how to get help, and how to manage the tasks of the group setting.
- **Spend time in.** Spend time with undivided focus on the child's eye level. Have personal conversation about the child's family and personal life outside the program. When you are near, give a gentle touch, a hug, or lap time. Include older infants and toddlers in special helping tasks, like feeding the fish, watering plants, putting napkins on the table. When you are with infants, talk with them about daily routines and spend individual playtime together.
- **Respect boundaries.** Respect boundaries for children's bodies, belongings, feelings, space, wants, needs, and words. When a child says, "no," honor "no." This is the child using words to communicate. For example, if a child says, "My shirt itches," find something else that feels more comfortable.

  Before you go into a cubby, take the child with you and ask, "May I get a diaper from your cubby?" "May I check your diaper?" The time spent up front will pay off in children's respect of others. When children feel respected, they are more likely to respect the boundaries and rights of others.
- **Remove power struggles.** The lingering belief that children should do what they are told results in teachers making demands that often result in power struggles. When you make demands or threats, children may appear to be compliant, but they are simply dependent on you to make the behavior happen—with a threat or fear of punishment. Instead, draw their attention to the most effective ways to manage a situation.

  A power struggle is an ultimatum, because it is a "do it or else" command. The child can say no or simply refuse to comply. For example, "If you don't stop waving the book around, I will take it away." Threats to take away something are not in the child's best interest because they teach the child to respond to threats but not to notice needs—like how to use the book gently. It is in the child's best interest to have the book.

The goal is for children to participate willingly and realize the joy of being helpful and cooperative. Reframe behavior guidance as teaching. "Let's take care of the book and hold it carefully." "The toys all fell out. Let's put them in the basket together." This approach invites connection and communicates value for the child and instills habits of responsibility and self-awareness.

- **Be prepared.** Stock meal and diapering supplies, feeding equipment (bottles, dishes, food), toys and materials, and family handouts ahead of time. Planning ahead allows you to be physically and emotionally present for supervision, play, and caring.
- **Stay in close proximity.** Sit on the carpet with the children or sit on a small pillow or stool during play. Close proximity allows you to attend to individual children who are more active and those who are quiet or need additional stimulation. You will be able to step in and assist before frustrations escalates, as well as to problem-solve and assist.
- **Use data.** Pay attention to changes in daily patterns. The schedule you set when children are 5 months will not be the same as that when they are 9 months. Keep track of time fluctuations, and record incidents that are easy or challenging for a child. This information allows you to adjust your level of assistance or the schedule next time.
- **Maintain consistent rituals, self-care routines, and schedules.** Consistency is the greatest teaching tool for infants. They learn to trust what will happen in the moment and what will happen next. The normal sounds, routines, and patterns of their day will feel comforting and reassuring to them. Infants need and enjoy repetition. Their faces light up when you use the same silly finger play during diapering and say the same words before feeding, "Let's get your bottle and blanket. Time for snuggles." Their bodies relax when they hear the same lullaby their momma sings at home while you prepare them for sleeping. The steady familiarity of words, sounds, and melodies becomes the internalized pattern for their sense of safety and trust.
- **Keep boundaries secure.** Even when play spaces have been meticulously checked for safety, children need protection from other children, secure spaces for solitary play, and appropriate freedom to move and explore. Infants and toddlers move quickly, and circumstances can change in an instant. Monitor safety at all times.
- **Encourage communication.** Preverbal infants are learning language skills that will become the foundation of social–emotional development. Notice and respond to their vocalizations. Let them hear you describing what you are doing, what they are doing, and what other children are doing. Playful repetition and familiarity is the key. "Where is the ball? It's hiding under the blanket." Hand the ball to the child, and encourage engagement. "Can you hide the ball under the

blanket?" Listen as much as you talk—connecting through reciprocal responses and shared positive emotions.

Strategy Toolbox: Implementing Effective Guidance

Once you prepare the setting, what can you say and do with the children to help them adjust to daily experiences? The following are strategies that can be used daily:

1. **Prepare children for what is coming next.** "First, we will wash hands. Then we will eat lunch." Be consistent every time. Only say what you plan to do.
2. **Notice and narrate what works.** Draw children's attention to effective strategies. "You were patient and moved the box to get the puzzle." "You are a good problem-solver. You found another ball for Jack." "You are a good helper. You looked under the table to find Andrea's doll shoe." Specific narration is an important *replacement* for random praise like "Good job."
3. **Keep instructions simple.**
   - For a child wanting to play at naptime, say, "Naptime. I will pat your back," rather than "Honey, if you don't sleep now, you will be tired when Mamma comes, and I promised her I would help you take a good nap."
   - For a child waving a book around, say, "Book on your lap. Let's read together," rather than "If you wave that book around, you will bop yourself on the head and get hurt."
4. **Ask instead of tell.** Instead of "Put your feet on the floor," ask, "Where are your feet? Instead of "Put the paper in the trashcan," ask, "Where does the wastepaper go?"
5. **Give positive feedback.** Narrate what you see. "How kind. You shared your wagon with Skye." "You stepped over Bryon's puzzle. Good for you to see what he was doing and tell your body where to go."
6. **Teach and model self-talk.** Words are powerful. "Tell your hands to be gentle." "Tell your brain, I can stop myself." "Tell your feet to steer around Nathan." Also narrate your own thinking. "I'm pushing my drink back so it won't spill."
7. **Use effective redirection.** Rather than tell a child to stop doing something, describe a safe, positive choice or solution. Effective redirection draws attention to positive outcomes and empowers children to notice the needs of themselves and others.
   - To a child throwing balls, say, "You can throw the balls into the basket." Offer the basket and play with the child.

- To a child reaching for another child's toy, say, "Marina has her streamer. Here is one for you."
- To a child steering in the direction of another child's ride-on toy, say, "Drive around Tommy." (Rather than "Don't hit Tommy.")

8. **Offer choices.** Describe the needed task and then add two choices to shift responsibility to the child.
   - "Naptime. Do you want to snuggle with your blanket or teddy bear?"
   - "Time to pick up toys. Do you want to pick up the cars or the bears?" Follow through using co-regulation—meaning "do the task with" the child.
9. **Ask the children.** Asking children what they think results in surprising insights and helps you know them better. "How do you think we can fix it?" "What do you think you can do to solve the problem?" When children are preverbal, narrate your own brainstorming, so they learn how to focus on solutions.

The complexity you use when you talk with children must match the emotional, physical, language, and developmental understanding of each child. With one child, you may need to offer physical or verbal assistance. With another child, you may need to problem-solve and offer choices. Since most infants and toddlers are nonverbal or just learning language, guidance should be simple and consistent, deescalating frustrations and encouraging positive solutions. Guidance requires your flexibility, patience, self-reflection, and appropriate developmental expectations. You must learn about each child's unique growth patterns and continually seek to adjust expectations to fit with their context, strengths, and abilities.

The strategies presented in this chapter are not magic. You need to know the individual child, develop a close relationship with the child and family, evaluate the specific situation, and attend to each child's level of energy and sensory needs. You need to monitor over- or understimulation, notice whether they need a break from peers, and recognize whether they are hungry or need rest or quiet play. The goal is not compliance but to help children learn authentic skills for cooperation, honoring the needs of self and others.

Children love to be with you, to see you smile, and to share laughter. Each day should be a time of celebration, where children feel special and loved. Move children forward quickly from minor frustrations and toward experiences that bring them joy. The goal of behavior guidance is to increase children's self-agency and sense of confidence as they develop new skills.

PRACTICING SELF-REFLECTION

Ms. Olive reflects with her program director.

> The most important moments of the day are the few minutes I spend daily with Ms. Iris before the children arrive. We keep a written schedule posted on a whiteboard, so additional notes can be added. This way, we have a visual roadmap for the day. We also take five minutes at the end of each day to discuss what went well and talk about what can be adjusted. We try to be clear about "who is responsible for what," so that our daily conversations can be focused on teaching the children. We have a four-part checklist: what to prepare, what's happening with behavior guidance, who is leading learning, and how caring routines are going. We place our schedule with notes on the board so the families can see and feel our planning and intentionality about the daily life in our classroom.

Because of the blurred boundaries between personal and professional mindsets when caring for infants and toddlers, the practice of self-reflection is absolutely essential to provide effective behavior guidance. Behavior guidance requires reflection about your perceptions about children, your expectations, and your own emotional and physical monitoring. Children are watching your face and body movements, so staying calm and thoughtful influences their responses, as well.

- **Behavior guidance requires flexibility and patience.** Guidance is part of social–emotional teaching, as teachers recognize that developmental skills are interdependent and seek to support children's understanding and growth. When children need assistance, imagine what you and the situation look like and feel like from the child's perspective. Are you smiling? Does your face look anxious or upset? Is there anything else you need to know about this particular situation, such as what led up to it? Have you evaluated the underlying regulatory and processing skills that may need support? What intervention, adjustment, and support can create a successful outcome for the child?
- **Behavior guidance requires sensitivity.** Be careful about using a child's name only when redirecting behavior and speaking to children from across the room. Other children may associate this child's name with being corrected. Instead, go to the child and quietly support success by getting in the child's eye level, speaking softly, offering options, and staying with the child to assist.
- **Behavior guidance requires self-awareness.** Take stock of your own mental, physical, and emotional responses when you encounter complex or challenging behaviors. Without conscious evaluation,

there may be subconscious feelings that cause you to react rather than select the best kind of support for a particular child. For example, when a child throws food or becomes angry and strikes an adult, very strong emotions may result. Stay objective, offering compassionate support for children's stress and also for your own.

- **Behavior guidance requires developmentally appropriate expectations.** Effective guidance with infants and toddlers requires examining underlying beliefs you hold about what is important for children to be able to do. Yet national parent surveys show that adults have unrealistic ideas about a toddler's ability to control their emotions, demonstrate self-control, and share, when these skills do not develop until the preschool years (Zero to Three, 2016a). You will need to honor the individual developmental patterns of each child, recognizing that behaviors will not be consistent from day to day or even week to week. A child's ability to manage may be affected by many factors, such as illness, a change of schedule, or other experiences. You will need to evaluate each child's skills; their family, language, and cultural contexts; make room for daily variations—and then make intentional decisions that will be in the best interest of that specific child. Respecting individual differences and building on children's strengths is a necessary part of decision-making.
- **Behavior guidance requires self-reflection.** As you think about or talk about the following questions with your coteachers, consider that infants and toddlers are completely dependent on you to guide and support them.
    - » What kind of interactions require the greatest patience and consistency?
    - » Describe a common behavior challenge. How have you responded in the past? What can you do differently to intervene sooner or approach the situation more effectively next time?
    - » What personal experiences may influence your ability to remain calm and evaluate what children need objectively?
    - » How does family communication enhance your understanding of children?
    - » What lessons have you learned about yourself as you interact with children who are frustrated, tired, needy, or upset? What have you learned about the children?

Research Revisited: Addressing Behavior Contexts

Guiding behavior effectively requires understanding of child development in context, including the need for protection from screen time and media, nutrition, physical activity, and sleep. The following are guidelines families and teachers together can use to advocate for children's health and wellness.

Screen time. Studies indicate that excessive screen time for infants and toddlers is associated with delays in communication, fine motor, personal, social, and thinking skills, due to lowered interaction between children and caregivers (Muppalla et al., 2023; Takahashi et al., 2023). A national study found that children who spend more than 2 hours a day of screen-time activities score lower on language and thinking tests (NIH, 2019). In early childhood programs, children under age 2 should have no exposure to screens. Children over age 2 may have 30 minutes per week in the child care setting, with no screen time at meals and snacks. The total exposure in early childhood programs and home settings combined should be limited to 1 hour per day of high-quality programming viewed with an adult who can help children apply what they are learning to the world around them (NRC, 2017; Zero to Three, 2016b).

Sleep. Insufficient sleep in very young children is linked with mental and behavioral health issues, including attention, behavior, and learning challenges (Claussen et al., 2023). Shorter and poorer-quality sleep in infancy is linked to emotion and behavior issues in toddlers (Morales- Muñoz et al., 2020). The American Academy of Sleep Medicine recommends that infants between 4 months and 12 months sleep between 12 and 16 hours a day, including naps (Paruthi et al., 2016). One- to 2-year-old children sleep 11 to 14 hours each day. Beginning at age 3, children sleep between 10 and 13 hours a day, including naps. Newborns sleep about 16 to 17 hours per day, usually in durations of 1 to 2 hours. Families and programs together must prioritize healthy sleep routines for infants and toddlers.

Physical activity. In spite of toddlers' need for active play, they spend a significant percentage of the day without active movement (Alhassan et al., 2021; Bruijns et al., 2020). Many studies suggest children in child care programs do not engage in adequate active play, yet physically active play is linked to improved motor and cognitive development, physical health, and psychosocial health (Carson et al., 2017). The American Academy of Pediatrics (2020) recommends 180 minutes of aerobic activity (active physical play) per day or 3 hours per day for toddlers, with a minimum of 30 minutes of tummy time for infants.

Nutrition. During children's time in the program, teachers model healthy eating habits and support families' nutrition goals for their children. Research shows that childhood eating patterns persist into adulthood (Scaglioni et al., 2018). With increasing incidence of obesity in younger children, establishing healthy patterns in the early years is a priority (Cunningham et al., 2022). Nutrition and access to foods without coloring and artificial ingredients are critical for children's behavior, including reducing behavior challenges (Bartolini, 2024).

Q&As FROM THE FIELD: MANAGING CHALLENGING BEHAVIOR

Question: *What do we do about biting?*

Answer: When children bite, pinch, or push, they are signaling that they don't have the skills to manage a situation and need your help to provide safe ways to get what they want or need. Biting can be solved best with a multilayered approach to supervision and appropriately challenging activities.

Stay calm and evaluate what leads to a situation. Don't wait for patterns to occur. Adjust the timing of activities, the spaces, materials, peer choices, and supervision to reduce the likelihood of issues reoccurring. Replace the urge to bite with safe oral sensory experiences. Offer a soft basket of items the children can bite, like teething necklaces, teething bracelets, and gum soothers.

There are a number of books that older infants and toddlers enjoy, including *Teeth Are Not for Biting*, by Elizabeth Verdick and *Hands Are Not for Hitting*, by Martine Agassi. Use puppets to act out situations children encounter, and have them model solutions like going to a teacher and saying, "Help me," and saying to a peer, "No, thank you." Use the many techniques in this chapter to assist children in managing emotions and redirecting to satisfying solutions before frustrations occur.

Question 2: *Sometimes families tell me what they don't want children doing at home—like unrolling toilet paper rolls and throwing things. I want to explain that skills like rolling and throwing are part of children's natural ways of playing and developing.*

Answer: Information from families can help you plan activities that will be a perfect fit for individual children. For example, if a child has flooded the bathroom sink while playing with water at home or doesn't want to get out of the bathtub, this is key information for your planning. This shows you the child's need for sensory water play—which you can provide. As well as cups and pitchers in the water table, add tubes and cars, boats with little people, animals with "islands" to climb on, and other open-ended items. Consider making the water temperature warm enough to feel comfortable to children's hands. Offer gloves to children who prefer not to touch the water directly.

When a child has repeatedly squeezed out toothpaste at home, provide sensory toys that "squeeze" in the classroom, such as toys that can be pressed to make sounds, play dough to push through a press mold or extruder, and add squeeze bottles, turkey basters, and plastic syringes to the water table. Provide spray bottles for water with a "squeeze trigger" for "washing" the windows, spritzing the plants, or for outdoor play (i.e., children squirt the trees and bushes with water).

Rather than trying to suppress normal developmental curiosity, seek to satisfy sensory needs by offering safe ways to practice developmental skills. You can prepare a range of experiences that are satisfying and enjoyable to the specific children. Applying what you learn about children at home reflects a strengths-based approach and individualizes support for children's development.

FOR YOUR INFORMATION: TENDING TO CHILDREN'S WELL-BEING

- The American Academy of Pediatrics offers information on trauma-informed care: https://www.aap.org/en/patient-care/trauma-informed-care/
- The Child Care Technical Assistance Network provides trauma-responsive care information for infants and toddlers: https://childcareta.acf.hhs.gov/trauma-responsive-care-infants-and-toddlers
- Zero to Three explores the way infants and toddlers develop self-control: https://www.zerotothree.org/resource/developing-self-control-from-0-12-months/
- Zero to Three offers mindfulness practices to use and share with families: https://www.zerotothree.org/resource/mindfulness-practices-for-families
- The Centers for Disease Control provides information about infant and toddler nutrition: https://www.cdc.gov/infant-toddler-nutrition/about/
- The American Academy of Pediatrics gives recommendations for sleep: https://www.healthychildren.org/English/healthy-living/sleep/Pages/default.aspx
- For more information on licensing regulations in your state, see https://licensingregulations.acf.hhs.gov/

REFLECTION QUESTIONS

1. As you reflect on your own and others' interactions with children and families, think about a situation you have witnessed or an experience you have had when you misjudged a child or their family. What did you learn that helped you reorient your understanding?

2. What are some behaviors teachers should model consistently that will change the way children respond?
3. What behaviors do you find challenging? Which strategies in the toolbox list can you use to create positive outcomes?
4. How does using positive guidance change children? How does it change teachers?

CHAPTER 7

Setting Priorities for High-Quality Teaching

This chapter addresses priorities for high-quality teaching across all areas of children's development and learning. It offers strategies for intentional practices that focus more deeply on each area of development, including language, communication, second-language acquisition, book reading, social–emotional learning, cognitive development and thinking skills, inquiry learning, and physical development and well-being.

Learning Goal 1: Evaluate high-impact strategies for language and multilingual development, with in-depth competencies for shared book reading and strategies to boost children's joyful connection to learning.
Learning Goal 2: Understand the connection among interrelated areas of infant and toddler development, including social-emotional learning; cognitive development; and inquiry exploration through science, technology, engineering, arts, and math (STEAM).
Learning Goal 3: Explore the important foundations for physical development, recommended practices for health and well-being, and the impacts of outdoor play on coordination, multi-sensory integration, and learning.

SUPPORTING LANGUAGE AND COMMUNICATION

Ms. Erin bounces 10-month-old Quinn and 9-month-old Abey gently—one child on each knee—while sitting on the floor. She chants, "Trot, trot to Boston, trot, trot to Dover. Watch out Quinn and Abey—that you don't fall over!" As she tips them to the right, they giggle, "More! More!" Ms. Erin repeats the rhyme, leaning the girls to the left. Finally, she chants, "Giddy-up, giddy-up ride to town, giddy-up, giddy-up, up and down. Giddy-up FAST, Giddy-up SLOW, Giddy-up, giddy-up, giddy-up WHOOAH!"

Ms. Erin introduces a soft animal book. "Here is a little brown squirrel." She makes a chirping sound. Quinn pulls on the tail and pats the fur. "Here is a sweet bunny with its fluffy white ears." Quinn touches the bunny's paws. Ms. Erin holds up the last page, which has a shiny mirror. "And there is Quinn! Peek-a-boo Quinn. I see you! There is Abey. Peek-a-boo Abey. I see you!" Abey pulls the book toward her and presses her nose on the mirror.

Ms. Erin knows that rhyming songs and chants with gestures and motion wire the brain for language. She reads every day—many times—to the children. They like the soft books with animal textures they can touch. They like board books that show people, families, and children doing everyday things.

When Ms. Erin reads and engages the children in finger play, she provides language nutrition. Language nutrition is the "use of language sufficiently rich in engagement, quality, quantity, and context that it nourishes the child neurologically, socially, and linguistically" (Head Zauche et al., 2017, p. 494). Language nutrition can involve more than talking, listening, and responding. Rhythmic chants, singing, and motion together wire the brain for language, as each incorporates a range of stimuli, including timing, pitch, volume, and tone quality, while requiring whole body coordination (Chiara Pino et al., 2023; Fiveash et al., 2021).

Language nutrition is like food for the brain. As children listen and interact, their brains take note of the sequences, sounds, and properties of language (Feldman, 2019). Before they produce words, they are already developing a catalog of sounds and labels that are connected to their daily life experiences and interactions with others. Even when infants and toddlers are nonverbal, they communicate meaningful cues, sounds, and behaviors that teachers can notice and respond to. They don't simply absorb language when it is part of the environment, like overhearing other people's conversations. They learn through interactions that are personal—focused on them.

Conversations with children should move beyond asking a question or making a comment. Conversational turns are the back-and-forth interaction between you and a child that can take place even before children begin to talk. To support language development, you will engage with children in frequent, sustained, meaningful interactions that have multiple turn-taking responses throughout the day. Research shows that greater the numbers of serve-and-return interactions between 18 and 24 months, the greater increase in IQ, verbal comprehension, and receptive and expressive vocabulary even a decade later (Gilkerson et al., 2018). That represents a significant influence, indeed.

Meaningful interactions happen when teachers respond to children's cues, wait and listen, encourage turn-taking, and build on what children say through expansions and extensions (Degotardi & Han, 2020; Degotardi et al., 2018). An expansion completes a child's sentence in a way that is slightly more complex. An extension provides additional information or explanation about what the child says. Extensions pull conversations forward beyond one-word responses or a single exchange.

Language skills are self-reinforcing because they boost children's ability to connect with others, inviting even more opportunities to develop understanding about social situations. In turn, strong social skills boost learning success as children interact during group experiences. This is why teachers need to be strategic and intentional about listening and responding to individual children throughout the day.

Strategy Toolbox: Talking With Children

- ❑ **Notice and narrate nonverbal cues.** Respond to facial expressions, body language, and vocalizations. Where does a child look or point? "Do you want to roll the ball?"
- ❑ **Make connections to home.** When reading, "Do you take a bath like Little Rabbit?" When diapering, "Does daddy play *This Little Piggy*, too?"
- ❑ **Wait and listen.** When expecting an infant's vocal sounds or a toddler's answer, pause and give enough time for a response.
- ❑ **Replace pronouns with specific words.**

Typical response:	Much better:
• "Put that over there."	"Put the red truck on the ramp."
• "Put them in there."	"Put the red shapes into the sorter box."
• "Please put it down."	"Please put the ball in the basket."
• "Let's do it."	"Roll the ball to me. I will catch it in my hands."
• "Here you go."	"We have beans, potatoes, and chicken for lunch."
• "Hang it over there."	"Hang the shopping bag on the hook."
• "Whatcha doin'?"	"Baby looks cold. Did you cover baby with a blanket?"
• "How was that?"	"Did you like your bagel with cream cheese?"

- ❑ **Complete a sentence or add missing words to what children say (expansion).**
  - Child: "I gotta car." Teacher: "Yes. You have a car. Where are you going?"
  - Child: "Lin Soo cry." Teacher: "Yes. Lin Soo is crying. Let's sit with her."
- ❑ **Add meaningful information to what children say (extension).**
  - Child: "I got a big piece."

    Typical response: "Yummy, yummy!"

Much better: "Yes, you have a big square of graham cracker. It sounds crunchy. Do you hear the cracker crunch when you bite into it?"

- Child: "Wheee! I gotta fire truck."

  Typical response: "You sure do. It makes a lotta noise."

  Much better: "Yes, you have a ladder truck. Look here in *The Little Fire Truck* book. Do you see the fire people climbing the ladder to rescue the kitten? The ladder helps them reach up higher in the tree."

- Child: "Bean."

  Typical response: "Mmmm, beans."

  Much better: "The green beans are vegetables. Remember we had crunchy carrots at snack? Carrots are vegetables too."

❑ **Reframe information by asking a question (recast).**

- Child: "Baby sleeping." Teacher: "Is your baby sleeping?"
- Child: "Gotta ball." Teacher: "Are you rolling the ball?"

❑ **Use word repetition and expression.** Children learn through repeated exposure. Say, "Up, up, up"—as you adds blocks to a tower. Emphasize, "Down, down, down"—as the blocks fall.

❑ **Use descriptive words.** Introduce details. When patting a stuffed animal, describe texture. "The bunny is soft and smooth. Can you feel the silky ears?" When reading, point and say, "That's an enormous elephant. Enormous means big!"

❑ **Teach simple signs.** Pair high-frequency words with sign language, like *drink*, *more*, and *all done* to support communicating wants and needs.

❑ **Integrate finger play and rhyming songs.** Children learn phonemic awareness (recognizing sound differences and similarities) through rhymes, rhythms, and repetition. "The itsy-bitsy spider went up the waterspout. Down came the rain and washed the spider ___."

❑ **Narrate children's actions.** Focus on effective choices and strategies. "You and Becca worked hard. You pulled the chair to the table. That was teamwork."

❑ **Use open-ended questions and prompts.** "What did you and daddy see on the nature walk?" "Why does the boy in the picture feel sad?" A prompt may include nonverbal cues like pointing or nodding, or a verbal cue like providing the first part of a sentence. "The father gives the puppy a . . . (bone)." "I'm hungry. It's time to . . . (eat)."

❑ **Play with words.** When children are eating a muffin, ask, "Are you eating a pancake?" (They will laugh and say no.) "Are you eating a popsicle (pickle, popcorn)?" "Is it a muffin?" They will respond, "Yes." Then ask, "What kind of muffin are you eating?" Play "I spy, with my little eye. . . ."

ENCOURAGING MULTILINGUAL LEARNING

Two-year-old Keej seems happy, smiling at the other children while sitting next to Ms. Leah. Ms. Leah knows Keej's family speaks the Miao-Yao language at home. With the help of a Hmong liaison from the community, she creates picture cards with verbal prompts to support his participation, like hao *for drink,* noj *for eat, and* chav dej *for bathroom. Keej points to pictures and nods yes and no.*

When Ms. Njuwu, an experienced coaching consultant, visits the classroom, she notices Keej watching quietly while the other children are playing. She explains to Ms. Leah that Keej is used to adults planning and directing his activities at home. "Let's introduce some objects that Keej plays with at home, including cloth balls and blocks. Pair him with other children when you show him how to use materials. He will learn as much from his peers as from you."

Whether you are bilingual and share the language of families or you speak English only, like Ms. Leah, keep communication open with families and seek information from a specialist or cultural broker. Learn about the languages spoken in your community and state, even when these are not yet represented in your program. Early childhood programs, cultural and linguistic brokers, and community organizations together provide a system of support to close the gaps in communication and ensure children can participate fully in the life of programs.

Bilingual and multilingual children learn best in a multisensory, language-rich setting with caring relationships and meaningful play. Just like monolingual language learning, the amount of infant-directed speech and turn-taking has a direct connection to children's speech and language development (Fibla et al., 2022). Responding to infants' cooing and smiling using back-and-forth rhythm, including the use of more exaggerated pitch, speed, and melodic emphasis, as well as facial expression, supports language learning across cultures (Michnick Golinkoff et al., 2015).

Below are effective approaches that promote language learning for all children and are key practices for supporting multilingual development with infants and toddlers.

- Prioritize high-quality exposure to both languages, and create connections between the two languages. For example, introduce the word label *book* in English and the home language together.
- Introduce frequently used words in the child's home language and in English during caring routines, like words for blanket, milk, diaper, hug, peek-a-boo. body parts, eating, and drinking.
- Laminate family photos and use the special names for family members as you point and talk about the pictures with children.
- Use colorful picture cards. Show children how to point to what they need, such as a drink, a hug, or a bottle.

- Ask families to record songs and books in home languages. Even when you speak the family's home language, including family voices and contexts this way benefits children.
- Use a range of strategies to communicate the meaning of words, like gestures, physical objects, and vocal and facial expression, which provide a rich context for children's understanding.
- Introduce colorful laminated photos of routines, read picture books about routines, and model the steps in routines using dolls and stuffed animals.
- Enjoy daily shared book reading, connecting words to pictures and photos of familiar objects, people, and places. Include books and stories in the home language and in English. Invite families and others who share the home language to read to children.
- For teachers seeking to include words and phrases with infants and toddlers, apps like Speak and Translate, Google Translate, and Microsoft Translator can assist (Lake & Beisly, 2019).

Research Revisited: Supporting Multilingual Strengths

Simultaneous bilingual development and bilingual first-language acquisition are terms used for children who learn two or more languages from birth or who start within 1 year of being born (De Houwer, 2021). Teachers may use English and the home language together, as children learn both at the same time.

Children's brains from birth to age 3 are especially sensitive to the differences in language sounds, and high-quality, high-frequency experiences offer steady support for learning (Fibla et al., 2022). You can expect infants and toddlers to use multiple languages together (called code-switching or code-mixing) (Byers-Heinlein & Lew-Williams, 2013). Infants and toddlers have the capacity to make sense of the complexities of two languages just by listening to the sounds and rhythms of the languages (D'Souza & D'Souza, 2021; Pino et al., 2023).

One in three children from birth through age 5 in the United States are dual-language learners, with at least one parent speaking a language other than English at home, and some states having higher percentages, including 59% in California, 49% in Texas, 47% in New Jersey, 44% in New Mexico, 43% in Nevada, 42% in Florida (Migration Policy Institute, 2022). Importantly, the numbers are higher for children living in low-income communities.

While the greatest number of dual-language families speak Spanish (59%), Chinese, Tagalog, Vietnamese, and Arabic are also common (Park et al., 2018). However, across the United States, more than 400 languages are represented, so understanding and supporting bilingualism is a critical priority (U.S. Department of Education, 2017).

FOR YOUR INFORMATION: RESOURCES FOR MULTILINGUAL TEACHING

- Explore additional strategies in *Supporting Emergent Bilingual Children in Early Learning*: https://www.edc.org/sites/default/files/uploads/Supporting-Emergent-Bilingual-Children_English.pdf
- Explore Storybooks Canada, where the multicultural pictures are paired with stories translated into a range of languages: https://www.storybookscanada.ca/
- Check out NAEYC resources for dual-language learners: https://www.naeyc.org/resources/topics/dual-language-learners
- WIDA offers multiple resources to promote home languages: https://wida.wisc.edu/teach/learners/engagement
- The Center on the Developing Child offers five steps for promoting serve-and-return interactions: https://developingchild.harvard.edu/resources/how-to-5-steps-for-brain-building-serve-and-return/
- Learn about the many benefits of dual-language learning and development at Zero to Three: https://www.zerotothree.org/resource/dual-language-development-double-the-benefit/

INVITING ENGAGEMENT IN SHARED BOOK READING

Ms. Sanchez donates some books to Ms. Ruth's toddler classroom. In the set are Max Goes to the Library, Max Goes to the Playground, Max Goes to the Doctor, *and* Max Goes to the Zoo, *by Adria F. Klein. Ms. Ruth isn't sure the children will like these, but as soon as she reads them, the children ask for them over and over. Today, Nedra and Joshua want her to read* Max Goes to the Zoo.

Ms. Ruby asks, "Why are Max and Lily laughing?" Nedra points to the picture, "He sprayed water." "Yes! The elephant sprayed water. He was taking a shower," says Ms. Ruth. She turns the page and reads. Then she asks, "Why are Max and Lily laughing?" "Bear fell in," says Joshua. "Yes. The polar bear leaped into the water," says Ms. Ruth. "Leap is another word for jump. Can you see the polar bear leaping?" When they reach the end, Ms. Ruth says, "Max and Lily have blue tongues. Do you get a blue tongue when you eat a popsicle?" Joshua says. "I gotta blue tongue."

Ms. Ruth rotates books frequently, and the children have favorites. They often want her to read the same book over and over. She uses voices for the characters and points to the pictures. The children enjoy books that tell stories about places they go—to the store, the library, the zoo, the playground, and the doctor. Ms. Ruth wants to know about their visits, too.

Meaningful literacy experiences are part of high-quality infant and toddler teaching. Infants and toddlers who read with adults will reach independently for books to self-entertain. They will turn the page and look at the pictures. When preverbal, they will babble as they look at the pictures, imitating adults who read to them. They associate using books with the feelings of closeness they experience with the adults who read to them. Instilling love of reading is a priority, as it sets a strong foundation for brain development, cognition, and greater mental health later in life (Sun et al., 2023). What are some ways to instill a love of reading? The following tips can jump-start your focus.

- **Read joyfully.** Model your own love of stories and pictures. Read with expression to engage children with the events and characters depicted.
- **Select infant and toddler books with positive messages.** Books offer mirrors—images and stories with experiences that are special and valued by the children—and windows—introductions to people, places, events, and ideas that are new to children and represent a range of diversities, cultures, races, ethnicities, and abilities (NAEYC, 2020).
- **Choose books that appeal to children.** Select photos and images that depict realistic objects children recognize. Choose designs with bright, simple images that invite conversation. Include predictable books with rhythms, rhymes, and memorable stories.
- **Create personal books using photos and drawings from families.** Create a book for each child, labeling family members, relatives, friends, and pets. Include places the child visits and other special activities in the child's life.
- **Make book reading interactive.** Make reading a lively back-and-forth exchange about the stories and characters in the books. Point out illustrations. Ask questions. "The girl is helping her family. How do you help your family?" Since reading with infants and toddlers takes place individually or in a small group, it can be personal.
- **Read creatively.** Add props, costumes, puppets, and flannel board (felt) figures to reenact stories. Emphasize the feelings and experiences of the characters and events.

FOCUSING ON SOCIAL–EMOTIONAL LEARNING

Ms. Claire holds Clancy Cat puppet in one hand and Timmy Turtle in the other. Clancy Cat says, "Meow. I want to play with the puzzle." Timmy Turtle says in a low voice, "It's my puzzle." Ms. Claire looks at the three toddlers and says, "Hmm. What does Clancy Cat feel when Timmy Turtle has the puzzle?" Nadine says, "Sad." "Yes. We feel sad when we can't play. Can Timmy and Clancy get another puzzle?" Lucas says, "Get a puzzle." Ms. Claire agrees. "Yes. There are enough puzzles for everyone to play."

Ms. Claire notices that the children often get frustrated at the low puzzle table. She tries introducing some puzzles on the floor. She rearranges the puzzle racks to make access easier. But she still finds that the children often want the same puzzles. By modeling with the puppets, she thinks the children can recognize that there are enough puzzles for everyone. She often uses Clancy Cat and Timmy Turtle to talk with the children about ways to solve problems.

When teachers focus on social–emotional learning, it lowers their own stress while helping children better adjust (Mader, 2023). Social–emotional learning helps children recognize, identify, and manage their emotions; develop empathy; and solve social problems. Over time, they can verbalize what they need and ask for help. Emotional learning takes root in the infant and toddler years through consistent modeling and encouragement. Children depend on co-regulation, with teachers who supervise closely, listen carefully, and intervene early to assist them in managing social situations. The following are approaches you can easily incorporate in your setting.

- Talk about children's feelings. "Are you happy to see Ms. Frankie? She is glad to see you. We feel happy when friends come to visit."
- Label emotions. "I know you are sad when mommy leaves. Let's wave bye-bye together."
- Draw attention to the feelings of others "Macy is excited to see the birds. Look, she's clapping!" "Haven is frustrated. Her ball got stuck in the tube. Let's help her."
- Model problem solving using puppets. "Polly Parrot is putting away the toys. She likes to be a helper." "Gerry Giraffe wants to play. What should he say to Lyla Lion?"
- Read (or tell) social stories. Include books like *Baby's Feelings* by Little Hippo Books, *Making Faces* by Abrams Appleseed, and *What Do I Feel?* by Annie Kubler. Ask children what the characters in the book feel. Point to the pictures to label and narrate the feelings.
- Respond to frustration with empathy and encouragement. "I'm sorry you dropped the puzzle. I can see you are upset. Let's pick it up together."
- Provide physical comfort. Prepare soft sensory experiences. Invite time for snuggling and relaxation. Help children engage in comforting routines with dolls and plush animals.

Teachers model self-care and empathy for self and others by the ways they respond to infants and toddlers with gentleness and encouragement. Children learn through teachers' consistent responding that they are safe seeking help and comfort. Early experiences that demonstrate safety, comfort, and nurturing create a template for healthy practices of self-care and stress management. Children learn they can turn to others for comfort, a skill necessary for resilience (NCTSN, 2016). These behaviors are also the foundations for healthy social–emotional development.

ENHANCING COGNITIVE DEVELOPMENT AND FINE MOTOR SKILLS

Dakari is almost 3. He spends a lot of playtime lining up toys. Today, he makes a line of magnetic tiles that stretches from the closet door to the table. Ms. Tova sits next to Dakari. "You've been working hard. You made a pattern. You used all the yellow tiles. See? Then all the orange tiles." "Yep. Making a road." "Who is going on your road?" asks Ms. Tova. "I got dinosaurs. They goin' on a trip." Ms. Tova watches as he dumps the plastic figures out of the box. He picks through them and puts the largest figure first, followed by the smaller ones. Ms. Tova points to the first one. "Is this dinosaur the Supersaurus?" "Yep," says Dakari. "He's the super-duper one."

Dakari has older brothers who like dinosaurs, too. Ms. Tova reads him *My First Book of Dinosaurs*, by Erin Waters. On his own, he turns the pages to look at the pictures in the *ABCs of Dinosaur: A Powerfully Prehistoric Alphabet* book, by Sienna Nightingale. He enjoys the detailed drawings. Ms. Tova has learned more about dinosaurs from following Dakari's interest in them.

Dakari is highly focused in his play, often preferring to play alone. Ms. Tova communicates frequently with his family to understand the context for his play. She knows his choices at the program are similar to his play at home. Dakari is left-handed and is still figuring out how to manage crayons and markers. Ms. Tova offers him pebble and muffin crayons that are easier for him to grasp. While he is very advanced in gross motor skills and language, he is taking time to develop fine motor skills.

Offering children experiences with grasping, squeezing, pinching, and twisting are important fine motor activities that can be introduced with successive levels of challenge. Infants begin with random movements and gradually coordinate bringing their hands to their mouths. As they gain strength, they push up with their arms and close their fingers around objects. They begin to shake and bang objects, use the pincer grasp with their fingers, and then turn objects around. They put objects in and take them out of containers. Over time, they use fine motor skills to communicate as they wave bye-bye and point. They engage eagerly with rattles, teething objects, hanging rings, activity boxes, and—most importantly—with the interactive play they enjoy with teachers.

For mobile infants and toddlers, provide a range of challenges. Shape sorters, knob puzzles, stacking and nesting cups/rings, geoboards, child-safe magnetic tiles, large pop beads, commercial brick and peg sets, rod and tube connectors, stringing beads, pounding games (pegboard with hammer), and other open-ended object play are great options. Sand play with buckets, molds, shovels, and thematic toys and water play with funnels, tubes, squeeze bulbs, and containers encourage fine motor skills.

Note that *all materials for infants and toddlers must be evaluated for ingredients that are nontoxic, labeled safe for ages birth to 3, and inspected for size using a choke tube.*

Smaller blocks are considered to be fine motor materials, while larger blocks require more space for building. Construction and block play promote carrying, stacking, lifting, balancing, lining up, bridging, pushing, and comparing skills. Like Dakari, toddlers begin by lining up blocks on the floor and gradually experimenting with stacking, bridging, and creating taller and more complex structures. Fine motor and block experiences are greatly enhanced through teacher modeling and active facilitation. As children begin to test emerging skills, they often require support and encouragement as they play.

Strategy Toolbox: Boosting Higher-Level Thinking Skills

What concepts can be developed for infants and toddlers? The following provide some examples.

- ❑ Connect new ideas to experiences children already know.
  - During water play: "Soap bubbles make the water slippery. When you are in the bathtub at home, you have to hold on tight, because bathwater is slippery, too."
  - During mealtime: "Apples are crunchy. What other food is crunchy? Carrots, celery, and apples are crunchy."
  - While getting dressed to go outdoors: "Gloves are like mittens with fingers."
- ❑ Invite reasoning about processes in daily life.
  - Where do things come from? "Water comes from rain, waterspouts, and hoses." "Milk comes from mamma, the refrigerator, or from cows."
  - Where do things go? "Cars go on the road." "Water and soap go in the bath." "Toys go in the box." "Juice pours into a cup." "Squirrels go up in the tree." "Mamma goes to work."
  - What things go together (grouping)? "Socks go with shoes." "Hammers go with the pegboard." "Mittens and boots come in pairs." "Shapes go in the hole with a matching outline." "Balls go in the hoop." "Cups stack together."
  - What happens when . . . (cause and effect)? "Doors on hinges swing open and shut." "Round objects roll." "Light switches make spaces dark and light." "A breeze and the wind make things move."
  - How are things arranged in order? "Books are placed by size on a shelf." "Cars line up by size or color." "Crayons fit into a container." "People go first and second in a game and conversation."
  - How do things work? "Cooked things are hot. Snow is cold." "Gears turn other gears around." "Pushing a cart makes it go."
  - How are things similar and different? "Dogs are the same and different. This dog has black fur and a big bushy tail. This dog is tiny and has white hair. Dogs come in many sizes. Some are big and some are small."

❑ Facilitate exploration of questions and wonderings.
- What does the child think? "What's a good way to cook the potatoes? Should we stir or mash?" "What should we put on first—socks or pants?" "Where does the rabbit go when it sleeps?"
- Why do things happen? "Why did the robin fly away?" "How did the squirrel get on the feeder?" "Why did the milk spill? Was the cup too close to the edge?"

❑ Use teaching moments when children show interest.
- While looking outside the window: "The worker moves the dirt with a shovel. He scoops up the dirt and dumps it into the wheelbarrow."
- While playing with magnetic tiles: "We made a long line putting the tiles side by side. Let's stack them up and see how high they reach."
- When rolling cars down a ramp: "The balls roll down the track fast. I will roll the car. You roll the ball. Let's see which one rolls faster."

INTRODUCING INQUIRY THROUGH STEAM

Ms. Jesse enjoys brainstorming with Mr. Kim about investigations for toddlers. She explains to Mr. Kim, "I was afraid to bring nature into my classroom, thinking the children would simply throw things. I am always amazed they put objects in containers, take them out, sort and stack them, and treat them with respect. They take pride using the trays and especially the tweezers and magnifying glasses. Mr. Kim responds, "They certainly like watering plants and feeding the fish every day. The outdoor seed box worked, especially now that wildflowers are growing." Ms. Jesse responds, "The nature walks are awesome. They fill their bags to bring treasures back." Mr. Kim adds, "And the families are amazing. Mr. Corral's gear and magnet projects were something special. The children still play with them daily. I'm super excited and wonder how we can extend these through other construction projects?"

Ms. Jesse and Mr. Kim work in an underresourced community in the city. They know that early inquiry experiences for infants and toddlers can be as simple as outdoor exploration and bringing natural objects indoors. They are committed to inquiry learning by fostering curiosity, asking questions, and helping children develop a mindset for comparing, contrasting, noticing details, and testing their ideas. They have daily conversations about the world around them to invite children's interest, ideas, and excitement about discovery learning.

Introducing science, technology, engineering, arts, and mathematics (STEAM) to infants and toddlers exemplifies a critical equity issue—because early experiences with STEAM provide a solid foundation for future success in school and in careers (Clements et al., 2020; Wade et al., 2023). Early inquiry experiences promote curiosity, engagement, and self-agency, dispositions that are the foundation of future academic success.

What ideas come to mind that make sense for your specific children and your unique location? Consider exploration of light and shadow with light tables, flashlights that shine through a variety of materials, boxes with holes, translucent mobiles, and window light catchers (University of Northern Iowa, 2020). Explore the wind on a breezy day, as leaves flutter, a ball rolls away, and hair stands on end. In the classroom, introduce objects that move when you blow on them, and explore the way air feels when it moves across the children's skin. Investigations lead to conversations about why children feel cold and how clothing and blankets (and snuggling) keep them warm. Nature and science are all around—and children are natural explorers.

Toddlers want to know why they have shadows, why objects are heavy or light, where animals eat and sleep, and how their bodies work. Older infants and toddlers develop a sense of ownership and pride in caring for the earth. Great ideas for toddlers include growing seeds, using butterfly kits and bug catchers, and creating an indoor sensory garden with fragrant herbs. Provide wooden bowls to fill with pine cones, seedpods, bark, and twig bits. Invite children to collect interesting leaves, dandelions, pebbles, and flowers. How does this work for children who have never had these experiences before?

- Invite children to find and choose materials.
- Introduce magnifying glasses, flexible tweezers, and sorting trays.
- Demonstrate ways to use materials, like affixing collections to paper or cartons.
- Add picture books that provide visual information to support children's understanding.
- Inspire children's curiosity through daily "I spy" conversations about the community, playground, and classroom. "I spy a ladybug." "I spy a feather."
- Follow safety guidelines for all materials and supervise carefully.

Science play includes learning how the body works, inviting interactive water play (using tubes to transport water, turning waterwheels, using sieves and cups for pouring and filling, testing materials for sinking and floating), and observing how materials change in response to temperature (ice/water) and physical action (pressing/squeezing). Nature activities include learning about animals, plants, and the weather. These are not formal activities but simply responding naturally to the events and patterns observed daily and following children's initiation and interest.

Engineering activities include play with ramps, gears, and loose parts. Mathematics concepts (counting) and patterns (more/less, big/small, heavy/light) are part of children's daily sensory experiences. Technology is incorporated as children look at photos, talk about videos of their own play, and listen to sound recordings. Appropriate digital apps allow them to learn more about an insect or animal they have seen. Creative and artistic play encourages creating, comparing, matching, fittings things together, and taking them apart. Open-ended materials invite children to build, construct, experiment, and pretend. In all these ways, science, technology, engineering, art, and math become integrated during play.

FOR YOUR INFORMATION: INFANT AND TODDLER RESOURCES FOR STEAM

- *Exploring Light and Shadow with Infants and Toddlers* (University of Northern Iowa): https://regentsctr.uni.edu/sites/default/files/inline-uploads/LightandShadowInfantsToddlers_ExperienceSheet.pdf
- NAEYC, *Breaking Down STEAM for Young Children*: https://www.naeyc.org/resources/pubs/tyc/feb2020/breaking-down-steam
- Head Start ECLKC, *Understanding STEAM and How Children Use It*: https://eclkc.ohs.acf.hhs.gov/publication/understanding-steam-how-children-use-it
- Start Early, *STEM/STEAM Education for Toddlers?* https://www.startearly.org/post/stem-for-toddlers/
- Head Start ECLKC, *Infant/Toddler STEAM Series*: https://eclkc.ohs.acf.hhs.gov/school-readiness/teacher-time-series/infanttoddler-steam-series
- Child Care Technical Assistance Network STEAM Resources: https://childcareta.acf.hhs.gov/resource/steam-resources

STRENGTHENING PHYSICAL DEVELOPMENT

In the indoor gross motor room, 2½-year-old George and Marlow are playing copycats on the soft mat surface. Marlow jumps across the mat, with George close behind. They run across the room together until they bump into the wall. Giggling, they run back to the mat and flop down. Mr. Nate offers them the exercise balls. They lean over the top of the balls, with legs dangling. Mr. Leo rocks them gently back and forth for a few moments. "Rocking feels good. Take a few deep breaths." When the children slide off, Mr. Leo says, "Run over to the wall again. I'll roll the balls to you." The children take off running.

Mr. Nate stays close to the children, fully engaged in supervising and engaging the toddlers' energies. He leads them in a game of crab walk and frog hop, which draws in other children. Some of the children try to roll across the mat but aren't able to stay on a straight course. They end up bumping into each other and laughing. Mr. Leo recognizes when George and Marlow are highly stimulated. By introducing a calming activity, he refocuses them before reengaging their energy.

Children need indoor and outdoor spaces with stationary and portable equipment to strengthen physical skills and to introduce new challenges.

Infants enjoy tummy time, lap time, and floor time while interacting with teachers. Toddlers respond to simple games, like throwing and rolling balls and knocking over bowling pins. They enjoy balance equipment, playing on soft mats, using hoops, and steering ride-on and push toys. They need climbing and portable equipment, with daily opportunities to play freely. Active play requires sustained aerobic energy that results in sweating and deep breathing. Dancing movements are generally not active enough to increase heart rate and breathing or to adequately challenge muscles.

Infants use their fingers, hands, and limbs to reach, grasp, and manipulate objects. Over time, they develop greater accuracy and make precise movements, like pinching and grasping. They soon transfer objects from one hand to another and drop and pick up toys. While infants begin to move their limbs with purpose, toddlers learn to balance, jump, kick, and roll. While each child is unique and the timing of skill development varies, positive interactions with teachers encourage and support physical development.

In addition to active indoor play, the American Academy of Pediatrics (2020), the World Health Organization (2019), and Head Start Guidelines (2024) provide recommendations for physical activity for infants and toddlers.

- Children from age 1 should have 3 or more hours of daily physical activity or about 15 minutes every hour they are awake (Iacobucci, 2019). Infants from birth to 1 year of age and toddlers should be taken outside two to three times per day, as tolerated.
- Infants should have 30 minutes or more of tummy time for physical activity like pulling and pushing, reaching and gasping, and moving (NHS, 2022).
- Toddlers need up to 3 hours (180 minutes) of active play daily, spread out through the day and including daily outdoor play (NHS, 2022). Toddlers age 12 to 35 months should be allowed 60 to 90 total minutes of outdoor play. When outdoor play is limited during adverse weather conditions, indoor activity should be increased to compensate.

Part of physical development is the necessary coordination of body systems. Children develop awareness of and coordination of their bodies in space (proprioception) and the ability to maintain balance through visual tracking and torso control (vestibular sense). What do children need to integrate these systems? They need many opportunities to move. Throughout the toddler years, active play, including running, jumping, moving, twirling, climbing, balancing, dancing, and jumping, strengthen physical development.

In spite of these developmental benefits, toddlers spend between 74–89% of their day in sedentary activities with little physical activity (Alhassan et al., 2021). During routines, play, and outdoor time (when they may be confined to a stroller or may be sitting in a sandbox), children are often stationary. In contrast, taking a walk, climbing, playing with outdoor equipment, running, jumping, or navigating an obstacle course can provide needed aerobic exercise.

PROMOTING OUTDOOR PLAY

Eighteen-month-olds Lilianna and Toby are crunching leaves in their fingers and throwing them in the air. Mr. Carlos rakes more of the leaves together, and the children run and fall into the pile. Ms. Abena catches a grasshopper and brings it in her hands to Ada and Kenan. They lay on their bellies and reach out to touch it. It hops onto the mossy patch of grass. "Look at it go. It's so fast!" says Ms. Abena. "Look! It's hopping!" shrieks Kenan. He and Ada scramble up to run after the grasshopper.

This is a city program, where the teachers use all the resources around them to introduce the children to the joys of the natural world on the playground and on their walks to the park. Every day that weather permits, the teachers bring them outdoors at least twice a day, knowing that their many conversations about birds, insects, tree bark, squirrels, and chipmunks help them become curious observers of their world. They also know that active exploration makes their book reading come to life and inspires their active play.

The AAP (2022) encourages curriculum that promotes a lifelong love of the outdoors and nature. Natural features of outdoor play spaces should include "looping pathways, shade, trees, edible landscapes, vegetable gardens, loose parts and outdoor classrooms and storage" (Kemp & Josephidou, 2023, p. 147). Children need unhurried time to enjoy fresh air and sunlight with freedom to interact with open spaces, trees, plants, and nature. The Children and Nature Network (2024) promotes equitable access to safe outdoor spaces for all children.

Outdoor play is influenced by cultural norms and beliefs about supervision, health, safety, sleeping and play approaches, and by views about nature and physical play (Kemp et al., 2023). Adults need to facilitate outdoor experiences, as well as communicate openly with families to ensure collaboration and shared goals. "We suggest a need for more inclusive narratives which value the outdoors as a place for babies, and which recognize additional 'ways of being' outdoors for the youngest children" (Dinkel et al., 2019, p. 139). Creating and protecting safe green spaces is especially critical to overcome socio-environmental inequities (Guedes Vidal & Castro Seixas, 2022).

Research Revisited: Recognizing the Benefits of Outdoor Play

Outdoor play is an important lever for combatting health inequities, including reducing childhood obesity and promoting a wide range of physical and cognitive benefits. Outdoor nature play has a range of direct benefits for children and is essential for children's health, fitness, and motor skills, well-being, mental health, and gross motor development. Children need to be active daily, including infants who sit and crawl and toddlers who need to run, climb, jump, and explore (Josephidou et al., 2021). The American Academy of Pediatrics (AAP) (2021) notes the impact of outdoor play on all areas of child development. Outdoor play:

- Offers necessary multisensory stimulation for the nervous system more comprehensive than possible in indoor settings (Kemp & Josephidou, 2023).
- Improves sensory integration skills and academic success, and offers time for diverse friendships (Yogman et al., 2018).
- Lowers obesity rates and myopia (nearsightedness), increases vitamin E, reduces stress and aggression, and increases impulse control (Glassy & Tandon, 2023).
- Increases social and emotional resilience, has positive outcomes on mental health and academic learning, and lowers children's risk for obesity (Dankiw et al., 2020).

From My Experience: *We keep extra sets of sweaters, mittens, hats, socks, shoes, and boots in what we call our in-and-out supply. Having extra basics has eliminated wasted time. We simply wash and reuse clothing as needed. The shoes and boots are needed when children's own shoes or boots are wet. We also schedule diapering or potty time just before going outdoors.*

Q&As FROM THE FIELD: EXPANDING YOUR IMPACT

Question 1: I am very creative and enjoy preparing integrated themes. The families are ready to collaborate and contribute. What do I do with materials from activities afterward to stay organized?

Answer: When a specific theme is complete, place the props and materials in a storage tub, labeling the front and attaching a photograph. Insert the lesson plan, planning chart, and materials lists. Include photos documenting successful parts of each activity, with notes about what you want to do next time. Over the years, you will develop prop boxes for a variety of themes, with materials and ideas that can be reused in the future.

Question 2: *I'd really like to be more creative and focus more on vocabulary and reading. What's a good first step? How should we get started?*

Answer: Begin with a theme, like exploring nature on the playground. Gather colorful books that fit with your infants or toddlers and your specific setting. Great ideas include *The Busy Tree* by Jennifer Ward and *Toddler Books About Nature: Going on a Nature Hunt,* by Busy Hands Books. Show children how to look for treasures and gather natural collections. Use puppets (e.g., a squirrel puppet) to introduce the books. Wear a sun hat and encourage the children to wear caps or hats when they become "explorers" on outdoor walks. Invite them to feel the textures of bark on different trees and to collect small sticks, seedpods, and leaves. Identify vocabulary words like smooth, rough, bumpy, and soft. Arrange the materials where they can respond by arranging, carrying, or examine them using magnifying glasses. Integrated themes inspire new ways to play, like making a squirrel nest of blankets, searching for "nuts," and bringing them back to the next. Infants will enjoy the hats, puppets, and dropping objects into bags or boxes, and toddlers will enjoy the active and creative exploration.

RESOURCES FOR OUTDOOR PLAY

Given the importance of outdoor play for motor development, body coordination, and self-regulation, the following resources can help you reimagine outdoor and nature experiences that will inspire a lifelong interest in and stewardship of the natural world.

- Childhood by Nature introduces resources and ideas for outdoor exploration and activities for toddlers: https://www.childhoodbynature.com/
- NAEYC provides ideas for outdoor play: https://www.naeyc.org/resources/topics/outdoor
- Early Childhood Outdoors offers nature play ideas for infants and toddlers: https://www.earlychildhoodoutdoors.org/nature-play-for-babies-and-toddlers/

REFLECTION QUESTIONS

1. As you think about your previous experience in the classroom, what is one area of teaching you really enjoy and are "good at"? What is it you do that makes you effective in this area? What skills does this require?

2. In what developmental or learning domain do you want to try new strategies? What strategies from this chapter are especially interesting to you and why? What difference do you think using the strategies will make?
3. What do you notice about the individual strengths of each child? Why is a strengths-based lens a foundational anchor for high-quality teaching?

CHAPTER 8

Setting Priorities for Professional Growth

This chapter focuses on the positive outcomes of reflective practice and the rich opportunities to pursue collaborative growth and learning as part of your professional journey. It provides strategies, encouragement, and inspiration for your work with infants, toddlers, and their families, as you take new steps toward influence and impact.

Learning Goal 1: Explore the processes of self-evaluation, reflective thinking, and shared inquiry that lead to continuous learning and greater effectiveness in teaching.
Learning Goal 2: Develop deeper and more complex understanding of the contexts and strengths of children and families with strategies and insights for reflective practice, personal growth, and positive change.
Learning Goal 3: Explore opportunities for professional growth, strategies for advancing your professional journey, and pathways to becoming a highly effective and influential advocate for children and families.

LEARNING THROUGH REFLECTIVE PRACTICE

Mr. Daniel and Ms. Camila watch 2½-year-old Abigail and Harper push the buggies. The children tuck dolls under their arms and then stuff them into the buggies. Mr. Daniel says, "It's cold outside. Let's get your babies buckled in and covered up." He turns Abigail's baby right-side up and helps tuck a small blanket around the doll. "I'm going to push a baby, too." He shows them how to steer the buggies around the "Park Walk," which is a sidewalk mapped out on the floor. It ends under the paper-bag tree that's been attached to the wall, with a child-sized park bench underneath and a soft green carpet.

During naptime, the teachers talk about the morning "I'm wondering if I should have asked Abigail if she wanted my help with her doll. I could have asked how her momma does it." Ms. Camila responds, "I think it's okay that you assisted her this time. Let's see what she does alone tomorrow."

Ms. Camila and Mr. Daniel share their thinking and ask questions almost daily. Sometimes, conversations are brief. Other times, they wonder more deeply about the children and concerns they have. They talk about their expectations for specific children, whether they are challenging children enough during learning, and whether they are anticipating and responding to children's social behaviors effectively and fairly (Blackson et al., 2022). They consider the best ways to support the children.

Reflective practice must be a daily habit for preparing the classroom, deciding on curriculum, and planning lessons. What has worked well before? What do you still need to know about children to make informed decisions? What do you need to understand about the ways specific children learn? What communication or clarification with families is needed? What else do you need to consider as you plan for specific children? What have you learned about yourself and your setting that can help you make effective teaching decisions? These questions guide teaching as a journey of reflection and action—balanced by shared collaboration with others.

From My Experience: *When I have a challenge, my instinct is to work it out alone, but our director encouraged us to seek support right away. We started a weekly staff feedback meeting. We often share the same questions and issues. We identify reading resources and reach out to our coach. But most of the time, I learn best from the meaningful insights of my colleagues.*

REFLECTIVE PRACTICE IN ACTION

Ms. Alma sits next to 9-month-old Safa and sees she stops playing with the rattles and begins to suck on her fingers. She fusses a little and rubs her eyes. "Can I get the bottle for you?" Ms. Miral offers. "Thank you so much," responds Ms. Alma. "But Safa's parents want us to hold off until noon for her second feeding. Let me distract her for a few minutes." Ms. Miral walks Safa over to the window and puts on some music. She bobs and sways with Safa to the music and afterward sits to read Stomp, Wiggle, Clap, and Tap: My First Book of Dance, *by Rachelle Burk. She reads the rhymes with emphasis and rocks back and forth when she reads, wiggling her shoulders. Safa laughs and wiggles too.*

Later, when Safa has been fed and is asleep, Ms. Miral asks, "I noticed you dancing and reading with Safa. I can see how much she enjoyed it. Maybe we can do this more purposefully with the other children. Do you want to work on a song list with me? I feel like we can coordinate songs with the books better." Ms. Alma agrees. "Great idea. Let's ask families if they have suggestions, too."

Ms. Miral and Ms. Alma talk daily when they have a few minutes and connect at the end of the day as they are cleaning and getting the room set for the following day. They often discuss how their planning worked, how the children responded, and what they can do to be more effective. They also bring families in on the conversations, asking for advice and input. The daily experience of reflective practice in action also helps them identify potential challenges before patterns develop. They trust each other's feedback, ideas, and opinions.

Reflective practice includes evaluation, reflective thinking, and critical analysis as a means of questioning accepted practices (Ruming & McFarland, 2022). It also includes celebration of strategies that work well. You may take time to evaluate challenges, talk about plans, get feedback, and consider next steps. Sometimes, ideas are proactive, like planning to coordinate songs and books. At other times, you may take several days or weeks to work on more complex issues, like supporting a child who frequently cries or adjusting routines to be sure children are engaged.

Continuous quality improvement begins with reflective practice as you identify areas for growth. You may gather feedback from colleagues or participate in more formal program evaluation using a checklist or an outside observer. Once you identify areas you want to address, you will identify research-based strategies that can make a difference. You will select and implement the strategies that make the most sense for your specific children and setting and then document the impact. What happened when you tried a new approach? How did the children respond? How did the change feel to you? Is this approach something you can sustain? Is there anything else you learned about yourself or the children? These questions are part of the ongoing journey of reflective practice in action.

Finally, you can decide on your next steps for growth. Has the issue been resolved, or do you want to make additional adjustments? In what areas can children be better challenged or supported? Are there other areas of creativity, learning, language, or positive guidance you want to work on? Personalize the process to be most meaningful and helpful to you.

Strategy Toolbox: Reflect, Plan, and Grow

There are many ways to reflect, plan, and grow. The following strategies can help guide your planning.

- **Start where you are.** Reflect on your current areas of focus. What are you learning about children and families? What's working well and why? What challenges are you experiencing? What "aha!" moments during teaching have been meaningful to you? What cultural perspectives challenge your assumptions and ideas?

- **Identify areas for growth.** Talk with colleagues to learn what they are experiencing. What insights do they have about themselves and teaching? What concerns, wonderings, or deeper understanding do you both want to explore? What priorities are most important to you?
- **Use feedback.** What information have you gained from families that you can incorporate in planning and teaching? What feedback from colleagues or coaches is important to consider? What strategies from this book make sense for your setting and situation?
- **Try new strategies.** Identify action steps that make sense for your planning and teaching. Decide who will be involved and when you will implement the changes.
- **Set a timeline.** How long will you use the new strategies before reassessing the situation? This may be several days, a week, or a month, depending on the complexity of the issue.
- **Talk about what happened.** How did things turn out? What do you need to adjust? What did you learn? What do you want to do next? What did you learn about yourself, the families, and the children?
- **Join or facilitate a community of practice.** You and your colleagues may come together to pursue deeper learning about topics of shared interest. You will share resources, reflect on your own teaching, hold deeper conversations to address challenges, pursue continuous quality improvement, and promote professional growth (START Project, 2024).

ENGAGING IN CONTINUOUS LEARNING

In the toddler classroom, Ms. Rachel uses a parrot puppet to announce it's time to wash hands and come to the table. When Mr. James finishes handwashing with Sean and Noel, the puppet leads a thank-you song for the food. While the children are eating, Mr. James says, "My watermelon is juicy and sweet. Is your watermelon juicy and sweet?" Nora answers, "Mmmm. Juicy." Ms. Rachel follows up with Sean, "I can see your pretzel is salty." Sean says, "I like curly pretzels." Ms. Rachel says, "Yes, pretzels can be curly and round or straight like sticks. Both are salty."

Mr. James reminds the children, "Do you remember baby crocodile eats a watermelon, and his watermelon has seeds? Does our watermelon have seeds?" The children look at the fruit they are holding. Tamara says, "No seeds." Mr. James responds, "Our watermelon does not have seeds, but baby crocodile's watermelon had seeds." Tamara says, "A watermelon growed in his ear." "Oh," responds Mr. James with a smile. "The watermelon did not *grow in baby crocodile's ear."*

This group of toddlers usually takes a break and eats a snack as a choice when they are hungry during free playtime. But today, the children need extra support for the juicy, slippery snack, so the teachers eat with them as a group. The children are also offered pretzels and cheese cubes. The teachers know the children are hungry by the way they focus on eating and finish every bit.

To integrate learning, the teachers have read *The Watermelon Seed*, by Greg Pizzoli, which is one of the children's favorite stories. They ask for it over and over. They also read *My First Book of Growing Food*, by duopress labs. The children grow seeds on a sunny windowsill in the classroom.

The teachers work together to make meals and snacks intentional times of conversation and learning. They know mealtimes are one of the most important learning experiences for the children. In this rural program, there is a high degree of poverty. Food availability and nutrition are a high priority. A number of families experiencing homelessness have joined the program, and the program has responded to ensure high-quality, nutritious food for the children and to connect families with community resources.

Mr. James and Ms. Rachel understand that teaching is much more than sharing knowledge and modeling love of learning. They try new ideas, integrating themes in ways that are meaningful and interesting to the children. They make meal and snack times personal, warm, and safe, so that children associate eating with security, caring, and connection. By creating cohesiveness across the day, the teachers achieve important goals, including building relationships, soothing stress, and creating meaningful opportunities for learning. They understand and build on the following anchors of developmentally appropriate practice.

- **Exploring child development through the lens of family, culture, and community.** The teachers value families as the source of identity and strength to the children. Consider your own family identity and the experiences that mattered to you as a child. Who and what made you feel important and loved? What important values were instilled? What words of encouragement helped you feel safe and empowered you to rebound from stress and develop confidence? Recognizing the importance of your own early experiences, consider how honoring family, culture, and the experiences of the community allows teaching to be meaningful and personal. It communicates, "I'm here for you. You belong here."
- **Using meaningful communication with families.** The teachers view families through the lens of cultural humility. They really listen—desiring to know the families well. They are committed to cultural continuity and seek to understand, respect, and build on the cultural and linguistic strengths of the children's homes. They observe families with children to understand more about their interactions and

perspectives. They respond with compassion to families experiencing transition and stress, making sure those families are welcome and included in the life and decisions of the program.

- **Promoting play as children's natural way of learning.** The teachers approach each child as an individual, providing activities and designing spaces to appropriately challenge and engage them. They facilitate outdoor play, sharing their love of nature and introducing children to experiences that inspire curiosity and engagement. They integrate new vocabulary and concepts that build on what children already know and understand to make meaningful connections during play.
- **Creating consistent routines and transitions**. The teachers want the program to feel like home to the children—a safe place to explore and learn. They respond with sensitivity to children's need for consistency, soothing, and stress management. They understand that caring routines depend on encouraging and responsive relationships, where teachers respect the unique developmental progress and strengths of each child.
- **Nurturing identity through creativity and self-expression.** The teachers design curriculum that nurtures each child's developing sense of self and reflects their unique and special traits. Children's art projects are displayed, along with photos of the families and children at play. Children explore music, art, dancing, puppets, and dress-up to enhance their creative learning experiences.
- **Using skill-affirming behavior guidance.** The teachers encourage and support children as they learn new skills. They are gentle and patient; understanding that children do their best to navigate daily challenges and are naturally inconsistent day-to-day. They know children respond best to consistent affirmation, reassurance, and caring. They use assisted regulation strategies, knowing the children learn social and emotional skills in partnership with sensitive and responsive adults.
- **Setting goals for high-quality teaching.** The teachers learn from children. They use intentional observation and documentation to identify and understand children's emerging skills. As teachers record and evaluate the children's progress, they adjust the curriculum to support the interests, skills, cultures, languages, and engagement of each child, ensuring each has the best opportunities to learn, grow, and thrive. They model love of learning and nurture authentic relationships with children and their families.

Importantly, the teachers reflect on their teaching. They evaluate the setting through the eyes of the children and the families. What will feel personal and safe? What activities and interactions will feel comfortable and encourage the children's sense of confidence? These practices are priorities for high-quality teaching with infants and toddlers, including promoting child development, strengthening love of learning, and nurturing self-agency, security, and trust.

SETTING GOALS FOR YOUR PROFESSIONAL JOURNEY

Charissa owns a family child care that enrolls children from her neighborhood. She enjoys planning activities to support the children's learning—especially outdoor experiences and music. She knows the toddlers have a lot of energy and finds once they engage in active play, they are ready for more focused activities. Over time, she organizes containers for music that include dress-up tutus, wands and streamers. She stores them on a shelf next to musical instruments and the CD player.

When the children dance, 10-month-old Parker wants to be held. He cries when Charissa puts him down. Over the next week, she finds she needs to hold Parker while preparing meals and supervising the other children. Parker has attended the program for 4 months, and his family tells her everything is normal at home.

Charissa talks with her family child care support group about Parker. Another family child care leader, Mary Ann, laughs. "Oh—that's definitely typical 10-month-old behavior. Around 8 months, babies develop object permanence, so they remember when people and things are gone. It's typical to need holding and reassurance, especially if he is held a lot at home. Just keep the pace of the day the same. Every child is different, and it won't spoil him to hold him. Soon, he will want to crawl and play again."

Charissa is interested in this conversation about child development. She decides to take an online course at the local community college on Saturday mornings. There she learns more about children's development and decides to move forward with pursuing an associate's degree. Her local community college offers credit for her teaching experiences, and her state early childhood system offers scholarships. She enjoys knowing that 10-month-old Parker inspired her to move ahead in her training.

Like Charissa, you may be motivated to learn more when you face a challenge or need more information for your current work. A mentor or colleague may affirm your special skills or impact. Maybe you are required to take ongoing coursework or training as part of your participation in local or state quality improvement initiatives. Perhaps you are reflecting on your work, desire to better understand children and families, and are ready to take the next steps. You may take pride in making a positive difference in the lives of colleagues, families, and children—and want to know and do more.

Professionalism begins with a commitment and sense of purpose. Your goals may include pursuing a Child Development Associate® (CDA) Credential, an associate's degree, a bachelor's degree, a specialist certificate, a master's degree, or a doctorate. The field of early childhood education offers a range of opportunities and career pathways that align with "where you are" in your journey.

Strategy Toolbox: Moving Forward on Your Professional Journey

- ❑ Stay connected to current updates, trends, and research in the field.
- ❑ Advocate for high-quality infant and toddler teaching.
- ❑ Apply for scholarships to support additional training or coursework.
- ❑ Speak up for and share the impact of your program and the profession.
- ❑ View the classroom as a learning laboratory, using daily moments to learn about and with children, families, and colleagues in reflective practice.
- ❑ Document your growth. Create an action plan, journal about what you are learning, and connect with colleagues to share your ideas and plans.
- ❑ Connect with other professionals through local community and area early childhood collaborations and learning groups.
- ❑ Join and take part in the National Association for the Education of Young Children (NAEYC) conferences—and opportunities provided by your state NAEYC affiliate. Explore the organization's many resources available on the web.
- ❑ Tap into community resources for yourself, for families, and for your program.
- ❑ Stay informed about policy and legislation as these impact work in your community and state. Learn how to get involved to advocate for others.

In the midst of change and challenge, there are many ways to balance work, keep a healthy perspective, and thrive. Some helpful approaches are basic and practical, while others require adjustments to time management, planning, and patterns of thinking. Start with the following priorities and apply them in ways that make sense for your own journey.

Take Self-Initiative for Growth. If you don't have a professional mentor, find one. If you aren't yet a mentor to someone else, seek the opportunity to encourage and support others in the field. Ask colleagues to meet with you virtually or in person once a month for a book study. Join a community of practice, where you celebrate strengths and work with others to learn and grow. Meet with your program director to explore opportunities for collaborative growth. Invite colleagues to grow with you.

Manage Your Own Wellness and Well-Being. Take time to evaluate your priorities and needs. Your personal and professional well-being are interrelated. A well-balanced life fosters renewed energy and vision. Take good care of yourself, so you can be fully present with the children you teach.

Ensure High Expectations for Every Child. Nurture and empower every child, family, and colleague. Affirming words are powerful. Your encouragement, strengths-based perspective, and high expectations for all make a positive difference.

Use Challenges as Opportunities to Learn. Respond to daily experiences with flexibility, being willing to learn, adapt, and develop deeper understanding about yourself and others. Reach out to community resources and cultural brokers to learn more about responsive practices and ways to more effectively serve families. The more you know, the more sensitive you will become to the personal stories, values, hopes, and dreams of others.

Be Your Best Self. Stay inspired and use your influence to inspire others. The caring, responsive relationships you offer children become a lasting blueprint for the way they feel about themselves, the expectations they carry forward about learning, and the belief that they can contribute positively to the lives of others. Together with your colleagues, you are making a lasting difference in the lives of infants and toddlers and their families.

AIMING FOR ADVOCACY

"I always wanted to be a teacher, but now I'm thinking about being an infant-toddler specialist," Ms. Mona shares. Ms. Anne responds, "That makes sense. You always encourage me to try new things. In the future, I'd like to be a program director in a setting that serves infants and toddlers. I'm feeling confident about our ability to make a difference."

Ms. Anne and Ms. Mona enrolled together and completed the requirements of the CDA credential. They attended a state conference and met with legislators to share the successes and challenges of their program and to ask support for workforce funding. As a result of these inspiring experiences, they both enrolled in an early childhood bachelor's degree program. By joining with the state early childhood organization, they learned more about career options and extending their circle of influence.

Advocacy begins with *identity*—understanding the importance of your role as an educator. It includes sharing the impact of your own work in the lives of infants, toddlers, and families. It means explaining the importance of high-quality early learning experiences and the impact of your program.

Advocacy also expands your *influence*. You will join with colleagues, community members, and other professionals to participate in fundraising, educational events, and advocacy for systems that support the health, education, and well-being of children.

Advocacy has *impact.* You may write letters, send an email, write an article, or meet in person with community leaders or legislators to share your story and explain how your work impacts families, children, and the life of your community. Joining with state and national organizations allows you to learn about and support current issues and initiatives.

Advocacy shares *information.* You may collaborate with local early childhood organizations, community family service agencies, libraries, health services, and educational sources to distribute research-based information about the importance of the early years and high-quality programing. You will continue to learn about and share the benefits of culturally and linguistically responsive curriculum and the importance of understanding child development in context.

As you collaborate with others, you will continue to create positive changes within your program and contribute to circles of influence that radiate into your community and beyond. As you explore the next steps in your professional journey, you will be able to invite children, families, and colleagues into relationships of belonging and affirmation that will change their lives and your own.

Q&As FROM THE FIELD: GROWING AS A PROFESSIONAL

Question 1: I really want to practice continuous quality improvement. What is the best way to get started?

Answer: First, talk with your program director and colleagues. Collaborative growth is inspiring and meaningful. Together, reach out to your local or state quality improvement system, which will connect you with professional training, information about career pathways, scholarship opportunities, coaching resources, and much more.

- Child Trends offers resources for engaging in cycles of continuous improvement: https://www.childtrends.org/publications/supporting-continuous-quality-improvement-in-programs-and-services-for-young-children
- Quality improvement resource links are available at in the QRIS Resource Guide: https://ecquality.acf.hhs.gov/states

Question 2: How do I learn more about advancing my education? Where can I find the career pathway for my state?

Answer: First, maximize opportunities for training and early childhood credentials offered by your Child Care Resource and Referral Agency and state professional development system. Connect with your local community college or university to explore the CDA credential, associate's, bachelor's, and other advanced degrees in early childhood education. Your state quality improvement system and institutions of higher education can share information about scholarships and resources to support your professional journey.

FOR YOUR INFORMATION: RESOURCES FOR ADVOCACY

Take time to explore the wealth of resources offered by the following organizations:

- The National Association for Family Child Care offers information about advocacy events and issues: https://nafcc.org/
- The Center on the Developing Child at Harvard University provides research-based information to anchor your communication with others: https://developingchild.harvard.edu/
- Zero to Three *Take Action Now* provides links to state and federal policymakers: https://stateofbabies.org/take-action/
- The NAEYC page *Build Your Advocacy Skills*, offers resources, connections, and action steps: https://www.naeyc.org/our-work/public-policy-advocacy/build-your-advocacy-skills-and-knowledge
- Quality Recognition and Improvement Systems (QRIS) provide links to advocacy resource guides for each state: https://ecquality.acf.hhs.gov/states
- The Council for Professional Recognition provides opportunities to get started on a career pathway through the Child Development Associate® (CDA) Credential: https://www.cdacouncil.org/en/
- Zero to Three offers a range of resources for professional growth and advocacy: https://zerotothree.org

REFLECTION QUESTIONS

1. Inspire your professional journey with self-knowledge. What are the reasons you entered the field? What goals and aspirations do you have for yourself as an early childhood professional?
2. How would you describe your experiences so far as a professional? Where do you envision yourself being over the next 5 to 10 years?
3. What next steps do you want to take in advocacy? What people, events, and organizations can help you reach your goals?
4. What does professionalism mean to you in your daily practice? What next steps do you want to take to grow as a professional?

References

Abbott, R. (2022). The anxious child: A new orientation. *Exceptional Parent, 52*(8), 34–36.

Accavitti, M., & Newland, R. (2023). Exclusionary discipline: Missed opportunities for youngest learners. *The Brown University Child and Adolescent Behavior Letter, 39*(5), 1–4.

Administration for Children and Families, U.S. Department of Health and Human Services (ACF USDHHS). (2015, June 25). *Caring for our children basics: Health and safety foundations for early care and education*. https://www.acf.hhs.gov/sites/default/files/documents/ecd/caring_for_our_children_basics.pdf

Administration for Children and Families. (2023). *Toxic stress*. Administration for Children and Families. https://www.acf.hhs.gov/trauma-toolkit/toxic-stress

Ainsworth, M., Blehar, M., Waters, E., & Wall, S. (1978). *Patterns of attachment: A psychological study of the strange situation*. Erlbaum. https://mindsplain.com/wp-content/uploads/2021/01/Ainsworth-Patterns-of-Attachment.pdf

Ajodhia, A., & CohenMiller, A. S. (2024). Can arts-informed pedagogy facilitate communities of learning and belonging for minoritised early years children? An integrative review of research. *International Journal of Early Years Education, 31*(1), 52–67.

Alhassan, S., Cox, M., St. Laurent, C., Burkart, S., Amalbert-Birriel, M., & Sudarsky, L. (2021). Understanding the perceptions, practices, and barriers of physical activity opportunities in toddler classrooms: A qualitative study in toddler childcare providers. *International Journal of Early Childhood, 53*(3), 315–331.

Allen, R., Meek, S., Alexander, B., Palomino, C., Blevins, D., Catherine, E., McIntosh, K., Hemmeter, M. L., Powell, T., & Soto-Boykin, X. (2022). A holistic approach to ending exclusionary discipline for young learners: A review of the data, research, and multidimensional solutions. *The Children's Equity Project,* 1–27. https://childandfamilysuccess.asu.edu/sites/default/files/2022-09/exclusionary-discipline-093022-1.pdf

Allen, V. (2023, December 1). Why nursery rhymes are best for your child's brain: Speaking in a sing-song voice helps babies to learn language, study finds. *Daily Mail: Science and Tech.* https://www.dailymail.co.uk/sciencetech/article-12814279/Why-nursery-rhymes-best-childs-brain-Speaking-sing-song-voice-helps-babies-learn-language-study-finds.html

Amadon, S., Lin, Y., & Padilla, C. (2023). *Turnover in the center-based child care and early education workforce: Findings from the 2019 National Survey of Early Care and Education*. Office of Planning, Research, and Evaluation.

American Academy of Child & Adolescent Psychiatry (AACAP). (2019). *Diversity and culture in child mental health care. Family and youth facts for families, #188.* https://www.aacap.org/AACAP/Families_and_Youth/Facts_for_Families/FFF-Guide/Diversity_and_Culture_in_Child_Mental_Health_Care-118.aspx

American Academy of Pediatrics (AAP). (2019). *Caring for our children, national health and safety performance standards* (4th ed.). American Academy of Pediatrics. https://nrckids.org/files/CFOC4%20pdf-%20FINAL.pdf

American Academy of Pediatrics. (2019, October 7). *Sensory integration therapy.* https://www.healthychildren.org/English/health-issues/conditions/developmental-disabilities/Pages/Sensory-Integration-Therapy.aspx

American Academy of Pediatrics. (2020). *Making physical activity a way of life: AAP policy explained.* Healthy Children. https://www.healthychildren.org/English/healthy-living/fitness/Pages/Making-Fitness-a-Way-of-Life.aspx

American Academy of Pediatrics. (2021). *Power of play in early childhood.* https://www.aap.org/en/patient-care/early-childhood/early-childhood-health-and-development/power-of-play/

American Academy of Pediatrics. (2022). *Potty training.* https://www.healthychildren.org/English/ages-stages/toddler/toilet-training/Pages/default.aspx

American Academy of Pediatrics. (2023a). *Food and media: Not a healthy mix.* https://www.healthychildren.org/English/family-life/Media/Pages/Food-and-TV-Not-a-Healthy-Mix.aspx

American Academy of Pediatrics. (2023b). *American Academy of Pediatrics renews its call to end corporal punishment in schools.* https://www.aap.org/en/news-room/news-releases/aap/2023/american-academy-of-pediatrics-renews-its-call-to-end-corporal-punishment-in-schools/

American Academy of Pediatrics. (2024a). *Choking prevention for babies & children.* Healthy Children. https://www.healthychildren.org/English/health-issues/injuries-emergencies/Pages/Choking-Prevention.aspx

American Academy of Pediatrics. (2024b). *Toddler food and feeding.* https://www.aap.org/en/patient-care/healthy-active-living-for-families/toddler-food-and-feeding/

American Psychological Association (APA). (2019). *Resolution on Physical Discipline of Children by Parents.* https://www.apa.org/monitor/2019/05/physical-discipline

American Psychological Association. (2023). *Parents and caregivers are essential to children's healthy development.* https://www.apa.org/topics/families/parents-caregivers-kids-healthy-development

Amodia-Bidakowska, A., Laverty, C., & Ramchandani, P. (2020, September). Father-child play: A systematic review of its frequency, characteristics, and potential impact on children's development. *Developmental Review, 57,* 100924.

Andrade-Guirguis, R., & Plotka, R. (2019). Engaging Latino families in early childhood programs: Barriers, misconceptions, and recommendations. *Dimensions of Early Childhood, 47*(2), 14–20.

Banghart, P., Halle, T., Bamdad, T., Cook, M., Redd, Z., Cox, A., & Zaslow, M. (2020). *Executive summary: A review of the literature on access to high-quality care for infants and toddlers.* Child Trends. https://www.childtrends.org/wpcontent/uploads/2020/05/HighQualityCare

Barrett, K., Moding, K., Flesher, A., & Johnson, S. (2023). "The kale is green" and other things caregivers say when feeding infants and toddlers are associated with child rate of acceptance. *Journal of Nutrition, 153*(4), 1297–1304.

Barrish, K. (2020). The role of play in contemporary child psychotherapy: A developmental perspective. *Journal of Infant, Child, and Adolescent Psychotherapy, 19*(2), 148–158.

Bartolini, S. (2024). *Toddler nutrition 101: How nutrition affects behavior.* https://kabrita.com/blogs/nourish-blog/toddler-nutrition-101-how-nutrition-affects-behavior

Bassok, D., Markowitz, A., Bellows, L., & Sadowski, K. (2021). New evidence on teacher turnover in early childhood. *Educational Evaluation and Policy Analysis, 43*(1), 172–180.

Behrens, K., & Umemura, T. (2020). Japan-US comparison of mothers' wishes for their children's futures in the context of attachment. *Journal of Family Studies, 26*(3), 329–344.

Bembich, C. (2016). Parenting and educational aims in a cross cultural perspective: How culture affects early interactions with the child. *Rivista Italiana di educazione familiare, 1*, 71–85.

Beneke, M., & Love, H. (2022). A DisCrit analysis of quality in early childhood: Toward pedagogies of wholeness, access, and interdependence. *Teachers College Record, 124*(12), 192–219.

Bennett, S., Gunn, A., Gayle-Evans, G., Barrea, E., & Leung, C. (2018). Culturally responsive literary practices in an early childhood community. *Early Childhood Education Journal, 46*(2), 241–248.

Benson McMullen, M. (2017). Continuity of care with infants & toddlers: Identifying benefits and addressing common concerns. *Child Care Exchange, 39*(11), 46–50.

Bento, G., & Dias, G., (2017). The importance of outdoor play for young children's healthy development. *Porto Biomedical Journal, 2*(5), 157–160.

Berg, A. (2005). The management of traumatic stress disorder in infants. *Journal of Child and Adolescent Mental Health, 17*(2), 88.

Bichay-Awadalla, K., & Butotsky-Shearer, R. (2022). Examining the factor structure of the Classroom Assessment Scoring System Toddler (CLASS-T) in Early Head Start and subsidized child care classrooms. *Early Education and Development, 33*(2), 309–325.

Bigelow, A., & Rankin Williams, L. (2020, September). To have and to hold: Effects of physical contact on infants and their caregivers. *Infant Behavior and Development, 61*, 101494.

Blackson, E., Gerdes, M., Segan, E., Anokam, C., & Johnson, T. (2022). Racial bias toward children in the early childhood education setting. *Journal of Early Childhood Research, 20*(3), 277–292.

Blaine, R., Davison, K., Hesketh, K., Taveras, E., Gillman, M., & Benjamin Neelon, S. (2015). Child care provider adherence to infant and toddler feeding recommendations: Findings from the baby nutrition and physical activity self-assessment for child care (Baby NAP SACC) study. *Child Obesity, 11*(3), 304–313.

Bornstein, M. (2015). Culture, parenting, and zero-to-threes. *Zero to Three, 35*(4), 2–9.

Brophy-Herb, H., Brinks, A., Cook, J., Stacks, A., Vallotton, C., Frosch, C., Carson, R., Wheeler, R., Perkins, H. A., & Jennings, P. (2023). Stress intensity and exhaustion among infant and toddler teachers: Descriptive analysis and associations with sources of stress and coping strategy use. *Early Education and Development, 34*(7), 1545–1564.

Bruijns, B., Truelove, S., Johnson, A., Gililand, J., & Tucker, P. (2020). Infants' and toddlers' physical activity and sedentary time as measured by accelerometry: A systematic review and meta-analysis. *International Journal of Behavioral Nutrition and Physical Activity, 17*(14), 1–14.

Buren, V., Müllensiefen, D., Roeske, T., & Degé, F. (2021). What makes babies musical? Conceptions of musicality in infants and toddlers. *Frontiers in Psychology, 12,* 736833. https://www.ncbi.nlm.nih.gov/pmc/articles/PMC8797144/

Byers-Heinlein, K., & Lew-Williams, C. (2013). Bilingualism in the early years: What the science says. *Learning Landscapes,* 7(1), 95–112.

California Department of Education (CDE). (2016). *Best practices for planning curriculum for young children: Family partnerships and culture.* https://www.cde.ca.gov/sp/cd/re/documents/familypartnerships.pdf

Calzada, E., Huang, K., Hernandez, M., Soriano, E., Acra, C., Dawson-McClure, S., Kamboukos, D., & Brotman, L. (2015). Family and teacher characteristics as predictors of parent involvement in education during early childhood among Afro-Caribbean and Latino immigrant families. *Urban Education, 50*(7), 870–896.

Campinha-Bacote, J. (2018). Cultural competemility: A paradigm shift in the cultural competence versus cultural humility debate—Part 1. *Online Journal of Issues in Nursing, 24*(1). https://doi.org/10.3912/OJIN.Vol24No01PPT20

Cantor, P., Osher, D., Berg, J., Steyer, L., & Rose, T. (2018). Malleability, plasticity, and individuality: How children learn and develop in context. *Applied Developmental Science, 23*(4), 1398649.

Carson, V., Lee, E., Hewit, L., Jennings, C., Hunter S., Kuzik, N., Stearns, J., Unrau, S., Poitras, V., Gray, C., Adamo, K., Janssen, I., Okely, A., Spence, J., Timmons, B., Sampson, M., & Tremblay, M. (2017). Systematic review of the relationships between physical activity and health indicators in the early years (0–4 years). *British Medical Journal Public Health, 17*(Suppl. 5), 854.

Cassidy, J., Jones, J., & Shaver, P. (2013). Contributions of attachment theory and research: A framework for future research, translation, and policy. *Developmental Psychology, 25*(4), 1415–1434.

Castle, S., Williamson, A., Young, E., Stubblefield, J., Laurin, D., & Pearce, N. (2016). Teacher–child interactions in Early Head Start classrooms: Associations with teacher characteristics. *Early Education and Development, 27*(2), 259–274.

Cebioğlu, S., & Broesch, T. (2021). Explaining cross-cultural variation in mirror self-recognition: New insights into the ontogeny of objective self-awareness. *Developmental Psychology, 57*(5), 625–638.

Cebioğlu, S., Marin, K., & Broesch, T. (2023). Variation in caregivers' references to their toddlers: Child-directed speech in Vanuatu and Canada. *Child Development, 93*(6), e622–e638.

Centers for Disease Control (CDC), (2024a). *Childhood obesity facts.* https://www.cdc.gov/obesity/childhood-obesity-facts/childhood-obesity-facts.html

Centers for Disease Control. (2024b). *Individuals with Disabilities Education Act (IDEA) services.* https://www.cdc.gov/ncbddd/actearly/autism/curriculum/documents/early-intervention-education_508.pdf

Centers for Disease Control and Prevention. (2023). *Fast facts: Preventing adverse childhood experiences.* https://www.cdc.gov/aces/prevention/index.html

Center for the Developing Child (2024). *A guide to executive function.* https://developingchild.harvard.edu/resource-guides/guide-executive-function/

Center for the Developing Child. (2021). *3 principles to improve outcomes for children and families: 2021 update.* https://harvardcenter.wpenginepowered.com/wp-content/uploads/2017/10/3Principles_Update2021v2.pdf

Chiara Pino, M., Giancola, M., & D'Amico, S. (2023). The association between music and language in children: A state-of-the-art review. *Children (Basel), 10*(5), 801.

Child Care State Capacity Building Center. (2022, August 29). Trauma-responsive care: A guide for infant and toddler professionals. https://childcareta.acf.hhs.gov/sites/default/files/new-occ/resource/files/trc_infographics_overview_.pdf

Choi, J. Y., Ryu, D., Van Pay, C., Meacham, S., & Beecher, C. (2021), Listening to Head Start teachers: Teacher beliefs, practices, and needs for educating dual language learners. *Early Childhood Research Quarterly, 54*(1), 110–124.

Claussen, A., Dimitrov, L., Bhupalam, S., Wheation, A., & Danielson, M. (2023). Short sleep duration: Children's mental, behavioral, and developmental disorders and demographic, neighborhood, and family context in a nationally representative sample, 2016–2019. *Preventing Chronic Disease: Public Health Research, Practice, and Policy, 20*(E58), 1–15. https://www.cdc.gov/pcd/issues/2023/pdf/22_0408.pdf

Clegg, J., Wen, N., & Legare, C. (2017). Is non-conformity WEIRD? Cultural variation in adults' beliefs about children's competency and conformity. *Journal of Experimental Psychology, 146*(3), 428–441.

Clements, D., Vinh, M., Lim, C., & Sarama, J. (2020). STEM for inclusive excellence and equity. *Early Education and Development, 32*(2), 1–23.

Coba-Rodriguez, S., Cambray-Engstrom, E., & Jarret, R. (2020). The home-based involvement experiences of low-income Latino families with preschoolers transitioning to kindergarten: Qualitative findings. *Journal of Child and Family Studies, 20,* 2678–2696.

Cole, J. (2023, September 12). *My block, my hood, my city.* [keynote address]. Leadership Connections Conference. National Louis University.

Cole, P., Trexberg, K., Schaffner, M., Maxfield, E., Pina, G., & Ryberg, R. (2023). *The state of babies yearbook: 2023.* Zero to Three. https://thinkbabies.org/state-of-babies/

Colliver, Y., Harrison, L., Brown, J., & Humburg, P. (2022). Free play predicts self-regulation years later: Longitudinal evidence from a large Australian sample of toddlers and preschoolers. *Early Childhood Research Quarterly, 59*(2), 148–161.

Connecticut Conference of Municipalities. (2020). Racial equity toolkit. https://www.ccmct.org/Portals/CCM/PDF/CCM_RacialEquityToolkit_2020_5.pdf

Cooper, A., Reschke, P., Porter, C., Coyne, S., Stockdale, L., Graver, H., Siufanua, M., Rogers, A., & Walle, E. (2023). "Oh no! What happened?" An investigation of parent-child conversations about self-conscious emotions. *Developmental Psychology, 59*(11), 2133–2147.

Cronk, K. (2023). Cultural responsiveness in pediatric screening: Developing a companion document to the ASQ-3 in Norton Sound Region, Alaska. https://anthc.org/wp-content/uploads/2021/11/Cronk-Cultural-Responsiveness-in-Pediatric-Screening-_-Developing-a-Companion-Document-to-the-Ages-and-Stages-Questionnaire-ASQ-3-for-Norton-Sound-Region-Alaska.pdf

Cunningham, S., Hardy, S., Jones, R., Ng, C., Kramer, M., & Narayan, V. (2022). Changes in the incidence of childhood obesity. *Pediatrics, 150*(2), e2021053708.

Curtis, K., Zhou, Q., & Tao, A. (2020). Emotion talk in Chinese American immigrant families and longitudinal links to children's socioemotional competence. *Developmental Psychology, 56*(3), 475–488.

D'Souza, D., & D'Souza, H. (2021). Bilingual adaptations in early development. *Trends in Cognitive Science, 25*(9), 727–729.

Dai, Q., McMahon, C., & Lim, A.K. (2020). Cross-cultural comparison of maternal mind-mindedness among Australian and Chinese mothers. *International Journal of Behavioral Development, 44*(4), 365–370.

Dankiw, K., Tsiros, M., Baldock, K., & Kumar, S. (2020). The impacts of unstructured nature play on health in early childhood development: A systematic review. *PLOS One*, 15(2), e0229006.

De Gioia, K. (2013). Cultural negotiation: Moving beyond a cycle of misunderstanding in early childhood settings. *Journal of Early Childhood Research, 11*(2), 108–122.

De Houwer, A. (2021). *Bilingual development in childhood.* Cambridge University Press.

De Witte, M., Spruit, A., van Horren, S., Moonen, Z., & Stams, G. (2020). Effects of music interventions on stress-related outcomes: A systematic review and two meta-analyses. *Health Psychology Review, 14*(2), 294–324.

Deater-Deckard, K., Godwin, J., Lansford, J. E., Bacchini, D., Bombi, A., Bornstein, M., Chang, L., Di Giunta, L., Dodge, K., Malone, P., Oburu, P., Pastorelli, C., Skinner, A., Sorbring, E., Steinberg, L., Tapanya, S., Alampay, L., Uribe Tirado, L., Zelli, A., & Al-Hassan, S. (2018). Within- and between-person and group variance in behavior and beliefs in cross-cultural longitudinal data. *Journal of Adolescence, 62*, 207–217.

Degotardi, S. (2017). Joint attention in infant-toddler early childhood programs: Its dynamics and potential for collaborative learning. *Contemporary Issues in Early Childhood, 18*(4), 409–421.

Degotardi, S., & Han, F. (2020). Quality of educator-infant conversational interactions among infants experiencing varying quantity of linguistic input. *European Early Childhood Education Research Journal, 28*(5), 743–757.

Degotardi, S., Han, F., & Hu, J. (2022). Infant educators' use of mental-state talk in Australia and China: A cross-cultural comparative study. *International Journal of Early Years Education, 30*(1), 87–105.

Degotardi, S., Han, F., & Torr, J. (2018). Infants' experience with "near and clear" educator talk: Individual variation and its relationship to indicators of quality. *International Journal of Early Years Education, 26*(3), 278–294.

Degotardi, S., Toor, J., & Nguyen, N. (2016). Infant-toddler educators' language support practices during snack-time. *Australasian Journal of Early Childhood, 41*(4), 52–62.

DeMeo Cook, K., Ferreira van Leer, K., & McPherran Lombardi, C. (2023). Exploring predictors and outcomes of racial/ethnic match between children and providers in Early Head Start. *Early Childhood Research Quarterly, 62(*1), 275–286.

Denham, S., Basset, H., & Miller, S. (2017). Early childhood teachers' socialization of emotion: Contextual and individual contributors. *Child Youth Care Forum, 46*, 805–824.

Dijkstra-de Neijs, L. Tisseur, C., Kluwen, L., van Berckelaer-Onnes, I., Swaab, H., & Ester, W. (2023). Effectivity of play-based interventions in children with autism spectrum disorder and their parents: A systemic review. *Journal of Autism and Developmental Disorders, 53*(4), 1588–1617.

Dinkel, D., Snyder, K., Patterson, T., Warehime, S., Kuhn, M., & Wisneski, D. (2019). An exploration of infant and toddler unstructured outdoor play. *European Early Childhood Education Research Journal, 27*(2), 257–271.

Doebel, S., & Lillard, A. (2023). How does play foster development? A new executive function perspective. *Developmental Review, 67,* 101064. https://www.sciencedirect.com/science/article/abs/pii/S0273229722000545

Dunn, D. (2021, December 15). *Understanding ableism and negative reactions to disability: Engaging in critical thinking can be helpful in altering beliefs and avoiding ableist conclusions.* American Psychological Association. https://www.apa.org/ed/precollege/psychology-teacher-network/introductory-psychology/ableism-negative-reactions-disability

Dym Bartlett, J., & Smith, S. (2019). The role of early care and education in addressing early childhood trauma. *American Journal of Community Psychology, 64*(3–4), 359–372. https://doi.org/10.1002/ajcp.12380

Ebbeck, M., Yim, H., Ho, S., & Sharma, M. (2022). Continuity of Care: Primary Caregiving in Singapore. *Early Childhood Education Journal, 50*(2), 291–300.

Edyburn, K., Quirk, M., & Oliva-Olson, C. (2019). Supporting Spanish–English bilingual language development among Latinx dual language learners in early learning settings. *Contemporary School Psychology, 23,* 87–100.

Einarsdottir, J., & Jónsdóttir, A. (2019). Parent-preschool partnership: Many levels of power. *Journal of International Research & Development, 39*(2), 175–189.

Escamilla, I., Kroll, L., Meier, D., & White, A. (2021). *Learning stories and teacher inquiry groups: Reimagining teach and assessment in early childhood education.* NAEYC.

Esteban-Guitart, M. (2021). Advancing the funds of identity theory: A critical and unfinished dialog. *Mind, Culture, and Activity, 28*(2), 169–179.

Evans, R., Dean, B., & Byett, F. (2022). The musical lives of young children in Aotearoa New Zealand. *British Journal of Music Education, 39*(3), 256–272.

Faircloth, C., & Murray, M. (2015). Parenting: Kinship, expertise, and anxiety. *Journal of Family Issues, 36*(9), 1115–1129.

Fantasia, V., & Delafield-Butt, J. (2023, September). Time and sequence as key dimensions of joint action development. *Developmental Review, 69,* 101091.

Farkas, C., Olhaberry, M., Pia Santelices, M., & Cordella, P. (2017). Interculturality and early attachment: A comparison of urban/non-Mapuche and rural/Mapuche mother-baby dyads in Chile. *Journal of Child and Family Studies, 26*(1), 205–216.

Faulkner, M., Gerstenblatt, P., Lee, A., Vallejo, V., & Travis, D. (2016). Child care providers: Work stress and personal well-being. *Journal of Early Childhood Research, 14*(3), 280–293.

Feldman, H. (2019). How young children learn language and speech: Implications of theory and evidence for clinical pediatric practice. *Pediatric Review, 40*(8), 398–411.

Fibla, L., Kosie, J., Kircher, R., Lew-Williams, C., & Byers-Heinlein, K. (2022). Bilingual language development in infancy: What can we do to support bilingual families? *Policy Insights from the Behavioral and Brain Sciences, 9*(1), 35–43.

Fielding, K., Maslin, K., & Murcia, K. (2023). "I can't draw, sing or dance to save my life!": Educator and parent implicit theories of creativity. *Australasian Journal of Early Childhood, 48*(2), 148–162.

Finnish National Agency for Education (FNAE). (2018). *National core curriculum for early childhood education and care.* https://www.oph.fi/sites/default/files/documents/National%20core%20curriculum%20for%20ECEC%202022.pdf

Fiveash, A., Bedoin, N., Gordon, R., & Tillmann, B. (2021). Processing rhythm in speech and music: Shared mechanisms and implications for developmental speech and language disorders. *Neuropsychology, 35*(8), 771–791.

Fleer, M. (2018). Conceptual play worlds: The role of imagination in play and learning. *Early Years: An International Journal of Research and Development, 41*(6), 1–12.

Fleer, M. (2023). Rising to the concrete: A cultural-historical study of concept development of infants and toddlers in imaginary situations. *Learning, Culture and Social Interaction, 46,* 100820. https://dx.doi.org/10.2139/ssrn.4633630

Franco, F., Suttora, C., Spinelli, M., Kozar, I., & Fasolo, M. (2021). Singing to infants matters: Early singing interactions affect musical preferences and facilitate vocabulary building. *Journal of Child Language, 49*(3), 552–577.

Frith, E., Loprinzi, P., & Miller, S. (2019). Role of embodied movement in assessing creative behavior in early childhood: A focused review of perceptual and motor skills. *Perceptual Motor Skills, 126*(6), 1058–1083.

Fulcher, L. (2002). Cultural safety and the duty of care. *Child Welfare, 81*(5), 689–708.

Fuller, B., Bridges, M., & Land, A. (2020). What policies advance infants and toddlers? Evidence to inform state and federal options. *Social Policy Report, 33*(1), 1–43.

Gardner-Neblett, N., Henk, J., Vallotton, C., Rucker, R., & Chazan-Cohen, R. (2021). The "what," "how," and "who" of early childhood professional development (PD): Differential associations of PD and self-reported beliefs and practices. *Journal of Early Childhood Teacher Education, 42*(1), 53–75.

Garner, A., & Yogman, M. (2021). Preventing childhood toxic stress: Partnering with families and communities to promote relational health. *Pediatrics, 148*(2), e2021052582.

Gee, D., & Cohodes, E. (2021). Caregiving influences on development: A sensitive period for biological embedding of predictability and safety cues. *Current Directions in Psychological Science, 30*(5), 376–383.

Gee, D., & Cohodes, E. (2023). Leveraging the developmental neuroscience of caregiving to promote resilience among youth exposed to adversity. *Development and Psychopathology, 35*(5), 2168–2185.

Gershoff, E., & Grogan-Kaylor, A. (2016). Spanking and child outcomes: Old controversies and new meta-analyses. *Journal of Family Psychology, 30*(4), 453–469.

Gilkerson, J., Richards, J., Warren, S., Kimbrough Oller, D., Russo, R., & Vohr, B. (2018). Language experience in the second year of life and language outcomes in late childhood. *Pediatrics, 142*(4), 220174276.

Giner Torréns, M., & Kartner, J. (2017). The influence of socialization on early helping from a cross-cultural perspective. *Journal of Cross-Cultural Psychology, 48*(3), 353–368.

Gitz-Johansen, T. (2022). Intersubjectivity in the nursery: A case-study from Denmark. *Childhood, 29*(1), 112–125.

Glassy, D., & Tandon, P. (2023). *Playing outside: Why it's important for kids.* American Academy of Pediatrics. https://www.healthychildren.org/English/family-life/power-of-play/Pages/playing-outside-why-its-important-for-kids.aspx

Glicksman, E. (2019, May). Physical discipline is harmful and ineffective: A new APA resolution cites evidence that physical punishment can cause lasting harm for children. *American Psychological Association, 50*(5), 22. https://www.apa.org/monitor/2019/05/physical-discipline

Goodhall, N., & Atkinson, C. (2020). An exploratory case study: Children's perceptions of play access in two schools (England and Wales). *Educational and Child Psychology, 37*(4), 37–52.

Goodman, J., & Cook, B. (2019). Shaming school children: A violation of fundamental rights? *Theory and Research in Education, 17*(1), 61–81.

Gopalan, M. (2019). Understanding the linkages between racial/ethnic discipline gaps and racial/ethnic achievement gaps in the United States. *Education Policy Analysis Archives, 27*(154), 1–34.

Greenberg, E., Adams, G., & Michie, M. (2016). *Barriers to preschool participation for low-income children of immigrants in Silicon Valley, Part 2* (Research Report). Urban Institute, Center on Labor, Human Services, and Population. https://www.urban.org/sites/default/files/publication/76991/2000586-Barriers-to-Preschool-Participation-for-Low-Income-Children-of-Immigrants-in-Silicon-Valley.pdf

Grisez, L. (2018, October 23). *Container baby syndrome: How equipment can hinder a child's development.* Nationwide Children's. https://www.nationwidechildrens.org/family-resources-education/700childrens/2018/10/container-baby-syndrome

Guedes, C., Cadima, J., Aguiar, T., Aguiar, C., & Barata, C. (2020, March–April). Activity settings in toddler classrooms and quality of group and individual interactions. *Journal of Applied Developmental Psychology, 67,* 101100.

Guedes Vidal, D., & Castro Seixas, E. (2022, April 4). Children's green infrastructure: Children and their rights to nature and the city. *Frontiers in Sociology, 7,* 804535.

Hallam, R., Fouts, H., Bargreen, K., & Perkins, K. (2016). Teacher–child interactions during mealtimes: Observations of toddlers in high subsidy child care settings. *Early Childhood Education, 44*(1), 51–59.

Hamby, S., Elm, J., Howell, K., & Merrick, M. (2021). Recognizing the cumulative burden of childhood adversities transforms science and practice for trauma and resilience. *American Psychologist, 76*(2), 230–242.

Hamilton, A., Jin, Y., & Krieg, S. (2019). Early childhood arts curriculum: A cross-cultural study." *Journal of Curriculum Studies, 51*(5), 698–714.

Harkness, S., & Super, C. (2020). Cross-cultural research on parents: Applications to the care and education of children introduction to the issue. *New Directions for Child and Adolescent Development, 170,* 7–11.

Harper, K. (2017, January 12). *5 things to know about racial and ethnic disparities in special education.* Child Trends. https://childtrends.org/publications/5-things-to-know-about-racial-and-ethnic-disparities-in-special-education

Harper, K., Ryberg, R., & Temkin Cahill, D. (2019). *Black students and students with disabilities remain more likely to receive out-of-school suspensions, despite overall declines.* Child Trends. https://www.childtrends.org/publications/black-students-disabilities-out-of-school-suspensions

Head Start. (2024). *Grow staff and family understanding of and comfort with outdoor play and learning.* https://eclkc.ohs.acf.hhs.gov/learning-environments/supporting-outdoor-play-exploration-infants-toddlers/grow-staff-family-understanding-comfort-outdoor-play-learning

Head Zauche, L., Darcy Mahoney, A., Thul, T., Zauche, M., Weldon, A., & Stapel-Waz, J. (2017). The power of language nutrition for children's brain development, health, and future academic achievement. *Journal of Pediatric Health Care, 31,* 493–503.

Hector Bruder, F. (2022, April 18). *Not just 9 to 5: Expanding child care options for parents working nontraditional hours.* https://iwpr.org/not-just-9-to-5-expanding-child-care-options-for-parents-working-nontraditional-hours/

Hoffman, J., Uretsky, M., Patterson, L., & Green, B. (2020). Effects of a school readiness intervention on family engagement during the kindergarten transition. *Early Childhood Research Quarterly, 53*(4), 86–96.

Hoicka, E., Mowat, R., Kirkwood, J., Kerr, T., Carberry, M., & Bijvoet-van den Berg, S. (2016). One-year-olds think creatively, just like their parents. *Child Development, 87*(4), 1009–1105.

Holst-Wolf, J., Yeh, I., & Konczak, J. (2016). Development of proprioceptive acuity in typically developing children: Normative data on forearm position sense. *Frontiers in Human Neuroscience.* https://doi.org/10.3389%2Ffnhum.2016.00436

Hooper, A. (2023). Sing and play your way to reading: Building emergent literacy skills in infants and toddlers through music. *Reading Teacher, 76*(4), 451–458.

Horm, D., File, N., Bryant, D., Burchinal, M., Raikes, H., Forestieri, N., Encinger, A., & Cobo-Lewis, A. (2018). Associations between continuity of care in infant-toddler classrooms and child outcomes. *Early Childhood Research Quarterly, 42,* 105–118.

Housman, D. (2017). The importance of emotional competence and self-regulation form birth: A case for the evidence-based emotional cognitive social early learning approach. *International Journal of Child Care and Education Policy, 11*(13), 1–19.

Housman, D. (2020). *The power of play: Building young children's resilience, healthy development, and learning.* Houseman Institute. https://www.housmaninstitute.com/blog/the-power-of-play-building-young-childrens-resilience-healthy-development-and-learning

Howard, J. (2017, November 8). How the world potty trains. *CNN* Health, Parenting Without Borders. https://www.cnn.com/2017/10/31/health/potty-training-parenting-without-borders-explainer

Hyun, S., McWayne, C., & Guetterman, T. (2022). Examination of Chinese immigrant parents' beliefs about children's social development through play: A mixed methods explanatory sequential study. *Developmental Psychology, 58*(2), 325–338.

Iacobucci, G. (2019). Children should have at least three hours of daily physical activity from age 1, WHO advices. *British Medical Journal.* https://doi.org/10.1136/bmj.l1884

Jacobi, B. (2019). Eurhythmics, sufficient space, and the role of the environment in the child's development. *Music Educators Journal, 105*(4), 37–44.

Jessen-Howard, S., Malik, R., & Falgout, M. (2020, August 4). *Costly and unavailable: America lacks sufficient child care supply for infants and toddlers.* Center for American

Progress. https://www.americanprogress.org/article/costly-unavailable-america-lacks-sufficient-child-care-supply-infants-toddlers/

Johns Hopkins Medicine. (2024). *Food allergies in children* and babies. https://www.hopkinsmedicine.org/health/conditions-and-diseases/food-allergies-in-children

Johnson, A., & Peterson, S. (2019). Supporting individual and community identity development in infant–toddler classrooms. *Zero to Three, 39*(3), 18–24.

Johnson, L., Radesky, J., & Zuckerman, B. (2013). Cross-cultural parenting: Reflections on autonomy and interdependence. *Pediatrics, 131*(4), 631–633.

Johnson, S., Moding, K, Flesher, A., Boenig, R., & Campain, J. (2024). I'll never give up: A qualitative study of caregivers' perceptions and decisional processes when feeding infants and toddlers novel and disliked foods. *Journal of Nutrition Education and Behavior, 56*(5), 287–299.

Jones Harden, B. (2015). Services for families of infants and toddlers experiencing trauma. A research-to-practice brief (OPRE Report # 2015–14). Office of Planning, Research and Evaluation (OPRE); Administration for Children and Families. https://www.acf.hhs.gov/sites/default/files/documents/opre/opre_nitr_brief_v07_508_2.pdf

Jones Harden, B., & Slopen, N. (2022). Inequitable experiences and outcomes in young children: Addressing racial and social-economic disparities in physical and mental health. *Annual Review of Developmental Psychology, 4*, 133–159.

Jordan, I. (2022). Both/and: Early childhood education needs both play and equity. *Young Children, 77(2)*, 51–52.

Josephidou, J., Kemp, N., & Durrant, I. (2021). Outdoor provision for babies and toddlers: Exploring the practice/policy/research nexus in English ECEC settings. *European Early Childhood Education Research Journal, 29*(6), 925–941.

Kaiser, B., & Rasminsky, J. (2019). Valuing diversity: Developing a deeper understanding of all young children's behavior. *Teaching Young Children, 13*(2), 20–22.

Karasik, K., & Kuchirko, Y. (2022). Talk the talk and walk the walk: Diversity and culture impact of development—A commentary on Kidd and Garcia. *First Language, 42*(6), 779–783.

Karasik, L., & Robinson, S. (2022). Milestones or millstones: How standards assessments mask cultural variation and misinform policies aimed at early childhood development. *Policy Insights from the Behavioral and Brain Sciences, 9*(1), 57–64.

Karasik, L., Tamis-LeMonda, C., Adolph, K., & Bornstein, M. (2015). Places and postures: A cross-cultural comparison of sitting in 5-month-olds. *Journal of Cross-Cultural Psychology, 46*, 1023–1038.

Keller, H. (2016). Attachment: A pancultural need but a cultural construct. *Current Opinion in Psychology, 8*, 59–63.

Keller, H. (2017). Cultural and historical diversity in early relationship formation. *European Journal of Developmental Psychology*, 14(1), 1–14.

Keller, H. (2018). Universality claim of attachment theory: Children's socioemotional development across cultures. *Proceedings of the National Academy of Sciences (PNAS), 115*(45), 11414–11419.

Keller, H., Bard, K., Morelli, G., Chaudhary, N., Vicedo, M., Rosabal-Coto, M., Scheideker, G., Murray, A., & Gottleib, A. (2018). The myth of universal sensitive responsiveness: Comment on Mesman et al. (2017). *Child Development, 89*(5), 1921–1928.

Kells, D. (2019). Music as the perfect serve-and-return interaction with infants. *Exchange May/June, 247*, 38–41.

Kemp, N., & Josephidou, J. (2023). Babies and toddlers outdoors: A narrative review of the literature on provision for under twos in ECEC settings. *Early Years: An International Research Journal, 43*(1), 137–150.

Kemp, N., Josephidou, J., & Bolshaw, P. (2023). *From weeds to tiny flowers: Rethinking the place of the youngest children outdoors.* The Open University, Froebel Trust. https://www.froebel.org.uk/uploads/documents/FT-From-Weeds-to-Tiny-Flowers-Miday-way-report-Nov-23-Kemp-Josephidou.pdf

Keren, M. (2019). Eating and feeding disorders in early childhood. In C. H. Zeanah (Ed.), *Handbook of infant mental health* (4th ed.). Guilford Press.

Kersey, K., & Masterson, M. (2013). *101 Principles for positive guidance with young children: Creating responsive teachers.* Pearson.

Keys Adair, J. (2015). *The impact of discrimination on the early schooling experiences of children from immigrant families.* Migration Policy Institute. https://www.migrationpolicy.org/sites/default/files/publications/FCD-Adair.pdf

Kim, H., Rajbhandari, A., Krile, R., Lang, I., Antonakos, C., & Colabianchi, N. (2023). Body mass index trajectories among the Healthy Communities Study children: Racial/ethnic and socioeconomic disparities in childhood obesity. *Journal of Racial and Ethnic Health Disparities, 11*, 203–215.

Kim, Y., & Calzada, E. (2019). Skin color and academic achievement in young, Latino children: Impacts across gender and ethnic group. *Cultural Diversity and Ethnic Minority Psychology, 25*(2), 220–231.

Kwon, K., Horm, D., & Amirault, C. (2021). *Early childhood teachers' well-being: What we know and why we should care*. Zero to Three. https://www.zerotothree.org/resource/journal/early-childhood-teachers-well-being-what-we-know-and-why-we-should-care/

Kwon, K., Jeon, S., Jeon, L., & Castle, S. (2019, August). The role of teachers' depressive symptoms in classroom quality and child developmental outcomes in Early Head Start programs. *Learning and Individual Differences, 74*, 101748.

LaForett, D., & Mendez, J. (2017). Children's engagement in play at home: A parent's role in supporting play opportunities during early childhood. *Early Child Development and Care, 187*(5/6), 910–923.

Lake, V., & Beisly, A. (2019). Translation apps: Increasing communication with dual language learners. *Early Childhood Education Journal, 47*(4), 489–496.

Lancy, D. (2015). *The anthropology of childhood: Cherubs, chattel, changelings.* Cambridge University Press.

Lang, S., Tolbert, A., Schoppe-Sullivan, S., & Bonomi, A. (2016, 1st Quarter). A cocaring framework for infants and toddlers: Applying a model of coparenting to parent–teacher relationships. *Early Childhood Research Quarterly, 34*, 40–52.

Lansford, J. (2022). Annual research review: Cross-cultural similarities and differences in parenting. *Journal of Child Psychology and Psychiatry, 63*(4), 466–479.

Lauren, D. (2018). One diaper at a time: Re-envisioning diapering routines with infants and toddlers. *Zero to Three, 39*(2), 11–20.

Lee, S. Y., Shin, M., & Recchia, S. (2016). Primary caregiving as a framework for preparing early childhood preschool students to understand and work with infants. *Early Childhood Research and Development, 27*(3), 336–351.

Leggett, N. (2017). Early childhood creativity: Challenging educators in their role to intentionally develop creative thinking in children. *Early Childhood Education Journal, 45*(6), 845–853.

Lense, M., Shultz, S., Astésano, C., & Jones, W. (2022). Music of infant-directed singing entrains infants' social visual behavior. *Psychological and Cognitive Sciences, 119*(45), e2116967119.

Lerner, C. (2017). *Parents under stress: What it means for babies.* Zero to Three. https://www.zerotothree.org/wp-content/uploads/2022/05/Parents-Under-Stress_-What-It-Means-for-Babies.pdf

Levine Coley, R., Spielvogel, B., Kruzik, C., Miller, P., Betancur, L., & Votruba-Drzal, E. (2021). Explaining income disparities in young children's development: The role of community contexts and family processes. *Early Childhood Research Quarterly, 55*(2), 295–311.

Lieberman, A. (2023, March 24). *Inequitable infant and toddler discipline practices and the need for better data.* First Five Years Fund. https://www.ffyf.org/inequitable-infant-and-toddler-discipline-practices-and-the-need-for-better-data/

Lim, N. (2016). Cultural differences in emotion: Differences in emotional arousal level between the East and West. *Integrated Medical Research, 5*(2), 105–109.

Liu, L., du Toit, M., & Weidemann, G. (2021). Infants are sensitive to cultural differences in emotions at 11 months. *PLOS One, 16*(9), e0257655.

Loebach, J., Sanches, M., Jaffe, J., & Elton-Marshall, T. (2021). Paving the way for outdoor play: Examining socio-environmental barriers to community-based outdoor play. *International Journal of Environmental Research and Public Health, 18*(7), 3617.

Loizou, E., & Loizou, E. K. (2022). Creative play and the role of the teacher through the cultural-historical activity theory framework. *International Journal of Early Years Education, 30*(2), 527–541.

Luo, A., Lahat, A., & Perlman, M., Howe, N., Recchia, H., Bukowski, W., Ross, H. (2022). Changes in social pretend play as toddlers form relationships with peers. *Merrill-Palmer Quarterly, 68*(4), 401–436.

Mader, J. (2023, March 21). *Toddlers need social emotional learning, teachers say.* Hechinger Report. https://hechingerreport.org/toddlers-need-social-emotional-learning-teachers-say/

Malloch, S., & Trevarthen, C. (2018). The human nature of music. Editorial: The impact of music on human development and wellbeing. *Frontiers in Psychology, 9.* https://www.frontiersin.org/journals/psychology/articles/10.3389/fpsyg.2018.01680/full

Mangione, P., Kriener-Althen, K., & Marcella, J. (2016). Measuring the multifaceted nature of infant and toddler care quality. *Early Education and Development, 27*(2), 149–169.

Markham Risica, P., Karpowicz, J., von Ash, T., Gans, K., Cooksey-Stowers, K., & Tovar, A. (2022). Feeding and activity environments for infants and toddlers in childcare centers and family childcare homes in Southeastern New England. *International Journal of Environment Research and Public Health, 18*(15), 9702.

Massing, C., Kirova, A., & Hennig, K. (2016). The role of first language facilitators in redefining parent involvement: Newcomer families' funds of knowledge in an intercultural preschool program. *Journal of Childhood Studies, 38*(2), 4–13.

McGlynn, K., & Kelly, J. (2019). Adaptations, modifications, and accommodations. *Science Scope, 43*(3), 36–41.

McWayne, C., Foster, B., & Melzi, G. (2018). Culturally embedded measurement of Latino caregivers' engagement in Head Start: A tale of two forms of engagement. *Early Education and Development, 29*(4), 540–562.

Meins, E. (2013). Sensitive attunement to infants' internal states: Operationalizing the construct of mind-mindedness. *Attachment & Human Development, 15*(5–6), 524–544.

Menashe-Grinberg, A., & Atzaba-Poria, N. (2017). Mother-child and father-child play interaction: The importance of parental playfulness as a moderator of the links between parental behavior and child negativity. *Infant Mental Health Journal, 38*(6), 772–784.

Mendez Smith, J. (2020). Early childhood education programs as protective experiences for low income Latino children and their families. *Adversity Resilience Science, 1*(3), 191–204.

Mendoza, J., & Fausey, C. (2022). Everyday parameters for episode-to-episode dynamics in the daily music of infancy. *Cognitive Science, 46*(8), 1–17.

Mesman, J., Minter, T., Angnged, A., Cissé, I., Deniz Salali, G., & Bamberg Migliano, A. (2018). Universality without uniformity: A culturally inclusive approach to sensitive responsiveness in infant caregiving. *Child Development, 89*(3), 837–850.

Mesman, J., van IJzendoorn, M., Behrens, K., Carbonell, O., Cárcamo, R., Cohen-Paraira, I., de la Harpe, C., Ekmekci, H., Emmen, R., Heidar, J., Kondo-Ikemura, K., Mels, C., Mooya, H., Murtisari, S., Noblega, M., Ortiz, J., Sagi-Schwartz, A., Sichimba, F., . . . Zreik, G. (2016). Is the ideal mother a sensitive mother? Beliefs about early childhood parenting in mothers across the globe. *International Journal of Behavioral Development, 40*(5), 385–397.

Michnick Golinkoff, R., Deniz, D., Soderstrom, M., & Hirsh-Pasek, K. (2015). (Baby) talk to me. The social context of infant-directed speech and its effects on early language acquisition. *Current Directions in Psychological Science, 24*(5), 339–344.

Migration Policy Institute (2022, October). *Learning more about dual language learners.* https://migrationpolicy.org/content/learning-more-about-dual-language-learners

Miller, K. (2018). An investigation of early childhood teachers' perceptions of families through a photo-sharing activity. *Journal of Early Childhood Teacher Education, 39*(2), 131–149.

Miller, P., Betancur, L., Coulanges, L., Kammerzell, J., Libertus, M., Bachman, H., & Votruba-Drzal, E. (2022). Time spent playing predicts early reading and math skills through associations with self-regulation. *Journal of Applied Developmental Psychology, 83*, 101470.

Morales-Muñoz, I., Lemola, S., Saarenpää-Heikkilä, O., Kylliäinen, A., Pölkki, P., Paunio, T., Broome, M., & Paavonen, E. (2020). Parent-reported early sleep problems and internalizing, externalizing and dysregulation symptoms in toddlers. *British Medical Journal Paediatrics Open, 4*(1), e000622.

Morris, C., Hunter, A., Fox, L., & Hemmeter, M. (2021, June 3). *The Pyramid Model and trauma-informed care: A guide for early childhood professionals to support young children's resilience.* https://challengingbehavior.org/docs/Trauma-Informed-Care_Guide.pdf

Mortenson, J., & Barnett, M. (2015). Teacher-child interactions in infant/toddler child care and socioemotional development. *Early Education and Development, 26*(2), 209–229.

Muppalla, S., Vuppalapati, S., Pulliahgaru, A., & Sreenivasulu, H. (2023). Effects of excessive screen time on child development: An updated review and strategies for management. *Cureus, 15*(6), 240608.

Murray, D., Rosanbalm, K., Christopoulos, C., & Hamoudi, A. (2015). *Self-regulation and toxic stress: Foundations for understanding self-regulation from an applied perspective* (OPRE Report #2015–21). Office of Planning, Research and Evaluation, Administration for Children and Families, U.S. Department of Health and Human Services.

National Academies of Sciences, Engineering, and Medicine (NASEM). (2015). *Parenting matters: Supporting parents of children ages 0–8.* National Academies of Sciences, Engineering, and Medicine NASEM, 2016.

National Association for Gifted Children (NAGC). (2024). *Identification.* https://nagc.org/page/identification

National Association for Gifted Children. (2019). *Asynchronous development.* https://home.lps.org/gifted/files/2019/03/Asynchronous-Development.pdf

National Association for the Education of Young Children (NAEYC). (2016, September 28). *Statement from NAEYC on implicit bias research.* https://www.naeyc.org/about-us/press-releases/statement-naeyc-implicit-bias-research

National Association for the Education of Young Children. (2019). *Early learning program accreditation standards and assessment items.* National Association for the Education of Young Children.

National Association for the Education of Young Children. (2020). *Position statement on developmentally appropriate practice.* National Association for the Education of Young Children.

National Association for the Education of Young Children. (2022). *Developmentally appropriate practice in early childhood programs serving children from birth through age 8* (4th ed.). National Association for the Education of Young Children.

National Association of School Psychologists (NASP). (2017). Implicit bias: A foundation for school psychologists. *Communique, 46*(3), 32–33.

National Center for Education Statistics (NCES). (2019). *Fast facts.* https://nces.ed.gov/fastfacts/display.asp?id=4

National Center for Learning Disabilities (NCLD). (2023). *Significant disproportionality in special education: Current trends and actions for impact.* https://ncld.org/wp-content/uploads/2023/07/2020-NCLD-Disproportionality_Trends-and-Actions-for-Impact_FINAL-1.pdf

National Center on Safe Supportive Learning Environments. (2018). Our nation's English learners. https://safesupportivelearning.ed.gov/resources/our-nations-english-learners

National Child Traumatic Stress Network (NCTSN). (2016). *Resilience and child traumatic stress.* https://www.nctsn.org/resources/resilience-and-child-traumatic-stress

National Health Services (NHS). (2022). *Physical activity guidelines for children (under 5 years).* https://www.nhs.uk/live-well/exercise/physical-activity-guidelines-children-under-five-years/

National Institutes of Health (NIH). (2019, November 25). *High amounts of screen time begin as early as infancy, NIH study suggests.* https://www.nih.gov/news-events/news-releases/high-amounts-screen-time-begin-early-infancy-nih-study-suggests

National Resource Center (NRC). (2017). *Updates to CFOC standards.* National Resource Center for Health and Safety in Child Care and Early Education. https://nrckids.org/CFOC

Nationwide Children's. (2018, October 23). *Container baby syndrome: How equipment can hinder a child's development.* https://www.nationwidechildrens.org/family-resources-education/700childrens/2018/10/container-baby-syndrome

Newton, R. (2020). Scaffolding of the brain: Infant parent psychotherapy during the primary biological entrainment period. *Journal of Infant, Child, and Adolescent Psychotherapy, 19*(1), 56–70.

Nguyen, T., Zimmer, L., & Hoehl, S. (2023). Your turn, my turn. Neural synchrony in mother–infant proto-conversation. *Philosophical Transactions of the Royal Society B: Biological Sciences 378*(1875), 1–9.

Oesch, N. (2019). Music and language in social interaction: Synchrony, antiphony, and functional origins. *Frontiers in Psychology, 10,* 1514.

Office of Disability Rights. (2022). *People first language.* https://odr.dc.gov/page/people-first-language

Oudgenoeg-Paz, O., Atun-Einy, O., & van Schaik, S. (2020). Two cultural models on infant motor development: Middle class parents in Israel and the Netherlands. *Frontiers in Psychology, 11,* 1–15. https://www.frontiersin.org/articles/10.3389/fpsyg.2020.00119/full

Owens, J. (2016). Early childhood behavior problems and the gender gap in educational attainment in the United States. *Sociology of Education, 89*(3), 236–258.

Owens, J. (2022). Double jeopardy: Teacher biases, racialized organizations, and the production of racial/ethnic disparities in school discipline. *American Sociological Review, 87*(6), 1007–1048.

Paley, B., & Hajal, N. (2022). Conceptualizing emotion regulation and coregulation as family-level phenomena. *Clinical Child and Family Psychology Review, 25*(1), 18–43.

Palmer Wolf, D. (2020). *Why making music matters: Music and early childhood development.* Carnegie Hall Education. https://www.carnegiehall.org/Explore/Articles/2020/12/09/Why-Making-Music-Matters

Papadimitriou, A., Smyth, C., Politimou, N., Franco, F., & Stewart, L. (2021). The impact of the home musical environment on infants' language development. *Infant Behavior and Development, 65,* 10165.

Park, M., Zong, J., & Batalova, J. (2018, February). *Growing superdiversity among young U.S. dual language learners and its implications.* Migration Policy Institute. https://www.migrationpolicy.org/sites/default/files/publications/SuperDiversityAmongDLLs_FINAL.pdf

Parkarinen, A., Hautala, L., Haman, L., Aromaa, M., Kallio, H., Liuksila, P., Sillanpää, M., & Salanterä, S. (2020). The association between the preference for active play and neurological development in toddlers: A register-based study. *International Journal of Environmental Research and Public Health, 17*(7), 2525. https://www.ncbi.nlm.nih.gov/pmc/articles/PMC7178213/

Paruthi, S., Brooks, L., D'Ambrosio, C., Hall, W., Kotagal, S., Lloyd, R., Malow, B., Maski, K., Nichols, C., Quan, S., Rosen, C., Troester, M., & Wise, M. (2016). Recommended amount of sleep for pediatric populations: A consensus statement of the American Academy of Sleep Medicine. *Journal of Clinical Sleep Medicine, 12*(6), 785–786.

Patel, C., Karasouli, E., Shuttlewood, E., & Meyer, C. (2018). Food parenting practices among parents with overweight and obesity: A systematic review. *Nutrients, 10*(12), 1966. https://www.preprints.org/manuscript/201811.0397/v1

Pelligra, R., Doman, G., & Leisman, G. (2014). A reassessment of the SIDS back to sleep campaign 12//23/2014. *The Scientific World Journal, 5*(July 21), 550–557. https://iahp.org/reassessment-sids-back-sleep-campaign-12232014/

Penalba, A., Martinez-Alvarez, L., & & Schiavio, A. (2020). The active musical room: Fostering sensorimotor discoveries and musical creativity in toddlers. *Journal of Research in Music Education, 69*(2), 002242942095306.

Perlman, M., Brunsek, A., Hepditch, A., Gray, K., & Falenchuck, O. (2017). Instrument development and validation of the infant and toddler assessment for quality improvement. *Early Education and Development, 28*(1), 115–133.

Perry, A. (2019, January 17). *Shaming students is keeping schools from teaching them.* The Brookings Institute. https://www.brookings.edu/articles/shaming-students-is-keeping-schools-from-teaching-them/

Perry, B., & Morris, E. (2014). Suspending progress: Collateral consequences of exclusionary punishment in public schools. *American Sociological Review, 79*(6), 1067–1087.

Pino, M. C., Giancola, M., & D'Amico, S. (2023). The association between music and language in children: A state-of-the-art review. *Children* (Basel), *10*(5), 801.

Poćwierz-Marciniak, I., & Harciarek, M. (2021). The effect of musical stimulation and mother's voice on the early development of musical abilities: A neuropsychological perspective. *International Journal of Environmental Research and Public Health, 18,* 8467. https://www.ncbi.nlm.nih.gov/pmc/articles/PMC8393253/pdf/ijerph-18-08467.pdf

Politimou, N., Dalla Bella, S., Farrugia, N., & Franco, F. (2019). Born to speak and sing: Musical predictors of language development pre-schoolers. *Frontiers of Psychology, 24*(10), 948.

Polk, C., & Bogard, K. (2016). Quality practices for working with infants and toddlers. *Zero to Three, 36*(4), 31–35.

Pugsley, L, & Acar, S. (2018). Supporting creativity or conformity? Influence of home environment and parental factors on the value of children's creativity characteristics. *The Journal of Creative Behavior, 54*(2), 598–609.

The Pyramid Model Consortium. (2021). *Checklist of early childhood practices that support social-emotional development through trauma-informed care.* National Center for Pyramid Model Innovations. https://challengingbehavior.org/document/checklist-of-early-childhood-practices-that-support-social-emotional-development-and-trauma-informed-care/

Rameka, L., Glasgow, A., Howarth, P., Rikihana, T., Wills, C., Mansell, T., Burgess, F., Fiti, S., Kauraka, B., & Iosefo, R. (2017). *Te Whātu Kete Mātauranga: Weaving Māori and Pasifika infant and toddler theory and practice in early childhood education*. http://www.tlri.org.nz/sites/default/files/projects/TLRI%20Summary_Rameka.pdf

Ramos, C., Pereira, A., Feher, A., & Baptista, J. (2023, November). How does sensitivity influence early executive function? A critical review on hot and cool processes. *Infant Behavior and Development, 73*, 101895.

Regueiro, S., Matte-Gagne, C., & Bernier, A. (2022). Paternal mind-mindedness and child executive functioning in the kindergarten classroom. *Early Childhood Research Quarterly, 58*, 27–34.

Reschke, K. (2019). Who am I? Developing a sense of self and belonging. *Zero to Three, 39*(3), 5–8.

Reschke, K. (2020, April 10). Who am I? Developing a sense of self and belonging. https://www.zerotothree.org/resource/journal/who-am-i-developing-a-sense-of-self-and-belonging/

Reyes, I., Da Silva Iddings, A., & Feller, N. (2016). Building relationships with diverse students and families: A funds of knowledge perspective. *Journal of Early Childhood Literacy, 16*(1), 8–33.

Richardson, C., & Romano, I. (2014). Supporting indigenous children and parents in early childhood settings. *Early Childhood Education, 42*(1), 4–11.

Riley, L., Rupert, J., & Boucher, O. (2018). Nutrition in toddlers. *American Family Physician, 98*(4), 227–233. https://www.aafp.org/pubs/afp/issues/2018/0815/p227.html

Rodriguez, M., & Kross, E. (2023). Sensory emotion regulation. *Trends in Cognitive Sciences, 27*(4), 379–390.

Rosanbalm, K., & Murray, D. (2017). *Co-regulation from birth through young adulthood: A practice brief* (OPRE Brief #2017–80). Office of Planning, Research, and Evaluation, Administration for Children and Families, U.S. Department of Health and Human Services. https://fpg.unc.edu/sites/fpg.unc.edu/files/resources/reports-and-policy-briefs/Co-RegulationFromBirthThroughYoungAdulthood.pdf

Rossetti, Z., Redash, A., Sauer, J., Bui, O., Wen, Y., & Regensburger, D. (2020). Access, accountability, and advocacy: Culturally and linguistically diverse families' participation in IEP meetings. *Exceptionality, 28*(4), 243–258.

Ruming, N., & McFarland, L. (2022). "When we sat together, it just worked": Supporting individual and collaborative reflective practice in a team of early childhood educators. *Australasian Journal of Early Childhood, 47*(1), 32–47.

Runco, M. A. (2019). Creativity as a dynamic, personal, parsimonious process. In R. Beghetto & G. Corazza (Eds.), *Dynamic perspectives on creativity* (pp. 181–188). *Creativity Theory and Action in Education, 4*. Springer. https://doi.org/10.1007/978-3-319-99163-4_10

Ruokonen, I., Tervaniemi, M., & Reunamo, J. (2021). The significance of music in early childhood education and care of toddlers in Finland: An extensive observational study. *Music Education Research, 23*(5), 634–646.

Ruprecht, K., Elicker, J., & Choi, J. (2016). Continuity of care, caregiver–child interactions, toddler social competence and problem behaviors. *Early Education and Development, 27*(2), 221–239.

Sabol, T., Kessler, C., Rogers, L., Petitclerc, A., Silver, J., Briggs-Gowan, M., & Wakschlag, L. (2021). A window into racial and socioeconomic status disparities in preschool disciplinary action using developmental methodology. *Annals of the New York Academy of Sciences, 1508*(1), 123–136.

Sacks, V., & Murphey, D. (2018, February 12). *The prevalence of adverse childhood experiences, nationally, by state, and by race or ethnicity*. Child Trends. https://www.childtrends.org/publications/prevalence-adverse-childhood-experiences-nationally-state-race-ethnicity

Sailer, A., & Guilmartin, L. (2019). A music class for babies? How making music with infants affects brain development. *Exchange, 264*, 61–67.

Salih, M. Abargil, M., Badarneh, S., Selle, N., Irani, M., & Atzil, S. (2023). Evidence for cultural differences in affect during mother–infant interactions. *Scientific Reports, 13*, 4831. https://www.nature.com/articles/s41598-023-31907-y

Salminen, J., Guedes, C., Lerkkanen, M., Parkaninen, E., & Cadima, J. (2019). Teacher–child interaction quality and children's self-regulation in toddler classrooms in Finland and Portugal. *Infant Child Development, 20*, 1–23.

Santamaría, L., & Santamaría, A. (2015). Counteracting educational injustice with applied critical leadership: Culturally responsive practices promoting sustainable change. *International Journal of Multicultural Education, 17*(1), 22–41.

Savage, P. E., Brown, S., Sakai, E., & Currie, T. E. (2015). Statistical universals reveal the structures and functions of human music. *Proceedings of the National Academy of Sciences of the United States of America, 112*(29), 8987–8992. https://doi.org/10.1073/pnas.1414495112

Scaglioni, S., De Cosmi, V., Ciappolino, V., Parazzini, F., Brambilla, P., & Agostoni, C. (2018). Factors influencing children's eating behaviours. *Nutrients, 10*(6), 706.

Schneider, M., Falkenberg, I., & Berger, P. (2022). Parent-child play and the emergence of externalizing and internalizing behavior problems in childhood: A systematic review. *Frontiers in Psychology, 13*. https://doi.org/10.3389/fpsyg.2022.822394

Schröder, L., Kärtner, J., Keller, H., & Chaudhary, N. (2012). Sticking out and fitting in: Culture-specific predictors of 3-year-olds' autobiographical memories during joint reminiscing. *Infant Behavior and Development, 35*(4), 627–634.

Sheppard, A., & Broughton, M. (2020). Promoting wellbeing and health through active participation in music and dance: A systematic review. *International Journal of Qualitative Studies on Health and Well-Being, 51*(1), 1732526. https://www.ncbi.nlm.nih.gov/pmc/articles/PMC7178871/pdf/ZQHW_15_1732526.pdf

Shorer, M., Swissa, O., Levavi, P., & Swissa, A. (2019). Parental playfulness and children's emotional regulation: The mediating role of parents' emotional regulation and the parent–child relationship. *Early Child Development and Care, 191*(2), 210–220.

Siddicky, S., Bumpass, D., Krishnan, A., Tackett, S., McCarthy, R., & Mannen, E. (2020, May 7). Positioning and baby devices impact infant spinal muscle activity. *Journal of Biotechnology, 104*, 109741.

Silver Williams, D., & Mulrooney, K. (2021). Guardians in the nursery: The role of early childhood educators in fostering infant and young children's positive mental health. *Zero to Three, 41*(3), 10–16.

Simons, C., Jones Harden, B., Lee, K., & Tirrell-Corbin, C. (2022). Infant-toddler teachers' early adversity, current wellbeing, and engaged support of early learning. *Early Childhood Research Quarterly, 61*(4), 158–169.

Skene, K., O'Farrelly, C., Byrne, E., Kirby, N., Stevens, E., & Ramchandani, P. (2022). Can guidance during play enhance children's learning and development in educational contexts? A systematic review and meta-analysis. *Child Development, 93*(34), 1162–1180.

Skiba, R. (2013). CCBD'S position summary on federal policy on disproportionality in special education. *Behavioral Disorders, 38*(2), 108–120.

Smith, L., & Osborn, C. (2024, March 1). *Top-down, bottom-up: Building a state child care center workforce.* Bipartisan Policy Center. https://bipartisanpolicy.org/report/building-state-child-care-center-workforce/

Sosinsky, L., Ruprecht, K., Horm, D., Kriener-Althen, K., Vogel, C., & Halle, T. (2016). *Including relationship-based care practices in infant-toddler care: Implications for practice and policy*. Policy Brief 2016-14. Office of Planning, Research and Evaluation, Administration for Children and Families, U.S. Department of Health and Human Services. https://acf.gov/sites/default/files/documents/opre/nitr_inquire_may_2016_070616_b508compliant.pdf

Souto-Manning, M. (2017). Is play a privilege or a right? And what's our responsibility? On the role of play for equity in early childhood education. *Early Child Development and Care, 187*(5–6), 785–787.

Spence, C., Rooks-Ellis, D., Ruiz, A., Fish, L., Jones, B., O'Grady, C., & Sulinski, E. (2022). The language we use: Providers' perceptions about families. *Early Childhood Education Journal, 50*(8), 1291–1302.

Staats, C. (2016). *Understanding implicit bias: What educators should know.* American Federation of Teachers. https://www.aft.org/ae/winter2015-2016/staats

Standley, J., & Gutierrez, C. (2020). Benefits of a comprehensive evidence-based NICU-MT program: Family-centered, neurodevelopmental music therapy for premature infants. *Pediatric Nursing, 46*(1), 40–46.

START Project. (2024). *Communities of practice (COP)*. Grand Valley State University. https://www.gvsu.edu/autismcenter/communities-of-practice-cop-529.htm

Steinberg, S., Liu, T., & Lense, M. (2021). Musical engagement and parent-child attachment in families with young children during the Covid-19 pandemic. *Frontiers in Psychology, 12*(641733), 641733.

Strand, P. (2020). The security-seeking impulse and the unification of attachment and culture. *Psychological Review, 127*(5), 778–791.

Sun, Y., Sahakian, B., Langley, C., Yang, A., Jiang, Y., Kang, J., Zhao, X., Li, C., Cheng, W., & Feng, J. (2023). Early-initiated childhood reading for pleasure: Associations with better cognitive performance, mental well-being and brain structure in young adolescence. *Psychological Medicine, 54*(2), 359–373.

Sundnes, A. (2018). Developing a context-sensitive understanding of infant toilet training: Cleanliness regimes adjusted for everyday life considerations. *International Journal of Early Childhood, 50*(3), 279–296.

Takahashi, I., Obara, T., Ishikuro, M., Murakami, K., Ueno, F., Noda, A., Onuma, T., Shinoda, G., Nishmura, T., Tsuchiya, K., & Kuriyama, S. (2023). Screen time at age 1 year and communication and problem-solving developmental delay at 2 and 4 years. *Journal of the American Medical Association Pediatrics, 177*(10), 1039–1046.

Taras, V., Steel., P., & Kirkman, B. (2016). Does country equate with culture? Beyond geography in the search for cultural boundaries. *Management International Review, 56*(4), 455–487.

Test, J. (2006). Infant and toddler teachers as transmitters of culture. *International Journal of Early Childhood, 38*(1), 47–63.

Test, J. (2015). The influence of culture in infant-toddler child care settings. *Zero to Three, 35*(4), 19–26.

Thiele, M., Hepach, R., Michel, C., & Haun, D. (2021). Infants' preference for social interactions increases from 7 to 13 months of age. *Child Development, 92*(6), 2577–2594.

Toader, C., Petru Tataru, C., Florian, J., Covache-Busuioc, R., Bratu, B., Giavan, L., Bordeianu, A., Dumitrascu, D., & Vlad Ciurea, A. (2023). Cognitive crescendo: How music shapes the brain's structure and function. *Brain Sciences, 13*(10), 1390.

Toub, T. S., Rajan, V., Golinkoff Michnick, R., & Hirsh-Pasek, K. (2016). Guided play: A solution to the play versus discovery learning dichotomy. In D. C. Geary & D. B. Berch (Eds.), *Evolutionary perspectives on child development and education* (pp. 117–141). Springer.

Trevarthen, C. (1992). An infant's motives for speaking and thinking in the culture. In A. H. Wold (Ed.), *The dialogical alternative: Towards a theory of language and mind* (pp. 99–137). Scandinavian University Press.

Trevarthen, C., & Delafield-Butt, J. (2014). The infant's creative vitality, in projects of self-discovery and shared meaning: How they anticipate school, and make it fruitful. In S. Robson & S. Flannery Quin (Eds.), *Routledge international handbook of young children's thinking and understanding*. Routledge.

U.S. Department of Education. (2024). *About IDEA*. https://sites.ed.gov/idea/about-idea/

U.S. Department of Health and Human Services, Administration for Children and Families (US DHHS). (2024). *Universal design for learning (URL)*. https://eclkc.ohs.acf.hhs.gov/publication/universal-design-learning-udl

U.S. Department of Health and Human Services Early Childhood Learning and Knowledge Center (USDHHS ECLKC). (2023). *Writing objective and accurate observation notes*. Head Start Early Childhood Learning and Knowledge Center. https://eclkc.ohs.acf.hhs.gov/child-screening-assessment/child-observation-heart-individualizing-responsive-care-infants-toddlers/writing-objective-accurate-observation-notes

UK in the World Values Survey. (2023). *Parenting priorities: International attitudes towards raising children*. The Policy Institute, Kings College London. https://www.kcl.ac.uk/policy-institute/assets/parenting-priorities.pdf

UNICEF. (2021, November). *Defining social norms and related concepts*. Child Protection Programme Team and Social and Behavior Change Team Programme Group. UNICEF. https://www.unicef.org/media/111061/file/Social-norms-definitions-2021.pdf

University of Northern Iowa. (2020). *Exploring light and shadow with infants and toddlers*. Iowa Regents Center for Early Developmental Education. https://regentsctr.uni.edu/sites/default/files/inline-uploads/LightandShadowInfantsToddlers_ExperienceSheet.pdf

Vélez-Ibáñez, C., & Greenberg, J. (2005). Formation and transformation of funds of knowledge among U.S.-Mexican households. In N. González, L. C. Moll, & C.

Amanti (Eds.), *Funds of knowledge: Theorizing practices in households, communities, and classrooms*. Erlbaum.

Vittrup, B. (2016). Early childhood teachers' approaches to multicultural education and perceived barriers to disseminating anti-bias messages. *Multicultural Education, 23*(3/4), 37–41.

Vonnegut, K. (2006, November 5). *Make your soul grow: 84-year-old Kurt Vonnegut's wonderful letter to a group of high school students*. https://www.highexistence.com/make-your-soul-grow-84-year-old-kurt-vonneguts-wonderful-letter-to-a-group-of-high-school-students/

Vu, K., Cheah, C., Sun, S., Zhou, N., & Xue, X. (2020). Adaptation and assessment of the child feeding questionnaire for Chinese immigrant families of young children in the United States. *Child: Care, Health and Development, 46*(1), 74–82.

Wade, C., Koc, M., Searcy, A., Coogle, C., & Walter, H. (2023). STEAM activities in the inclusive classroom: Intentional planning and practice. *Educational Science, 13*(11), 1161.

Walbam, K. (2023). A lot to maintain: Caregiver accommodation of sensory processing differences in early childhood. *Journal of Child and Family Studies, 32*(8), 2199–2213.

Wang, Q., & Wang, Y. (2019, October 30). Culture in emotional development: Introduction to the special issue. *Culture and Brain, 7*, 95–98.

Weir, K. (2016). Inequality at school: What's behind the racial disparity in our education system? *Monitor on Psychology, 47*(10), 42.

Welch, G. (2020). The challenge of ensuring effective early years music education by non-specialists. *Early Child Development and Care, 191*(1), 1–13.

Wen, N., Clegg, J., & Legare, C. (2019). Smart conformists: Children and adolescents associate conformity with intelligence across cultures. *Child Development, 90*(3), 746–758.

Whitebread, D., Neale, D., Jensen, H., Liu, C., Solis, S., Hopkins, E., Hirsh-Pasek, K., & Zosh, J. (2017). *The role of play in children's development: A review of the evidence: Research summary*. LEGO Foundation.

Williams, K., Barrett, M., Welch, G., Abad, V., & Broughton, M. (2015). Associations between early shared music activities in the home and later child outcomes: Findings from the Longitudinal Study of Australian Children. *Early Childhood Research Quarterly, 31*(2), 113–124.

Wise Lindeman, K., & McKendry Anderson, E. (2018). Inclusive early childhood classrooms: Voices from the field. *Exchange, 240*, 12–15.

World Class Instructional Design and Assessment (WIDA). (2022). *ABCs of family engagement: Key considerations for building relationships with families and strengthening family engagement practices*. Wisconsin Center for Education Research. https://wida.wisc.edu/sites/default/files/resource/ABCs-Family-Engagement.pdf

World Health Organization. (2019). *Guidelines on physical activity, sedentary behaviour and sleep for children under 5 years of age*. World Health Organization. https://iris.who.int/handle/10665/311664

Wright, B., & Counsell, S. (2018). *The brilliance of Black boys: Cultivating school success in the early grades*. Teachers College Press.

Wu, S. (2019). Researching children's learning and play in a Chinese context: Children's perspectives on their play and learning. *European Early Childhood Education Research Journal, 27*(4), 551–565.

Xiong, Y., Qin, L., Wang, Q., Wang, M., & Pomerantz, E. (2022). Reexamining the cultural specificity of controlling and autonomy-supportive parenting in the United States and China with a within-individual analytic approach. *Developmental Psychology, 58*(5), 935–949.

Yeager, K., & Bauer-Wu, S. (2013). Cultural humility: Essential foundation for clinical researchers. *Applied Nursing Research, 26*(4), 251–256.

Yildirim, Y., & Yilmaz, Y. (2023). Promoting creativity in early childhood education. *PLOS One, 18*(12), e0294915. https://www.ncbi.nlm.nih.gov/pmc/articles/PMC10699610/pdf/pone.0294915.pdf

Yildiz, S., Toruner, E., & Altay, N. (2018). Effects of different cultures on child health. *Journal of Nursing Research and Practice, 2*(2), 6–10.

Yogman, M., Garner, A., Hutchinson, J., Hirsh-Pasek, K., Michnick Golinkoff, R., AAP Committee on Psychosocial Aspects of Child and Family Health, AAP Council on Communications and Media. (2018). The power of play: A pediatric role in enhancing development in young children. *Pediatrics, 142*(3), e2018–2058.

Yoshida, S., & Funato, H. (2021). Physical contact in parent-infant relationship and its effect on fostering a feeling of safety. *iScience, 24*(7), 102721.

Zero to Three. (2016a). *Parent survey reveals expectation gap for parents of young children.* https://www.ilgateways.com/docman-docs/faculty-resources/itc-landing-pages/3317-hgd1-5-zero-to-three-parent-survey-reveals-expectation-gap/file

Zero to Three. (2016b, November 7). *Screen-time recommendations for children under six.* ZerotoThree.https://www.zerotothree.org/resource/screen-time-recommendations-for-children-under-six/

Zero to Three. (2016c). *Distillations: Beyond twinkle, twinkle: Using music with infants and toddlers.* Zero to Three. https://www.zerotothree.org/resource/distillation/beyond-twinkle-twinkle-using-music-with-infants-and-toddlers/

Zero to Three. (2022). *State of Babies Yearbook 2022.* https://stateofbabies.org/wp-content/uploads/2022/04/State-of-Babies-2022-Yearbook.pdf

Zhao, T. C., & Kuhl, P. (2016). Musical intervention enhances infants' neural processing of temporal structure in music and speech. *Proceedings of the National Academy of Sciences U.S.A., 113*(19), 5212–5217.

Zheng, W., Guo, Q., Huang, T., Lu, J., & Xie, C. (2021). The prosocial outgrowth of filial beliefs in different cultures: A conditional mediation model analysis. *Frontiers in Psychology. 12.* https://www.frontiersin.org/journals/psychology/articles/10.3389/fpsyg.2021.748759/full

Zheng, Z., Degotardi, S., & Djonov, E. (2021). Supporting multilingual development in early childhood education: A scoping review. *International Journal of Educational* Research, *110*(1) 1–11.

Žužek Lackovič, B., & Pšunder, M. (2019). Cooperation, effective classroom prevention and intervention strategies: Teachers' and parents' views. *New Educational Review, 56*, 233–243.

Index

About the Author

Marie L. Masterson is manager of ECE Competence and Practice for the Council for Professional Recognition. She holds a doctorate in early childhood education from Old Dominion University, is a licensed teacher, and is a national speaker and award-winning author of many books and articles that address research-based, practical skills for high-quality teaching, behavior guidance, quality improvement, and leadership. Dr. Masterson is a former higher education faculty teacher trainer, director of quality assessment for Illinois ExceleRate, and early childhood specialist for the Virginia Department of Education. A former Fulbright specialist, Dr. Masterson brings a wealth of experience in early childhood cross-cultural learning and a background in music and the creative arts to her perspectives about the capabilities of children and the essential role of families and teachers in nurturing relationships of security and resilience.